TWENTIETH CENTURY VIEWS

The aim of this series is to present the best
in contemporary critical opinion on major
authors, providing a twentieth century perspective on their changing status in an era
of profound revaluation.

Maynard Mack, *Series Editor*
Yale University

POPE

A COLLECTION OF CRITICAL ESSAYS

Edited by

J. V. Guerinot

Prentice-Hall, Inc. *Englewood Cliffs, N.J.*

A SPECTRUM BOOK

Library of Congress Cataloging in Publication Data

GUERINOT, JOSEPH V comp.
  Pope.

  (Twentieth Century Views) (A Spectrum Book)
  CONTENTS: Guerinot, J. V. Introduction.—Auden,
W. H. Alexander Pope.—Mack, M. Alexander Pope. [etc.]
  1. Pope, Alexander, 1688–1744—Addresses, essays,
lectures.
PR3634.G76   821'.5   72–8762
ISBN 0–13–687137–2
ISBN 0–13–687129–1 (pbk.)

10 9 8 7 6 5 4 3 2 1

PRENTICE-HALL INTERNATIONAL, INC. (*London*)
PRENTICE-HALL OF AUSTRALIA, PTY. LTD. (*Sydney*)
PRENTICE-HALL OF CANADA, LTD. (*Toronto*)
PRENTICE-HALL OF INDIA PRIVATE LIMITED (*New Delhi*)
PRENTICE-HALL OF JAPAN, INC. (*Tokyo*)

Contents

v

POPE

Introduction

by J. V. Guerinot

I

Thou shalt believe in Dryden and in Pope, commanded Byron in *Don Juan*. The nineteenth century was not inclined to take his advice, but our own century has at least in part returned to his creed and is fortunate enough to appreciate once more the power and precision of Pope's verse, its variety and range, and the moral seriousness of his vision of the City.

Pope talks to us about things that really matter—money, politics, sexuality, how to live in society—in verse that is at the very least, as well written as the best prose. He inherited the couplet from Dryden and exploited it so brilliantly that Johnson seems hardly to exaggerate in saying that "to attempt any further improvement of versification will be dangerous. Art and diligence have now done their best, and what shall be added will be the effort of tedious toil and needless curiosity." Like Shakespearean blank verse, the couplet in the manner of Pope was never to be quite usable again.

With his painfully acquired skill in writing well, Pope looked at his world lovingly and, like his age, ironically. Satire is a way of looking at the world—at the good and the nice and the bad. Pope crowded his poems with the people he observed: Belinda, the promtrotter; Clarissa, the good egg with a touch of vinegar; Duchesses and Lady Marys; Francis Chartres, the undercover agent and rapist; Theobald, the scholar; Cibber, the actor; the collectors of moss and butterflies; Addison; the terrible-tempered Dr. Bentley of Trinity College, Cambridge; and hundreds more. Some he found delightfully silly and forever fixed them taking tea or alcohol and talking fashionable nonsense. Some he found amusingly harebrained (like his close friend Martha Blount) but could hardly wish them otherwise; others he found dangerously disturbed and told them so in poems that also told everybody else. By those of his characters who were selfish and avaricious, an ulcerous influence on the body politic, he was moved to an eloquence of wrath few have equalled. For mindless hack writers, on the other hand, he invented suitable and less noxious pastimes such as urinating contests. Dr. Bentley, who was in some matters a pedant, he set to writing learned notes on the four-letter words in an obscene poem by Horace.

Pope was an appealing, even if dangerous man. He made the best out of the times in which he lived and out of the rag and bone heap that fate had given him for a body. He was interested in everything —the classics, the latest books of his friends, cooking, painting and architecture, his garden and house, the gardens and houses (both much larger) of his friends, his poetry, his grotto. From modest beginnings as the son of a well-to-do linen draper, he raised himself by his own abilities to become the greatest poet of his age, friend of the noblest and richest and most exciting men in England. This he did despite being (as a Roman Catholic) denied university enrollment and penalized by harsh laws, and despite being (as a hunchbacked dwarf four and a half feet high) almost never free from pain. What he accomplished is astonishing. His letters show him traveling to his friends' estates, advising them on their gardens, helping the needy, performing favors when he could, getting friends to render services when he could not, cherishing his friendships, worrying about other people, collecting shells for his grotto, and, of course, writing, editing, and publishing his poetry with infinite care.

Faults he all too notoriously had. If he was a friend such as not all men are lucky enough to find, he hated a few people with a shocking virulence. He occasionally passed off a lie as "genteel equivocation." He was not a safe man to get on the wrong side of and could be unforgiving, even malign. He dearly loved mystifications, evasions, tricks: sometimes, as with the publication of *The Dunciad,* these were high spirited and very funny; sometimes, as in bringing about the publication of his letters by Curll, they were not. More important to our understanding here, however, is a consideration of the complexity and beauty of his poetry, and—inseparable from it—his intense engagement with the moral and political problems of his time. Such were his concern and his humanity, and so well served was he by the neoclassical insistence on "Nature" (what all of us have in common and always have had) that he still speaks to our condition. One of his particular triumphs is that he can manage to say toward the end of his life—with some vanity and exaggeration, no doubt, but still with a feeling for the good community and the poet's function in it that we know he has earned:

> *Fr.* You're strangely proud.
>   *P.* So proud, I am no Slave:
> So impudent, I own myself no Knave:
> So odd, my Country's Ruin makes me grave.
> Yes, I am proud; I must be proud to see
> Men not afraid of God, afraid of me.
>   (*Epilogue to the Satires: Dialogue II*. 204–9)

II

Pope's poetry offers unusual opportunities and makes unusual demands. His lines "mean" intensely. I am not thinking here of his gift for the kind of epigram that ends in Bartlett's *Familiar Quotations,* remarkable and precocious as that gift was, but of other kinds of compression—in narrative, for example. What could be neater, speedier, and more complete than this? (The poet is speaking of a glutton named Helluo, whose death was brought on by a salmon's belly, not because *it* swallowed *him,* like Jonah, but because *he* swallowed *it*):

> A salmon's belly, Helluo, was thy fate,
> The doctor call'd, declares all help too late.
> Mercy! cries Helluo, mercy on my soul!
> Is there no hope? Alas!—then bring the jowl.
>   (*Epistle to Cobham*, 234–37)

Or this—spoken by a famous actress who even at her last gasp could not forget her public:

> 'Odious! in woollen! 'twould a Saint provoke,
> (Were the last words that poor Narcissa spoke)
> No, let a charming Chintz, and Brussels lace
> Wrap my cold limbs, and shade my lifeless face:
> One would not, sure, be frightful when one's dead —
> And—Betty—gave this Cheek a little Red.'
>   (*Epistle to Cobham*, 242–47)

Although the tone is very different, the same economy is evident in such a famous line as "P—x'd by her Love, or libell'd by her Hate" (*Satire II. i.* 84), which Pope unpardonably applied to Lady Mary Wortley Montague. Here the rigorous parallelism not only forces the participles and nouns upon us, but also "proves" (syntactically) that Lady Mary's love turns necessarily into the pox, her hate into libels. Or take a special triumph in this mode, in which each noun and adjective bears such weight that they all seem measured denunciations:

> Fair to no purpose, artful to no end,
> Young without Lovers, old without a Friend,
> A Fop their Passion, but their Prize a Sot,
> Alive, ridiculous, and dead, forgot!
> *(Epistle to a Lady*, 245–48)

Pope so trains us to expect the maximum concentration in each line that he can make any repetition explode with implications:

> So may the sons of sons of sons of whores,
> Prop thine, O Empress! like each neighbour Throne.
> *(The Dunciad* IV, 332–33)

Another pleasure Pope offers—one obviously appealing to readers weaned on the verse of our own day—is that of an easy colloquial style through which we can hear perfectly the speaking voice. He can begin a poem sounding rueful and surprised and disarmingly modest:

> There are (I scarce can think it, but am told)
> There are to whom my Satire seems too bold.
> *(Satire II. i.* 1–2)

Or talk to us soberly but simply of his recent and uncertain progress in prudence:

> Late as it is, I put my self to school,
> And feel some comfort, not to be a fool.
> Weak tho' I am of limb, and short of sight,
> Far from a Lynx, and not a Giant quite,
> I'll do what MEAD and CHESELDEN advise,
> To keep these limbs, and to preserve these eyes.
> Not to go back, is somewhat to advance,
> And men must walk at least before they dance.
> *(Epistle I. i.* 47–54)

Or in a more elevated tone now—rich in controlled emotion—eloquently justify his style of life:

> Oh let me live my own! and die so too!
> ('To live and die is all I have to do:')
> Maintain a Poet's Dignity and Ease,
> And see what friends, and read what books I please.
> Above a Patron, tho' I condescend
> Sometimes to call a Minister my Friend:
> I was not born for Courts or great Affairs,
> I pay my Debts, believe, and say my Pray'rs,
> Can sleep without a Poem in my head,
> Nor know, if *Dennis* be alive or dead.
>
> > *(Epistle to Arbuthnot,* 261–70)

In early Pope—in *The Pastorals, The Rape of the Lock, The Essay on Criticism*—there is little enough of what Wordsworth wanted: "the language really used by men"; but in the *Imitations of Horace,* which Pope worked on throughout the 1730s, the voice speaking to us is almost the most interesting thing about the verse. His handling of the living voice, contained miraculously in couplets that it always just threatens to burst, reaches its final perfection in the *Epilogue to the Satires, Dialogue II:*

> Who starv'd a Sister, who forswore a Debt,
> I never nam'd—the Town's enquiring yet.
> The pois'ning Dame—*Fr.* You mean—*P.* I don't.—*Fr.* You do.
> *P.* See! now I keep the Secret, and not you.
>
> > *(Epilogue to the Satires: Dialogue II.* 20–23)

Arnold, in a famous essay, when he needed a typical sample from Pope, chose:

> To Hounslow-heath, I point, and Bansted-down;
> Thence comes your mutton, and these chicks my own.
>
> > *(Satire II. ii.* 143–44)

Arnold was bent on proving Pope prosaic. Actually, the whole passage from which the lines come is a striking example of poetry made out of the most ordinary human occasions (here an invitation to dinner), the sort of thing that the nineteenth century neither valued nor knew how to do:

> Content with little, I can piddle here
> On Broccoli and mutton, round the year;
> But ancient friends, (tho' poor, or out of play)
> That touch my Bell, I cannot turn away.

> 'Tis true, no Turbots dignify my boards,
> But gudgeons, flounders, what my Thames affords.
> To Hounslow-heath I point, and Bansted-down,
> Thence comes your mutton, and these chicks my own:
> From yon old wallnut-tree a show'r shall fall;
> And grapes, long-lingring on my only wall,
> And figs, from standard and Espalier join:
> The dev'l is in you if you cannot dine.
> Then chearful healths (your Mistress shall have place)
> And, what's more rare, a Poet shall say *Grace.*
>
> (*Satire II, ii.* 137–50)

Yet the artlessness is only apparent. Pope is throughout these lines "imitating" Horace. The eighteenth-century reader, in fact, was given the poem with the Latin text printed facing it, and the Latin text translates as follows:

> I was not the man to eat on a working day, without
> good reason, anything more than greens and the
> shank of a smoked ham, and if after long absence
> a friend came to see me, or if in rainy weather,
> when I could not work, a neighbor paid me a visit—
> a welcome guest—we fared well, not with fish sent
> for from town, but with a pullet or a kid; by
> and by raisins and nuts and split figs set off our
> dessert.

Just behind Pope's lines, we can see, lie large and important concerns, of which he reminds us by his use of Horace. We are to think, for example, of the sacred duties of hospitality and of using up as little as possible in the living process, partly because to live more lavishly requires some sort of unacceptable compromise with those who wield power, partly because the good things of the earth are given for human stewardship, not for exploitation. Meals, particularly, from classical times to Peacock, have offered the satirist a handy symbol for dangerous luxury, happy moderation, or slovenly stinginess. Pope, the parallel with Horace implies, has turned his Twickenham villa into Horace's Sabine farm; he has made it a tranquil and virtuous retirement far from the city's vice and care, and brought to it a life of studied temperance and moral control, a wise detachment among simple pleasures. The security and poise of his identification with Horace is shown us by the vivid and realistic detail of the whole passage. Some of its implications are spelled out in a couplet from another Imitation:

Well, on the whole, *plain* Prose must be my fate:
Wisdom (curse on it) will come soon or late.
(Epistle II. ii. 198–99)

It is the same down-to-earth poet speaking, owning only to "plain" prose but off-handedly working in a double caesura in each line— daring to "waste" seven syllables on colloquial interjections and writing a second line one would have to be a brave man to scan with confidence.

The variety of Pope's styles is indeed remarkable. Pope was for too long offered in most collections as the author of *The Essay on Criticism* and *The Essay on Man* (presumably because they contained a digest of neoclassical poetics and a text in the history of ideas). The former is an astonishingly precocious and polished meditation on poetic theory—ambiguous and vital in ways we are just beginning to appreciate—but it is not a set of critical principles for undergraduates; the latter is a "philosophical" poem with passages of great power and beauty, but its theodicy makes us uncomfortable. Pope said many other things besides "Whatever is, is right." And his couplets achieve effects far more varied than simply the epigrammatic concentration of "The proper study of mankind is man." In those poems of Pope that most appeal to us today, there is a very odd, transfiguring imagination at work:

Till the freed *Indians* in their native Groves
Reap their own Fruits, and woo their Sable Loves,
Peru once more a Race of Kings behold,
And other *Mexico's* be roof'd with Gold.
(Windsor Forest, 409–12)

And the fresh vomit run for ever green!
(The Dunciad, 1743, II. 156)

Another Cynthia her new journey runs,
And other planets circle other suns.
(The Dunciad, 1743, III. 243–44)

To happy Convents, bosom'd deep in vines,
Where slumber Abbots, purple as their wines.
(The Dunciad, IV. 301–2)

One hesitates for a word—surreal? fantastic? The first passage images an apocalyptic, primitivist dream. "Other *Mexico's*" literally means the Mexico we know made new, but suggests an alternative geography: barely imaginable countries roofed entirely in gold, the

magnificence of an impossible, ultimate Baroque. "And the fresh
vomit run for ever green" is in its sounds and rhythms a lovely,
exulting line, as long as we forget the lexical meaning of "vomit,"
which we cannot do. It is like Dryden's "Through all the realms of
nonsense absolute," in which everything in the line suggests a dignified, reverential compliment—everything but the meaning of "nonsense." Pope makes the dunce's punishment for a moment beautiful.
His transfiguration in the third example is almost as odd; in the
passage from which it is taken, he is describing a spectacular pantomime. He is also transforming (Pope prefers never to do one thing
at a time) a line from the *Aeneid* describing Hades, where "They
knew their own sun and stars." What he makes out of this is an
evocation of mysterious planetary systems, alienating, eerie, in which
an unknown moon keeps her classical name. Although the Italian
convents in the fourth example are part of a description of sights
on the Grand Tour, no real convents have ever been so beautiful
and absurd. "Bosom'd (a slyly chosen participle) deep in vines" suggests pleasures of the senses that qualify the way in which the convents are "happy." Vines offer delightful shade but also produce
grapes. Abbots are sometimes dressed in purple, but here they
have themselves become that pleasing, vinous color and slumber
happily near their life-enhancing wines. The lines are too funny, too
ambiguous through their use of symbols of life and joy, to be anti-
monastic.

Even Pope's earliest poetry, in *The Pastorals*, shows a strange sur-
realist beauty:

> O'er Golden Sands let rich *Pactolus* flow,
> And Trees weep Amber on the Banks of *Po*;
> Blest *Thames's* Shores the brightest Beauties yield,
> Feed here my Lambs, I'll seek no distant Field.
>
> > (*Spring*, 61–64)

These verses seem to say exquisitely almost nothing whatever, to
achieve a poetry in which the content approaches zero. Or such is
a possible modern view. The pleasures offered appear to be only
sounds and rhythms and the imagistic beauty of golden sands and
tears of amber. But this surface is again deceptive. The poet is in
fact gathering up the motifs and images of the pastoral tradition—
the gold dust in the Pactolus, the amber tears of the Heliades—and
using them to transform the Thames valley into Arcady. The "I" of

the last line is, utterly unlike the "I" of the *Imitations*, a shadowy figure; he is the young poet making his own poetry out of the poetry of Theocritus and Virgil and imagining Thames's shores in their images. The lines pretend to distinguish the Pactolus and the Po from the Thames; what they really do is to unite them. The Thames idealized flows gently through the sinless, sunlit world of the pastoral.

III

The somewhat solipsistic and all-too-Virgilian poet of *The Pastorals* gave place during the 1720s to the mature man struggling with those problems of the City that the mature Virgil had imagined. It was Aeneas's task to found Rome, a city symbolic of justice, law, and civilization; it is the citizen's and satirist's job to struggle endlessly to preserve it against the forces of evil.

No correct reading of Pope can make him into a connoisseur of chaos. He is—however suspicious of this we may be—a poet of order, though not of a tidy, impossible, deistic order. If the typical modern poetic strategy is to set a scene of painfully achieved local order against a cosmic disorder, Pope's typical satiric strategy is to set a damaging local disorder against a background of cosmic order and meaning. Wallace Stevens must find in *Sunday Morning*, since there are no churches left for him to go to and Palestine is silent, what images of order he can to hold off emptiness:

> She hears, upon that water without sound,
> A voice that cries, 'The tomb in Palestine
> Is not the porch of spirits lingering.
> It is the grave of Jesus, where he lay.'
> We live in an old chaos of the sun,
> Or old dependency of day and night,
> Or island solitude, unsponsored, free,
> Of that wide water, inescapable.
> Deer walk upon our mountains, and the quail
> Whistle about us their spontaneous cries;
> Sweet berries ripen in the wilderness;
> And, in the isolation of the sky,
> At evening, casual flocks of pigeons make
> Ambiguous undulations as they sink,
> Downward to darkness, on extended wings.

Today it is the poem itself that creates such order as there is:

> I placed a jar in Tennessee,
> And round it was, upon a hill.
> It made the slovenly wilderness
> Surround that hill.
>
> The wilderness rose up to it,
> And sprawled around, no longer wild.
> The jar was round upon the ground
> And tall and of a port in air.

Pope would find such a claim for a poem startling. The rape of Belinda's lock had grievously upset the decorum of Hampton Court, but Pope ends the ludicrous battle by metamorphosing the ravished lock into a constellation, by having it become part of the very cosmic order itself, the army of unalterable law:

> Then cease, bright Nymph! to mourn thy ravish'd Hair
> Which adds new Glory to the shining Sphere!
> Not all the Tresses that fair Head can boast
> Shall draw such Envy as the Lock you lost.
> For, after all the Murders of your Eye,
> When, after Millions slain, your self shall die;
> When those fair Suns shall sett, as sett they must,
> And all those Tresses shall be laid in Dust;
> *This Lock,* the Muse shall consecrate to Fame,
> And mid'st the Stars inscribe *Belinda's* Name!   (V. 141–50)

Timon's huge villa, his tastelessness, and his senseless extravagance are contemptible, unnatural. But Timon, although he is a real social evil, cannot subvert the laws of Nature:

> Yet hence the Poor are cloath'd, the Hungry fed;
> Health to himself, and to his Infants bread
> The Lab'rer bears: What his hard Heart denies,
> His charitable Vanity supplies.
>   Another age shall see the golden Ear
> Imbrown the Slope, and nod on the Parterre,
> Deep Harvests bury all his pride has plann'd,
> And laughing Ceres re-assume the land.
>
>   (*Epistle to Burlington,* 169–76)

Auden has told us recently, "As I get older and the times get gloomier and more difficult, it is to poets like Horace and Pope that I find myself more and more turning for the kind of refreshment I require." Pope and Horace are poets of the centrally human, who talk to us in civilized voices of how men behave and how they ought to behave, of the nature of virtue and the good life. This need not make us sceptical about his realism: Pope's vision of evil is much too intense and concretely imagined to allow for coziness. His poems throng with frightening figures. Avidien and his wife ("him you'll call a dog, and her a bitch") are nauseating in their miserliness:

> One half-pint bottle serves them both to dine,
> And is at once their vinegar and wine.
> But on some lucky day (as when they found
> A lost Bank-bill, or heard their Son was drown'd)
> At such a feast old vinegar to spare,
> Is what two souls so gen'rous cannot bear;
> Oyl, tho' it stink, they drop by drop impart,
> But sowse the Cabbidge with a bounteous heart.
> *(Satire II. ii.* 53–60)

Elsewhere in the Satires, sisters are starved, legacies are left to cats, sad Sir Balaam (the ideal businessman, who loved the wages of unrighteousness) curses God and dies, and the Bishop of London, finding the Dean of Ferns and Leighlin picking up a prostitute in the park, cries:

> 'Proceed . . . proceed, my Reverend Brother,
> 'Tis *Fornicatio simplex,* and no other.
> *(Sober Advice from Horace,* 41–42)

The new all-powerful men of money—the swindling directors of the Charitable Corporation, the Governor of the Bank of England, the projectors of the South Sea Company—flaunt their inhumanity:

> Bond damns the Poor, and hates them from his heart:
> The grave Sir Gilbert holds it for a rule,
> That 'every man in want is knave or fool:'
> 'God cannot love (says Blunt, with tearless eyes)
> The wretch he starves'—and piously denies.
> *(Epistle to Bathurst,* 102–6)

A lady of fashion

> laughs at Hell, but (like her Grace)
> Cries, 'Ah! how charming if there's no such place!'
> *(Epistle to a Lady,* 107–8)

Educators boast,

> We ply the Memory, we load the brain,
> Bind rebel Wit, and double chain on chain,
> Confine the thought, to exercise the breath;
> And keep them in the pale of Words till death.
>   (*The Dunciad* IV. 157–60)

Partial evil may be universal good, but that does not alter the fact that Sporus is a Satan at the ear of Queen Caroline, that jealous Atticus and his fawning coterie corrupt the literary scene, and that Theobald and Cibber, however comic they sometimes seem, involve us all in a universal yawn of apathy and indifference to the body politic that is not funny at all. It is even hard at the end of *The Dunciad* to be sure whether the pessimism is mitigated in any way or, if it is, in any way other than through Pope's ability to make a work of art out of such a situation. Universal darkness covers all, or such is the terrible vision. Yet it just might be averted. Pope is ultimately optimistic, though there are no easy answers. The world is too full of poisoning Delias and bribed judges, wolfish money-lenders, venal placemen, and corrupt ministers.

More and more as the 30s went on, Pope moved from the problems of himself and his verse to an engagement in politics. The objects of his satire were important enough to justify his passionate concern. Political issues then revolved around the sleazy Hanoverian court of George II and the Lord Treasurer, Sir Robert Walpole. Walpole—with all that he stood for as a dramatization of the maxim that power corrupts—casts a large shadow on Pope's last poems. With spies and large sums of money, he controlled the press, bought what writers and votes in Parliament he needed, promoted the interests of the money men (the new capitalist class), and cared as little for intellectuals and what they thought as did his king, the nearly illiterate George II. Under such a government a poet could hardly help being in the Opposition. The older aristocracy and gentry—who, with their ancient classical and Christian sanctions, conveyed at any rate the illusion of valuing literature—were everywhere deteriorating, and the new City men, rootless and avaricious, were fast bringing to an end—as Pope believed (and he was not alone in this)—the only kind of world in which literature could thrive. "Get Mony, Mony still," says London's voice in one of his last epistles.

> Get Place and Wealth, if possible, with Grace;
> If not, by any means get Wealth and Place.
>   *(Epistle I. i.* 103–4)

In Pope's vision of Vice Triumphant at the end of the first *Epilogue to the Satires,* money draws the willing world in its golden chains. He is thinking of the financial panics he had lived through, the creation of a National Debt and of the Bank of England, usury, the fungoid "silent growth of ten per Cent,/In Dirt and darkness" *(Epistle I. i.* 132–33). Poets have intimations of immortality; they cannot be at home in a land where "Not to be corrupted is the Shame" *(Epilogue to the Satires: Dialogue I.* 160).

Yet the pursuit of money, as Pope well knew, was only the chief symptom of his country's malaise. The real causes lay deeper, in the failure of the nation's leadership to dignify any other pursuit. Although George II was not the worst of kings, and Robert Walpole, for all his corrupt dealings, was in many respects a very great first minister, neither man had the capacity—or the will—to capture the national imagination and invigorate it with a sense of firm direction and shared purpose. *Ad astra per aspera* ("To the stars no matter how rough the road") was a motto that no persuasive political figure in Pope's time ventured to lay claim to, and it is for this reason that the vision Pope gives us of his country in these later poems is so largely a vision of things ruining. Good manners, good morals, good arts, and, above all, the dream of the good community are being shoved to the wall, not for the most part by deeply villainous forces of destruction (though clearly Pope felt there were some of these in the picture), but more often by simple distraction, solipsism, cynicism, shortsightedness, and apathy—the failure to take high goals seriously, whether in literature (as by the Dunces), or in government (as by the Court party). It is not too much to say, I think, that in the whole corpus of English poetry there are no more apt lines for our meditation during the 1970s than those in which, at the close of his final poem, Pope traces the extinction of civilization, not to any sort of cataclysm, nuclear or otherwise, but to a yawn.

IV

Our twentieth-century view of Pope emerged in the 1930s. George Sherburn's *The Early Career of Alexander Pope* (1934) for the first time provided a meticulously accurate and convincingly sympathetic account of the man. His patient sifting of all the evidence cleared up dozens of vulgar errors. Pope, he could show, was far more tolerant of his enemies and was less impatient than any one had believed in two centuries. The other great landmark was the inception (1939) of the Twickenham Edition of Pope's poetry, which provides not only a definitive text but also the generous annotation that—such is Pope's allusiveness both to classical models and to almost forgotten contemporaries—any twentieth-century reader will find necessary.

At the same time, the critical revolution inaugurated by Hulme, Eliot, and Richards encouraged a revaluation of Pope's poetry. Stated briefly, what critics accomplished was to show us his varieties and surrogates of metaphor—his puns, allusions, pairings, rhymes. They read his couplets with an ear for their special rhythms, their subtle shifts in the caesura, and for the rhetoric of rhyme, alliteration, balance, and antithesis that enact their meaning. His satire they also read, but now with attention to the *persona;* that is, to the character speaking—who, since he is never quite identifiable with the historical Alexander Pope, saves us from reading the poem as a document in his biography. Several of the essays in this collection were signal contributions to this revaluation, especially the early Auden essay, which, though written long before most of the important work on Pope, remains a warm and balanced tribute from a critic who is a distinguished poet in his own right.

In general I have tried to select from the abundance available those essays that both illustrate the directions the study of Pope has taken in the past thirty-five years and offer the reader the most important critical insights. For this reason I have excluded articles dealing with scholarly questions of text or literary history. I am especially sorry that it has proved impossible to include even one essay on each of the major poems, or any essays at all on Pope as critic, translator, painter, and gardener.

Alexander Pope

by W. H. Auden

About 1705 Wycherley's visitors began to "meet a little Aesopic sort of animal in his own cropt hair, and dress agreeable to the forest he came from—probably some tenant's son of Wycherley's making court for continuance in his lease on the decease of his rustic parent—and were surprised to learn that he was poetically inclined and writ tolerably smooth verses." As is so often the case, just as Proust was a Jew, and Hitler is an Austrian, the man who was to epitomize Augustan culture was not of it by birth. The invalid self-educated son of a Roman Catholic linen merchant, it was not a very promising beginning for the man who was to become the friend of dukes, the gardener and gourmet, the poet to whom a mayor was to offer £4000 for a single couplet.

If Pope's social advantages were few his physical charms were even less. Only four feet six in height, he was already a sufferer from Pott's disease, "the little Alexander whom the women laugh at," and in middle age was to become really repulsive. ". . . so weak as to stand in perpetual need of female attendance; extremely sensible of cold, so that he wore a kind of fur doublet, under a shirt of a very coarse warm linen with fine sleeves. When he rose, he was invested in a bodice made of stiff canvas, being scarce able to hold himself erect till they were laced, and he then put on a flannel waistcoat. One side was contracted. His legs were so slender, that he enlarged their bulk with three pairs of stockings, which were drawn on and off by the maid; for he was not able to dress or undress himself, and neither went to bed nor rose without help. His weakness made it very difficult for him to be clean. His hair had fallen almost all away. . . ."

"Alexander Pope," by W. H. Auden. From *Anne to Victoria,* ed. Bonamy Dobrée (London: Cassell and Company, 1931). Reprinted by permission of Curtis Brown Ltd., London.

Nor, it must be admitted, even if not as sublimely odious as Addison, was he a prepossessing character. He was a snob and a social climber, who lied about his ancestry and cooked his correspondence; he was fretful and demanded constant attention, he was sly, he was mean, he was greedy, he was vain, touchy, and worldly while posing as being indifferent to the world and to criticism; he was not even a good conversationalist.

As a poet, he was limited to a single verse form, the end-stopped couplet; his rare attempts at other forms were failures. To limitation of form was added limitation of interest. He had no interest in nature as we understand the term, no interest in love, no interest in abstract ideas, and none in Tom, Dick and Harry. Yet his recognition was immediate, and his reputation never wavered during his lifetime.

If we are to understand his contemporary success, if we are to appreciate the nature of his poetry and its value, we must understand the age in which he lived.

At the beginning of the eighteenth century, although one quarter of the population was in receipt of occasional parish relief, England was the most prosperous country in Europe. According to Gregory King, out of a population of about 5 million, the two largest classes were cottagers and paupers, and the labouring people and out-servants, both of which the Act of Settlement of the Poor prevented from leaving the parishes in which they were born; about a quarter were tenant farmers or freeholders; an eighty-seventh small landed gentry with an income of from £250 to £450 a year; and the remainder the large landowners. One tenth of the population lived in London, which was more than fifteen times larger than her nearest rival, Bristol. The relative prosperity of the country was due, partly to colonies and Britain's favourable position on the Atlantic seaboard, partly to her export of cloth to Europe, partly to her free internal trade and partly to the comparative lack of friction, compared, for example, with France, between the landed aristocracy and business. Though the former professed to look down on the latter, they were ready to profit from them; the younger sons of the poorer gentry were frequently apprentices to business houses, and successful business men could and did become landed gentry. The Act of Toleration prevented religious difference from interfering with trade; and the establishment of the Bank of England and the National Debt drew financial and political interests close together.

The dependence on air and water for motive power preserved the balance between town and country; indeed, through the wish to escape obsolete borough restrictions, industry was less urban than in earlier times. There was therefore no emotional demand for "nature" poetry.

If a large number of the population were illiterate; if, by our modern liberal standards, their amusements of drinking, gambling, and cock-fighting were crude, their sanitation primitive, their politics virulent and corrupt, there had nevertheless been an improvement. There were more educated people than ever before, a greater interest in education—charity schools were being built everywhere —and England's increasing importance in, and ties with, Europe, gave her culture a breadth and balance hitherto unknown. The arts have hitherto flourished best where cultured society was large enough to provide variety and small enough to be homogeneous in taste. The eighteenth century in England fulfilled both these conditions. There was a growing consciousness of the value of refinement and good manners—a society for the Reformation of Manners is a symptom of a social rather than a Puritan conscience—and the age saw the development of these typical modern amusements—smoking —tea- and coffee-drinking—shooting birds on the wing instead of sitting—horse-racing—and cricket. Whether intentional or not, the wearing of wigs helped to delouse the upper classes, and in politics bribery may not be desirable but it is an improvement upon imprisonment and political murder.

You have, then, a society which, in spite of very wide variations in income and culture varying from the cottager with his bible and peddler's ballads, through the small squire with his *Hudibras* and Foxe's *Book of Martyrs,* through the Squire Westerns and the Sir Roger de Coverleys, up to the Duke with his classical library, his panelled room, his landscape garden, his china and mahogany furniture, and his round of London, Bath and his country estate, was at no point fundamentally divided in outlook and feeling. Owing to the fusing of landed and trade interests, owing to the fact that England was still rural, was a genuine economic unit, and rising in power, there was little clash between politics and economics, no apparent class conflict.

In studying the ideas and art of this period, therefore, we are studying firstly those of any rising class which has recently won power and security for itself—(perhaps the surest sign of victory in a political struggle is the removal of the Censorship; this happened in 1695)—and secondly those of a particular example of such a class in a small European island shortly before the Industrial Revolution. In consequence we may find certain characteristics which seem likely to recur through history, and others which are peculiar to the particular circumstance of the time, and can never happen again.

To take the more universal characteristics first; what should we expect to find? Those who have risen from a subordinate to a dominant position are, firstly, pleased with themselves, and, secondly, anxious to preserve the status quo. No one is so ready to cry Pax and All's well as he who has just got what he wants. They are optimistic, full of vitality, pacific, within their circle, and conservative.

> All Nature is but Art, unknown to thee;
> All Chance, Direction, which thou canst not see;
> All Discord, Harmony not understood;
> All partial Evil, universal Good;
> And, spite of Pride, in erring Reason's spite,
> One truth is clear, WHATEVER IS, IS RIGHT.

Secondly, they bring with them a sense of social inferiority; they are anxious to possess and develop the culture and social refinements of the class they have replaced. Contempt for art and manners is a symptom of a rising class that has not yet won power. When they have, they will welcome and reward handsomely art which teaches them refinement, and proves them refined. Because they have been successful, they are interested in themselves. The art of their choice will celebrate their activities, flatter their virtues, and poke fun at their fables.

Certain qualities of Augustan poetry, then, its air of well being, its gusto, its social reference,

> Correct with spirit, eloquent with ease.

are those which might occur after any social revolution. Others are more unique.

The Reformation split the conception of a God who was both immanent and transcendental, a God of faith and works, into two, into the Inner light to be approached only through the private conscience, and the Divine Architect and Engineer of the Physical Universe and the laws of Economics, whose operations could be understood but not interfered with. The religious life tended to become individualized, and the social life secularized. The evil effects of what a Catholic writer has described as

> Sundering the believer from his laicized body
> Sundering heaven from an earth evermore hireling, secularized,
>   enslaved,
> tied down to the manufacture of the useful.

are more apparent now than then, but of the importance of such an attitude to nature and historical law in the development of the physical sciences, there can be no doubt, and the secularization of education hastened the growth of culture among others than those in orders, and the creation of a general reading public.

At first the emphasis was all on the liberty of the individual conscience, and the Renaissance glorification of the individual, on anti-authoritarianism and anti-popery. But when those who believed in private illumination gained political and public power, they became, as they were bound to become, tyrants. After the Restoration, therefore, there was a swing over to the other pole, to a belief, equally one-sided, in reason against inspiration, in the laws of nature against enthusiastic private illumination, in society against the individual fanatic.

> For Forms of Government let fools contest;
> Whate'er is best administered is best:
> For Modes of Faith let graceless zealots fight;
> His can't be wrong whose life is in the right:
> In Faith and Hope the world will disagree,
> But All Mankind's concern is Charity:
> All must be false that thwart this one great end;
> And all of God, that bless Mankind or mend.

Anti-popery remained, reinforced by the events of 1688, Louis XIV's power in Europe, and his persecution of the Huguenots, but to it was added Anti-Dissent. Neither were violent enough to lead to real persecution or to prevent social intercourse; they were the natural distrust that people who are doing very nicely as they are, have for those who might interfere with them, with their social order, their pleasures, and their cash, but are in point of fact powerless.

The appreciation of law extended itself naturally enough to literature, and literary criticism became for the first time a serious study.

Suspicious of enthusiasm and inspiration, Dryden and his successors
based their psychology of creative work on Hobbes:

> Time and education beget experience.
> Experience begets Memory.
> Memory begets Judgement and Fancy.
> Memory is the world in which the Judgement, the severer sister,
> busieth herself in a grave and rigid examination of all the parts of
> Nature, and in registering by letters their order, causes, uses, differ-
> ences, and resemblances; whereby the Fancy, when any work of Art
> is to be performed, finding her materials at hand and prepared for
> her use, needs no more than a swift motion over them.
> Imagination is nothing else but sense decaying or weakened by
> the absence of the object.

Such a theory reduces imagination to a recording device, and
makes creative work a purely conscious activity. It has no place for
the solar plexus or the Unconscious of modern writers, nor for the
divine inspiration of the Ancients. Poetry becomes a matter of word-
painting of the objective world.

The difference is apparent if we compare Pope's invocation at the
beginning of his philosophical poem with those of a Catholic like
Dante, or a puritan like Milton.

> O good Apollo . . .
> Into my bosom enter thou, and so breathe as when thou
>   drewest
> Marsyas from out what sheathed his limbs.

> And chiefly thou, O spirit, that dost prefer
> Before all temples the upright heart and pure,
> Instruct me, for thou knowest . . .
>   . . . What in me is dark
> Illumine; what is low, raise and support.

> Awake, my St. John! leave all meaner things
> To low ambition and the pride of Kings.
> Let us (since life can little more supply
> Than just to look about us and to die)
> Expatiate free o'er all this scene of Man;
> A mighty maze! but not without a plan.

But it would be a mistake to say that the best poetry of Dryden
or Pope or any of the Augustans was deliberately written to their
theories. The writing of poetry is always a more complex thing than

any theory we may have about it. We write first and use the theory afterwards to justify the particular kind of poetry we like and the particular things about poetry in general which we think we like. Further, like most theories, it has its points. We, who have been brought up in the Romantic tradition, are inclined to think that whenever the Augustans wrote bad poetry, they were using their own recipe, and whenever they wrote good poetry they were using the Romantic recipe by mistake. This is false. Without their ideas on nature and the Heroic poem, we should miss *The Rape of the Lock* and the *Dunciad* just as much as we should be spared *Eloisa to Abelard* or Darwin's *Loves of the Plants*. The gusto, objectivity and perfection of texture of the one, owe quite as much to their theories, as does the bogus classicalism of the other.

All theories are one-sided generalizations; and are replaced by their opposite half-truth. When society has become too big to manage, when there is a class of persons whose incomes are drawn from investments without the responsibilities of landowners or employers, when the towns are congested, we shall hear other voices. Instead of Hobbes's psychology, we shall have Blake's "Natural objects deaden and weaken imagination in me." Instead of Pope's modest intention to please, the poets will proclaim themselves, and be believed in so far as they are listened to at all, as the Divine legislators of the world.

We, again, fancy we know better now; that the writing of poetry is a matter of neither a purely unconscious inspiration, nor purely conscious application, but a mixture of the two, in proportions which vary with different kinds of verse; that it is rarely the tortured madness which some of the Romantics pretended it was, and certainly never the effortless and thoughtless excitement the cinema public imagines it to be.

If the Augustans had the defects of their qualities, so did the Romantics. If the former sometimes came down, according to the late Professor Housman, to "singing hymns in the prison chapel," the latter sometimes went off into extempore prayers in the county asylum.

And on the whole, yes, on the whole, I think we agree with Byron "Thou shalt believe in Milton, Dryden and Pope. Thou shalt not set up Wordsworth, Coleridge and Southey." But then we know better now.

During the two centuries preceding Pope, the literary language

had undergone considerable change. We cannot tell how far Shakespeare's conversations in *The Merry Wives of Windsor* is a realistic
transcript, but it is remote from us in a way that the dialogue of
the Restoration dramatists is not. In Dryden's essay on *The Dramatic Poesy of The Last Age* he gives as the reason, "the greatest
advantage of our century, which proceeds from *conversation*. In the
age wherein these poets lived, there was less of gallantry than in
ours; neither did they keep the best company of theirs."

The change in social status is important. It is doubtful if the
Elizabethan dramatists would have been received in the best
drawing-rooms. The poets of a later age certainly were, and if poetry
lost that complete unity of language and sensation which the
Elizabethans at their best achieved,

> in her strong toil of grace

the rise of the writer into society was at least partly responsible.
A classical education and the company of ladies and gentlemen may
have advantages, but they make an instinctive vocabulary very difficult.

But it is the mark of a great writer to know his limitations. Had
Dryden attempted to continue the Elizabethan traditions, he would
have been no greater than Massinger. Instead, he did what Nature
has usually done in evolutionary changes, he turned to a form which,
though it had once been important, during the last age had played
second fiddle to blank verse.

The couplet had nevertheless had a continuous history, parallel
to and influenced by blank verse. The couplet of Chaucer's time
degenerated with the dropping of the final "e," and with the exception of Dunbar's *Freiris of Berwik,* is hardly seen, till it turns
up again in Spenser's *Mother Hubbard's Tale.*

> To such delight the noble wits he led
> Which him relieved as their vain humours fed
> With fruitless follies and unsound delights.

Its principal use was for narrative, as in Marlowe and Chapman's
Hero and Leander, with enjambement and spreading of sentences
over several couplets, a feature which developed in Donne and
Cowley to a point where the feeling of the couplet is almost lost.

> Seek true religion, O where? Mirreus,
> Thinking her unhoused here and fled from us,

> Seeks her at Rome, there, because he doth know
> That she was there a thousand years ago;
> And loves the rags so, as we here obey
> The state-cloth where the prince sate yesterday.
> Crants to such brave loves will not be enthrall'd,
> But loves her only who at Geneva's call'd
> Religion, plain, simple, sullen, young,
> Contemptuous yet unhandsome; as among
> Lecherous humours, there is one that judges
> No wenches wholesome, but coarse country drudges.
> Graius stays still at home here, and because
> Some preachers, vile ambitious bawds, and laws,
> Still new, like fashions, bid him think that she
> Which dwells with us, is only perfect, he
> Embraceth her, whom his godfathers will
> Tender to him, being tender; as wards still
> Take such wives as their guardians offer, or
> Pay values. Careless Phrygius doth abhor
> All, because all cannot be good; as one,
> Knowing some women whores, dares marry none.

But side by side with this, through the use of rhyming tags to round off dramatic scenes, through the conclusions of the sonnets, and occasional addresses, there is a development of the end-stopped epigrammatical couplet. Lytton Strachey in his essay on Pope has drawn attention to a series of couplets in *Othello*, ending,

> She was a wight if ever such wight were
> To suckle fools and chronicle small beer.

And there are plenty of other instances. Fairfax's Tasso and Sandys's Metamorphoses are no sudden new developments.

The evolution of the end-stopped couplet from Spenser through Drayton to them and Waller and Denham, and on to Dryden and Pope is continuous. It is only the pace of the development that alters.

The choice of a verse form is only half conscious. No form will express everything, as each form is particularly good at expressing something. Forms are chosen by poets because the most important part of what they have to say seems to go better with that form than any other; there is generally a margin which remains unsaid, and then, in its turn, the form develops and shapes the poet's imagination so that he says things which he did not know he was capable of saying, and at the same time those parts of his imagination which once had other things to say, dry up from lack of use.

The couplet was not Dryden's only instrument—the *Ode on St. Cecilia's Day, Annus Mirabilis,* the *Threnodia Augustalis* succeed in expressing things that the couplet could not have expressed—but it was Pope's.

Nor is the heroic couplet the only tune of the eighteenth century. There are the octosyllabics of Swift, the blank verse of Thomson, the odes of Gray and Collins. There is Prior:

> Now let us look for Louis' feather,
> That used to shine so like a star:
> The generals could not get together,
> Wanting that influence, great in war.

There is Gay, forestalling Byron.

> See generous Burlington with goodly Bruce
>   (But Bruce comes wafted in a soft sedan),
> Dan Prior next, beloved by every Muse,
>   And friendly Congreve, unreproachful man!
> (Oxford by Cunningham hath sent excuse;)
>   See hearty Watkins come with cup and can,
> And Lewis who has never friend forsaken,
>   And Laughton whispering asks "Is Troytown taken?"

or Dr. Johnson, forestalling Housman,

> All that prey on vice and folly
>   Joy to see their quarry fly;
> There the gamester light and jolly,
>   There the lender grave and sly.

and a host of popular songs and hymns.

> Come cheer up, my lads, 'tis to glory we steer
> To add something more to this wonderful year.

No, the poetry of the eighteenth century is at least as varied as that of any other, but Pope is labelled as the representative Augustan poet, and as he confined himself to the couplet, the couplet is labelled as the medium of Augustan poetry. As far as Pope personally was concerned, his limitation of form—he even denied himself the variety of an occasional Alexandrine—had its advantages. "Of this uniformity the certain consequence was readiness and dexterity. By perpetual practice, language had in his mind a systematical arrangement, having always the same use for words, he had words so selected and combined as to be ready at his call."

With this limit of form went a limit of interest. Pope was interested in three things, himself and what other people thought of him, his art, and the manners and characters of society. Not even Flaubert or Mallarmé was more devoted to his craft. "What his nature was unfitted to do, circumstance excused him from doing"; and he was never compelled to write to order, or to hurry over his work. He missed nothing. If he thought of something in the midst of the night, he rang for the servant to bring paper; if something struck him during a conversation, he would immediately write it down for future use. He constantly altered and rewrote, and always for the better. The introduction of sylphs and gnomes into the *Rape of the Lock,* and the conclusion of the *Dunciad* were not first thoughts.

> Let there be Darkness (the dread power shall say),
> All shall be Darkness, as it ne'er were day:
> To their first chaos Wit's vain works shall fall
> And universal Dullness cover all.
> No more the Monarch could such raptures bear;
> He waked, and all the Vision mixed with air.
>
> (1728)

> Lo! the great Anarch's ancient reign restored
> Light dies before her uncreating word . . .
> Thy hand, great Dullness! lets the curtain fall,
> And universal Darkness covers all.
> Enough! enough! the raptured Monarch cries;
> And through the ivory gate the Vision flies.
>
> (1729)

and finally,

> Lo! thy Dread Empire, Chaos! is restored,
> Light dies before thy uncreating word.
> Thy hand, great Anarch! lets the curtain fall,
> And universal darkness buries all.

The beauties and variety of his verse have been so brilliantly displayed by others, notably Miss Sitwell, that I shall confine myself to considering two popular ideas about Pope. That his language is either falsely poetic, or "a classic of our prose," and that his poetry

is cold and unemotional. The question of poetic diction was the
gravamen of the Romantic's charge. The answer is that Pope and
his contemporaries were interested in different fields of experience,
in a different "nature." If their description of cows and cottages
and birds are vague, it is because their focus of interest is sharp
elsewhere, and equal definition over the whole picture would spoil
its proportion and obscure its design. They are conventional, not
because the poets thought that "the waterpudge, the pilewort, the
petty chap, and the pooty" were unpoetic in their naked nature and
must be suitably dressed, but because they are intended to be conventional, a backcloth to the more important human stage figures.
When Pope writes in his preface to the *Odyssey*, "There is a real
beauty in an easy, pure, perspicuous description even of a low action," he is saying something which he both believes and practises.

> To compass this, his building is a Town,
> His pond an Ocean, his parterre a Down:
> Who but must laugh, the Master when he sees,
> A puny insect, shivering at a breeze!
> Lo! what huge heaps of littleness around!
> The whole, a laboured Quarry above ground;
> Two Cupids squirt before; a Lake behind
> Improves the keenness of the Northern wind.
> His Gardens next your admiration call,
> On every side you look, behold the Wall!
> No pleasing Intricacies intervene,
> No artful wildness to perplex the scene;
> Grove nods at grove, each Alley has a brother,
> And half the platform just reflects the other.
> The suffering eye inverted Nature sees,
> Trees cut to Statues, Statues thick as trees;
> With here a Fountain, never to be played;
> And there a Summer-house, that knows no shade;
> Here Amphitrate sails through myrtle bowers;
> There Gladiators fight, or die in flowers;
> Un-watered see the drooping sea-horse mourn,
> And swallows roost in Nilus' dusty Urn.
>
> Now lap-dogs give themselves the rousing shake,
> And sleepless lovers, just at twelve, awake:
> Thrice rung the bell, the slipper knocked the ground,
> And the pressed watch returned a silver sound.

There is no vagueness here. These are the images of contemporary life. This poetry, not Wordsworth's, is the ancestor of "the patient etherized on the table," of Baudelaire's,

> On entend ça et là les cuisines siffler,
> Les théâtres glapir, les orchestres ronfler;
> Les tables d'hôte, dont le jeu fait les délices,
> S'emplissent de catins et d'escrocs, leur complices,
> Et les voleurs, qui n'ont ni trêve ni merci,
> Vont bientôt commencer leur travail, eux aussi,
> Et forcer doucement les portes et les caisses
> Pour vivre quelques jours et vêtir leurs maîtresses.

Those who complain of Pope's use of periphrasis, of his refusal to call a spade a spade, cannot have read him carefully. When he chooses he is as direct as you please.

> So morning insects that in muck begun
> Shine, buzz, and flyblow in the setting sun.

And when he does use a periphrasis, in his best work at least, it is because an effect is to be gained by doing so.

> While China's earth receives the smoking tide.

To say that Pope was afraid to write, as Wordsworth might have written,

> While boiling water on the tea was poured

is nonsense. To the microscopic image of tea-making is added the macroscopic image of a flood, a favourite device of Pope's, and the opposite kind of synthesis to Dante's "A single moment maketh a deeper lethargy for use than twenty and five centuries have wrought on the emprise that erst threw Neptune in amaze at Argo's shadow."

There are places in Pope, as in all poets, where his imagination is forced, where one feels a division between the object and the word, but at his best there are few poets who can rival his fusion of vision and language.

> Chicane in furs, and casuistry in lawn
>
> Bare the mean heart that lurks beneath a star.
>
> How hints, like spawn, scarce quick in embryo lie,
> How new-born nonsense first is taught to cry,

Maggots half-formed in rhyme exactly meet,
And learn to crawl upon poetic feet.
Here one poor word an hundred clenches makes,
And ductile Dulness new maeanders takes;
There motley images her fancy strike,
Figures ill paired, and Similes unlike.
She sees a Mob of Metaphors advance,
Pleased with the madness of the mazy dance;
How Tragedy and Comedy embrace;
How Farce and Epic get a jumbled race;
How Time himself stands still at her command,
Realms shift their place, and Ocean turns to land.
Here gay Description Egypt glads with showers,
Or gives to Zembla fruits, to Barca flowers;
Glittering with ice here hoary hills are seen,
There painted valleys of eternal green;
In cold December fragrant chaplets blow,
And heavy harvests nod beneath the snow.

You will call this Fancy and Judgement if you are an Augustan, and
the Imagination if you are a Romantic, but there is no doubt about
it.

Like Dante, Pope had a passionate and quite undonnish interest
in classical literature. The transformation of the heroic epic into
The Rape of the Lock and the *Dunciad,* is not cheap parody; it is
the vision of a man who can see in Homer, in eighteenth-century
society, in Grub Street, similarities of motive, character and conduct
whereby an understanding of all is deepened. Rams and young bul-
locks are changed to folios and Birthday odes, and

Could all our care elude the gloomy grave,
Which claims no less the fearful than the brave,
For lust of fame I should not vainly dare
In fighting fields, nor urge thy soul to war

becomes

O if to dance all night and dress all day,
Charmed the small pox, or chased old age away;
Who would not scorn what housewife's cares produce,
Or who would learn one earthly thing of use?

Literature and life are once more happily married. We laugh and
we love. Unlike Dryden, Pope is not a dramatic poet. He is at his

best only when he is writing directly out of his own experience. I cannot feel that his Homer is anything but a set task, honourably executed: the diction gives it away. But show him the drawing-rooms where he longed to be received as a real gentleman, let him hear a disparaging remark about himself, and his poetry is beyond praise. The *Essay on Man* is smug and jaunty to a degree, until we come to Happiness and Fame.

> All that we feel of it begins and ends
> In the small circle of our foes or friends;
> To all beside as much an empty shade
> An Eugene living, as a Caesar dead.

Pope knew what it was to be flattered and libelled, to be ambitious, to be snubbed, to have enemies, to be short, and ugly, and ill and unhappy, and out of his knowledge he made his poetry, succeeded, as Rilke puts it, in

> transmuting himself into the words.
> Doggedly, as the carver of a cathedral
> Transfers himself to the stone's constancy.

and won his reward as he perceived

> . . . how fate may enter into a verse
> And not come back, how, once in, it turns image
> And nothing but image, nothing but ancestor,
> Who sometimes, when you look at him in his frame
> Seems to be like you and again not like you.

Alexander Pope

by Maynard Mack

Alexander Pope was born on the twenty-first of May, 1688, into the modest Roman Catholic household of a London linen tradesman and his second wife.[1] To be an English Catholic in Pope's day, and especially after the expulsion of the Catholic king, James II, in the year of the poet's birth, was to be in some important respects an alien in one's native land. Though the anti-Catholic laws were seldom rigidly enforced, Catholics were legally prohibited from practicing their religion openly, from taking degrees at public school or university, from entering several of the learned professions, from sitting in parliament or holding office. During much of Pope's lifetime, Catholics were also subject to double taxes and to restrictions that forbade their "taking any lands by purchase" or residing within ten miles of London.

These discriminations may have influenced Pope's eventual preference for the Tory party as against the Whig, since the latter embraced the most intolerant anti-Catholic groups in England, the commercial middle classes. But they cannot be said to have determined his career. It had been plain from earliest boyhood that his inclinations lay toward poetry, a study not easily impaired by legislation, and this interest was undoubtedly confirmed by the increasing delicacy of his constitution, manifested by the time he was fully grown in a crippling curvature of the spine, and later in chronic

"Alexander Pope" (editor's title) by Maynard Mack. From *Major British Writers*, Vol. I, ed. G. B. Harrison (New York: Harcourt Brace Jovanovich, Inc., 1959), pp. 749–59. Published originally as "Introduction to Alexander Pope." Reprinted by permission of the publisher.

[1] This introduction draws at some points on ideas I have presented more fully in "Wit and Poetry and Pope: Some Observations on His Imagery" in *Pope and His Contemporaries* (ed. by J. L. Clifford and L. A. Landa), 1950; in "The Muse of Satire" in *Studies in the Literature of the Augustan Age* (ed. by R. C. Boys), 1952; and in an essay on satire and society as yet unpublished.

headaches, asthma, and all the other disorders which made up what he calls in the *Epistle to Dr. Arbuthnot* "this long disease, my life."

Pope's literary career begins at Binfield in Windsor Forest, where his parents went to live when he was twelve, apparently in compliance with the ten-mile law. His education, which had been conducted up to this point not very efficiently by family priests and at two or three small Catholic schools, he now took under his own direction. He taught himself Homer's Greek, went up to London to learn Italian and French, pored over the Latin and English poets while he tried on for size a good many of their subjects and styles, and composed before he was sixteen a "kind of play," a tragedy, and a fragmentary epic which have happily not survived.

Even as a youth, however, Pope had too keen an interest in life and people to confine himself to books. He took long rambles on horseback in the Windsor countryside, pausing, as we may observe from his poem on the subject, to catch in the clear azure gleam of the Loddon the reflection of "the headlong mountains and the downward skies," or to watch, with the mixed feelings which that poem also records, the stag fleeing from the hounds, the struck pheasant fluttering in his blood. Later, as he grew on to manhood, he laughed and flirted in the gardens of nearby Mapledurham with the Blount sisters, "the fair-haired Martha and Teresa brown," young ladies who seemed sometimes encouragingly to forget, in their pleasure at his witty sallies, that he was only four feet six, known even to those who loved him as "little Pope," and to himself as "little Alexander that the women laugh at." Warm friendships were struck up, too, with men: with old Sir William Trumbull, a scholarly retired statesman, who watched with avuncular enthusiasm the progress of Pope's first memorable poems, the *Pastorals,* and suggested to him the writing of *Windsor Forest* and the translating of Homer; with John Caryll, who became his lifelong friend and correspondent, and whose concern a little later about a misunderstanding between the Petre and Fermor families supplied the germ of the *Rape of the Lock;* and with Wycherley the dramatist, a nodding ruin left over from the Restoration, through whose influence he began to come to the attention of the literary world.

When the *Pastorals* were published in 1709, Pope entered on the first of the two miraculous decades in his creative life. During the next eleven years, he wrote, apart from minor work, the *Essay on*

Criticism (1711), both versions of the *Rape of the Lock* (1712, 1714), *Windsor Forest* (1713), the *Temple of Fame* (1715), *Eloïsa to Abelard* (1717), and the entire six volumes of his translation of the *Iliad* (1715–20)—an output not to be matched in English poetry for a hundred years. In the early part of the decade, he met often with a little group of Tory boon companions, who before the fall of their party on the queen's death in 1714 were gathered around the ministry of Lords Oxford and Bolingbroke—Swift, Arbuthnot, Atterbury, Parnell. With these kindred spirits and his new friend John Gay, he helped found the so-called Scriblerus Club, a festive and vinous organization whose lucubrations on the pedantries of the age, taking shape around a learned blockhead named Martinus Scriblerus, left their mark years after on both *Gulliver's Travels* and the *Dunciad*. Though this association saw the beginning of some of Pope's most lasting friendships, it was itself unhappily short-lived. On the accession of the Hanoverians, Oxford was disgraced, Bolingbroke had to flee for his life to France, and Swift, his hopes of preferment in England forever dashed by the ascendancy of the Whigs, went back to his Irish deanery. From this exile, he was to return only twice to England, before passing in 1740 into the stonelike silence of the deaf and mad.

During these same early years, Pope was also courted by Steele and Addison on behalf of the Whig literary circles, which they dominated. This was the crucial period of transition to party government in English politics, when party leaders kept strings of writers as noblemen kept horses, and Pope was judged a likely prize by either side. But the friendship with Addison was doomed before it began. Even if Pope had had it in him to become a Whig, he did not have it in him to be a follower, and Addison could bear no brother near the throne. Pope was warm, impulsive, mischievous, sensitive as a snail's horn to criticism, and could be surreptitious and guileful when need required. Addison, by contrast, was prim, jealous, consciously exemplary, and always busy, like Pope himself at a later period, seeming more exemplary than he was. Pope had been guilty of some cruel horseplay in punishing one of Addison's enemies, which was likely to impugn the latter's reputation for imperturbable uprightness. Addison may have been guilty of first encouraging Pope in his translation of Homer and then transferring his support and praise to a rival version, which there is reason to believe he helped inspire. When the inevitable explosion came, it produced the famous lines on Atticus, written and sent to Addison possibly in 1716, but subsequently incorporated in the *Epistle to Dr. Arbuthnot*. It also terminated Pope's brief flirtation with the Whigs.

By 1716 Pope's literary affairs, which were multiplying with his fame, required a residence nearer London. Accordingly, the house in the forest was given up, and after an interlude of two years at Chiswick, where his father died, Pope in 1718 moved with his mother to Twickenham, a village on the Thames convenient to the capital but outside the forbidden limit. Here he leased a small dwelling with some five acres of ground about it, and set to work building, gardening, landscaping, till the place was gradually transformed. The result was not quite a Roman villa, though it had a temple of sorts, and a vineyard, and, after his mother's death in 1733, a small obelisk in her memory; nor quite a model in miniature of a great peer's estate, though by his example at Twickenham as well as by his influence with noble friends, Pope exercised a liberalizing influence on English landscaping. It was something betwixt and between—and, though he can hardly have intended it so, a residence well suited to the imagination that had already grasped in one grotesque yet thrilling vision Belinda's dressing table and the windy plains of Troy, and was soon to do likewise, in the satires of the second miraculous decade (inaugurated by the *Dunciad* of 1728–29), for the England of George Augustus II of Hanover and the imperium of Augustan Rome.

Pope lived at Twickenham, in this modern Tusculum, until his death in 1744. During the '20's, for the most part, his imagination lay fallow. He wrote little original poetry, busying himself instead with a collaborative translation of the *Odyssey* (1725–26), an edition of Shakespeare (1725), and his grotto. This last was a cavelike underpass which he caused to be constructed beneath a highway dividing his property. From its doors—so he wrote Edward Blount—you look "thro' a sloping arcade of trees and see the sails on the river passing suddenly and vanishing," and when you close the doors, "it becomes on the instant, from a luminous room, a *camera obscura*," on the walls of which, inset with bits of looking glass, "all objects of the river, hills, woods, and boats are forming a moving picture in their visible radiations." For Pope's imagination, this place of retirement and meditation became increasingly a symbol of the philosophic life and mind. It was a refuge that could be posed against the ways and motives of the materialism he saw around him, yet a refuge where these ways and motives could be flashed at will upon the screen of poetry, like the ever-moving picture on the wall.

With Bolingbroke's return from exile in 1725 and Swift's two visits to Twickenham in 1726 and 1727, Pope's poetic powers rekindled. Swift brought memories of Martinus Scriblerus, and snatched from Pope's fireplace, the story goes, an about-to-be-discarded satire on bad poets which grew thereafter rapidly into the *Dunciad* of 1728 and the *Dunciad Variorum* of 1729, while Bolingbroke, as everybody knows, generated in Pope the philosophical enthusiasm, though not necessarily the philosophy itself, which eventuated in the *Moral Essays* (1731–35) and the *Essay on Man* (1733–34). Through Bolingbroke, too, in the '30's, Pope's Muse took a political turn. The house and grotto at Twickenham became one of the meeting places of the Patriots, as they liked to call themselves —leaders both Whig and Tory of the parliamentary opposition to Walpole—and their views of the general disintegration of the nation under that "Great Man," while not always disinterested, unquestionably affected the poet's outlook, stiffening the accents of his satire after 1735 and deepening the "darkness visible" of the fourth book of the *Dunciad* in 1742.

By this time, and indeed well before it, "Mr. Pope" had become something very like a national institution. His financial independence had long been secured by the success of his Homer, establishing him as the first English man of letters since Shakespeare to make his fortune by his pen. He was loved by many, hated and feared by many, known to everyone. Through his house and garden for three decades passed an almost unending procession of friends, visitors, and acquaintances from every level of the realm: Bathurst, Burlington, Bolingbroke, Cobham, Chesterfield, Peterborough, Queensbury, Oxford, Marchmont, Lyttelton, Frederick, Prince of Wales, and many another—his friends among the great; the eminent physicians Mead and Cheselden; the lawyer Fortescue, Master of the Rolls, and the lawyer Murray, later Lord Chief Justice; the painters Kneller, Jervas, Richardson, Van Loo; the sculptor Roubiliac; the architects and landscapists Kent and Bridgman; the philosopher George Berkeley; the poet's intimates among the writers, Gay, Garth, Congreve, Arbuthnot, Swift; and his plain friends Bethell, Caryll, Ralph Allen, and Martha Blount. Here came Voltaire in 1726 to pay his respects to the British Homer. Here came often young Joseph

Spence of Oxford, whose jottings might have made him the poet's
Boswell if he had had a share of Boswell's dramatic instinct. Here
regularly, fresh with news of Grub Street, came the derelict poet
Richard Savage, Johnson's friend, to whose support Pope con-
tributed. And always, as we do not need the *Epistle to Dr. Arbuthnot* to tell us, there was the choir of apprentices and crackpots
which buzzes about the head of every successful writer, demanding
"my friendship, and a prologue, and ten pound."

In these last days, contemporary reports inform us, there was
likely to be an awed whisper of "Mr. Pope, Mr. Pope," when the
poet entered a public gathering. Hands reached out to touch him,
including the hand of Joshua Reynolds, then a boy. His voice, we
are told, was "naturally musical"; his manners, "delicate, easy, and
engaging"; in his house at Twickenham, "pleasure dwelt" and "elegance presided." But elegance did not preside alone. His body was
by this time "very humpbacked and deformed." His cheek muscles
were distended by frequent pain, "like small cords." He was so
sensible of cold that he wore "a kind of fur doublet under a shirt of
very warm coarse linen," and when he rose, was "invested in bodices
made of stiff canvas, being scarcely able to hold himself erect till
they were laced." His legs indeed were "so slender that he enlarged
their bulk with three pairs of stockings drawn on and off by the
maid, for he was not able to dress or undress himself."

The paraplegic who could objectify all this in humor:

> There are, who to my person pay their court:
> I cough like Horace, and, though lean, am short,
> Ammon's great son one shoulder had too high,
> Such Ovid's nose, and "Sir! you have an eye"—

or could dissolve his own pain in whimsical tenderness for the decay
of things in general:

> Years following years, steal something every day,
> At last they steal us from ourselves away;
> In one our frolics, one amusements end,
> In one a mistress drops, in one a friend:
> This subtle thief of life, this paltry Time,
> What will it leave me, if it snatch my rhyme?

is a man whose inner fortitude and magnanimity entitle him to our
respect, even though he was on all too many occasions (as some of

the notes and headnotes to the poems that follow will illustrate)
devious, testy, vain, and unforgiving, like the rest of us.

Pope's Poetry

I

Pope is a great poet because he has the gift of turning history into
symbol, the miscellany of experience into meaning. This is the gift
of all the great poets, but it is striking in Pope because the aspects
of experience he works with are so transparently mundane. He
makes his poetry out of the litter on a prom girl's dressing table
—"Puffs, powders, patches, Bibles, billets-doux"; amorous trophies
hanging from mirrors in bachelor rooms—"three garters, half a
pair of gloves"; elderly dowagers who "die, and endow a college or
a cat"; beat-up heroines of café society—"Still round and round the
ghosts of beauty glide,/And haunt the places where their honor
died"; or long weekends with dull relatives in the country, where
there is nothing to do but "muse, and spill [one's] solitary tea,/Or
o'er cold coffee trifle with the spoon."

These quotations are but a way of emphasizing that Pope is pre-
dominantly a social poet. His subject is human nature as it appears
when viewed against all the paraphernalia of its communal life, its
ephemera as well as its deeper concerns, its dignities, duties, pleasures, crimes. For this reason, his poems have much to say, either
directly or by implication, about politics and economics, about education and public taste, about literature and the other arts, and,
above all, about morals. Pope, Byron said, is "the moral poet of all
civilization"; and by this we must assume he meant not that Pope's
poetry is moral, since all poetry has its moral aspect, but that it is
a poetry which frankly stands guard over *morals:* the systematic
value codes of civilized behavior. The men and women in Pope's
poetry, we may note in this connection, are usually seen, and see
themselves, as the community sees them, either in their social sta-
tions as duchesses and serving-maids, or in their social functions as
doctors, lawyers, tradesmen, journalists, poets; and they are regularly measured, with a few exceptions like Eloïsa, in terms of their
contribution to the common stock of good or ill: they are sages and
fools, philanthropists and misers, connoisseurs and Philistines, good
citizens and scoundrels.

Pope's language too is social. In most of his poems, it is the speech of the coffeehouse, the street corner, the drawing room, though he has a selected language from which vulgarisms have been removed when he translates Homer, and sometimes, when he writes about nature, he has a second selected language, designed to bring out the moral significance of objects—"The fox *obscene* to gaping tombs retires"—rather than their sensory qualities; or else their place and rank in a universe which is conceived like civil state as a hierarchy of reconciled differences, from "the green myriads in the peopled grass" to the "rapt seraph that adores and burns." Even the well-known lines on the dying pheasant in *Windsor Forest*, which remind us that Pope was an amateur painter and brought a subtler palette of color to English poetry than had appeared in it before, are perhaps less a description of "nature" in the Romantic sense than a moral *exemplum*, less about the beauty of pheasants than the transience of all beauty: "Ah, what avail his glossy, varying dyes,/His purple crest, and scarlet-circled eyes . . . ?" The order of feeling in these lines is much closer to the order of feeling in such seventeenth-century poetry as "The glories of our blood and state/Are shadows not substantial things,/There is no armor against Fate . . ." than to anything written by the Romantic poets. When Wordsworth complained that the poets of Pope's day seldom wrote with their eye on the object, by which he meant with an eye for Romantic interpretation of nature, he was perfectly right. They had their eye on a different object.

II

But though primarily a moral and social poet in this larger perennial sense, Pope inherits certain characteristics from the Augustan age which are not always sufficiently understood by modern readers. Some of the qualities of his style, for instance, reflect the widespread intellectual effort of the period to bring the multiplicities and heterogeneities of observed reality under rational control, which for the Augustans usually meant the control of a general rule. The achievement of Newton in reducing the phenomena of motion to a single comprehensive formula was simply the greatest triumph, and the apparent confirmation, of a method universally applied. Hobbes had sought such a unifying principle for the phenomena of the state in egoism. Locke sought it for the mind in the operation of

sensation and reflection. The deists sought it for religion in a generic
creed—what would be left if the idiosyncrasies of existing creeds
were distilled away. The critics sought it in a comprehensive "art"
of poetry, based on the "rules" of individual genres. Even such
unlikely bedfellows as the newly invented calculus of the mathema-
ticians, the *carte du tendre* of the seventeenth-century lover, the
courtier's *point d'honneur,* or, closer home, Pope's hypothesis of a
ruling passion in men, all bear witness to the overwhelming desire
of the age to master a multiplicity of particulars by inducing from
them, or deducing them from, a general rule.

Expressed in the stylistic features of Augustan writing, this concern made itself felt in a variety of devices for reducing the complicated to the simple. The maxim was one of these: "A little
learning is a dangerous thing." The aphorism was another: "And die
of nothing but a rage to live." The portrait of a type was still
another: Atossa, Chloe, Atticus, Sporus; Sir Roger de Coverley, Squire
Western, Pamela Andrews. And for poetry, the closed couplet with
its neat lengths of thought set out in (usually) end-stopped lines
was the groundwork of them all. Just here, however, we touch on
one of the fundamental sources of strength in the Augustan style.
For the habitual strategy of the great masters of this style is to play
off against the apparent simplicity of their formulas, whether verbal like the couplet or psychological like the portrait, the real complexities of what is formulated. In this respect, Pope's achievement
in the couplet, holding, as Miss Sitwell aptly says, "all the waves,
and the towers and the gulfs of the world" in a narrow cage of
twenty syllables, has obvious relations to Swift's achievement in
Gulliver, where other waves, towers, and gulfs are held in the naïve
formula of a shipman's tale and in a prose so transparent that it is
intelligible in the nursery. Both achievements spring ultimately
from the habit of mind that brought the mathematical functions
under the law of the calculus, and the motions of bodies under the
law of gravitation.

An equally prominent influence on Pope's style and thought was
exercised by the Augustan metaphor of tension. This was in origin
a very ancient metaphor, going back at least to Heraclitus' image
for the world—"As with the bow and the lyre, so with the world: it
is the tension of opposing forces that makes the structure one"; and
to Cicero's for the state—"So the state achieves harmony by the
agreement of unlike individuals, when there is a wise blending of

the highest, the lowest, and the intervening middle classes, in the manner of tones; for what musicians call harmony in song is concord in a state." But in the age which had invented the spring-and-balance mechanism of the watch, explained the solar system by pitting the inertia of the planets against the attraction of the sun, formulated the concept of "balance" of power in international relations, the theory of "checks and counterchecks" in "mixed" government, the interpretation of experience in terms of tension seemed to have universal relevance. Thus when Pope has occasion to think about the universe, he thinks at once of opposing forces in equilibrium, sustained by "elemental strife." When he thinks of government, he thinks of "jarring interests," blended in "th' according music of a well-mixed state." When he thinks of human nature, he thinks of the passions whose "well-accorded strife" makes and maintains "the balance" of the mind; or perhaps he thinks of self-love, "the spring of motion," and reason's "comparing balance," as in a watch; or else of man's double duty to himself and society as twin Newtonian motions, whirling the planet-like individual simultaneously around his own axis and around the social sun. Even when he looks at the Windsor countryside, he sees instinctively a scene "harmoniously confused": "Here hills and vales, the woodland and the plain,/Here earth and water seem to *strive* again."

This way of thought is particularly noticeable in Pope's view of the structure of a work of art, and, accordingly, in his own poetic practice. The ideal garden for Pope is one so planted that "strength of shade contends with strength of light"; the ideal painting is one where darker and lighter colorings "invade" each other; the ideal building is "bold" but at the same time "regular"; the ideal poet-critic is one who, like Horace, "judged with coolness, though he sung with fire." For the same reasons, the ideal poem, if we try to define it from Pope's practice, is one in which maximum tension has resulted from a struggle of contraries of many kinds. The contraries may lie in style—the simile of the Alps *vs.* the anecdote of Don Quixote, in the *Essay on Criticism.* Or in theme—the life of Grace *vs.* the life of Nature, in *Eloïsa.* Or in tone—"Atticus" *vs.* "Sporus," in the *Epistle to Dr. Arbuthnot.* Or in matter *vs.* manner —in any of the mock heroic poems. Or in overt *vs.* implicit meaning—in the *Epistle to Augustus,* and the device of irony generally. Or in the subtlety of the things said *vs.* the simplicity of the formula for saying it, as noted earlier. Here once more, so far as poetry is

concerned, the closed couplet with its movement by thesis and antithesis is the groundwork of all.

This aspect of Augustan writing is one that modern readers must
be especially careful not to misapprehend. The Augustans did not
write antithetically simply because they liked symmetry and point,
though they did like these qualities, as all their arts show. They
wrote antithetically partly because the function of literature in their
view was to break apart the canned responses and the moral muddles
by which man as a social being disguises from himself the real nature of his activities. And the most dramatic way they knew of
doing this, whether in prose or verse, was through the explosive
mixture of contending attitudes that the structure of thesis and
antithesis affords: "The bookful blockhead, ignorantly read"; "And
wretches hang that jurymen may dine"; "I am not in the least pain
upon that matter, because it is very well known that they are every
day dying, and rotting, by cold, and famine, and filth, and vermin,
as fast as can be reasonably expected."

Finally, Pope shares with his age the habit of viewing contemporary reality in the light of traditional norms, usually norms derived
from classical literature and civilization. This was a habit that could
serve in two ways. On the one hand, it offered a means of taking
imaginative hold of the vigorous but new and crude mercantile society that lay around him and had produced him; enabled him to
distance and humanize it by imposing on it certain orders of value
drawn from the English and European past: the massive paradigm
of Rome in the satires; the heroic conventions of Homer in the
Rape of the Lock, the medieval cosmic ladder of degree in the
Essay on Man, the themes of *Paradise Lost* in the *Dunciad,* the
moral implications of British history in *Windsor Forest,* and many
more. All these, it is worth pausing to reflect, were mainly social
orders of value, therapeutics for the intense individualism that Pope
felt working centrifugally in the age. Similarly, in our own day, Mr.
Eliot can be said to have helped distance and humanize the raw
facts of an industrial culture, through the invocation of Grail mys-
teries, Greek myths, Dante's *Divine Comedy,* Catholic liturgy, and
the contemplative ladder of the mystics—in this case, mainly indi-
vidualist orders of value, correctives for the collectivist and totali-
tarian disposition of our century. Both poets have thus worked consciously or unconsciously to "redeem the time." A city crowd can
never be the senseless arbitrary fact it was, once it has been seen

through Mr. Eliot's eyes by way of Dante: "A crowd flowed over London Bridge, so many,/I had not thought death had undone so many." Nor could the then recently invented paper currency of a mercantilist society be quite the same, after it had been seen through Pope's eyes by way of Virgil: "A leaf, like Sibyl's, scatter[s] to and fro/Our fates and fortunes, as the winds shall blow."

The other utility of traditional norms for Pope was critical. If they helped him redeem the time, they also helped him measure it. They permitted him to place Belinda's world beside Homer's, the dunces beside Aeneas, George II beside Augustus Caesar, Sir Balaam beside Job, and to make all those other confrontations of the paltry and heroic that are a distinctive feature of his work. More especially, in the satires, they supplied him with his poles of value. For the structure of any of Pope's formal satires, it must be noticed, is a structure of debate between a way of life philosophically conditioned, based on classical precedents and the pursuit of "virtue," by which Pope usually means a sense of community responsibility, and another way of life economically conditioned, based on self-interest and the pursuit of gain. On one side of the argument stand the Hanoverian king, who has abdicated his function of moral and cultural leadership: "How shall the Muse, from such a monarch, steal/An hour, and not defraud the public weal?"; the court, with its flattering placemen of Walpole like Sporus: "Beauty that shocks you, parts that none will trust,/Wit that can creep, and pride that licks the dust"; and the trading City, many of its members infected, in Pope's view, with the *laissez-faire* philosophy of the new capitalism and hence indifferent, he feels, to communal obligation: "The grave Sir Gilbert holds it for a rule,/That 'every man in want is knave or fool.' "

On the other side stand the representatives of virtue. To this group belong men like the poet's father, who "walked innoxious thro' his age"; or like the Man of Ross, who is a kind of minor Moses of the Wye and Severn: "From the dry rock, who bade the waters flow?"; or like the Bathursts, Burlingtons, Cobhams, Oxfords, on whose hospitable estates, "English bounty yet awhile may stand,/ And honor linger ere it leaves the land." What is particularly characteristic of Pope's use of traditional norms in these poems is that the men of virtue, however urbane they may be in actual life, are endowed in the poetry with the rugged independence of the English countryman, and presented, more often than not, in country settings: Pelham in "Esher's peaceful grove," Burlington among his "cheerful tenants," Peterborough forming quincunxes and ranking vines, the satirist himself in his secluded villa at Twickenham, living frugally "on broccoli and mutton, round the year."

In this alignment of values, it is clearly Pope the Tory who speaks; for the Tories, the country or landed interest, saw in the money power of the Whigs a threat to their way of life. But it is also Pope the poet who speaks. Like his predecessors, Spenser, Shakespeare, and Milton, he was haunted throughout his life (as a study of poems as far apart in time and spirit as *Windsor Forest* and the *Dunciad* makes clear) by a vision of England as the ideal commonwealth to be realized on earth—a Prospero's island, House of Temperance, Garden of Alcinoüs, and demi-Eden, all rolled in one. Pope knows that the vision is only a vision, but it is a cherished vision, and its enemies are real, looming far above the local frictions of Whig and Tory. It is for this reason that he dares invoke beside Cibber in his laureate's chair—emblem of a court's corrupted taste —the great shadow of Milton's Satan on his throne in hell; or beside the dapper Sporus—emblem of a court's corrupted morals— the shadow of the original Tempter, "at the ear of Eve, familiar toad." To Pope's satires, in this sense, we may apply what Miss Marianne Moore has finely said of poems generally: that they are "imaginary gardens, with real toads in them."

III

The enjoyment of Pope, like the enjoyment of the other poets in these volumes, depends to a large extent on bringing to his poetry appropriate expectations. Spenser, as the reader has found already, is not Chaucer, and Milton is not Donne; nor will Browning be like Wordsworth, or Arnold like Yeats. In Pope's case, the expectancies most helpful to a reader coming to his work for the first time can be summarized as follows. First, the experiences which Pope records, though they spring inevitably from his own subjective sensibility, are always reformulated in his poetry in representative terms; to do this is indeed the aim of poetry in Pope's view of it: "What oft was thought, but ne'er so well expressed." Second, Pope's relationship to his audience is invariably dramatic, like Chaucer's. Even when it seems most confessional and confidential, it is fully conscious, the performance of an accomplished public speaker or an actor on the stage. Third, Pope is in no sense a poet of supreme moments, whether of tragic agonies *de profundis* or of soaring exaltations. He is a poet of the long diurnal haul. This is his limitation, but it is also his strength. His poetry neither laments the limits of the human situation nor seeks to transcend or challenge them. It simply accepts them wryly, with a smile.

Perhaps the best way to grasp the representativeness of Pope is to compare his work with Donne's. Donne's poetry, if we may oversimplify to make the point, is intimate. Even if the poem was meant for publication, which is infrequently the case with Donne, the emphasis is on the privacy of the poetic situation. The poet is close-closeted with his mistress, or, in absence, addressing her ear only, or apostrophizing blossoms, or a flea, or that busy old fool, the unruly sun, or talking to his God, or performing any of the other verbal acts which presuppose that the speaker of a poem is "alone," and that the fiction to be maintained in poetry is that of a mind in the actual processes of thought, emotion, speech. Pope's poetry, on the other hand, is public. It is acutely conscious of the social audience beyond the immediate addressee. Its tacit assumption is that the social audience is the real audience, no matter whom the speaker professes to be addressing; and therefore its characteristic fiction is not that of a man undergoing an experience, but that of a man who has already undergone the experience and is now conveying what is representative in it, what is socially viable, to his peers. Donne's typical poem, in other words, and Pope's, are dramatizations of different stages in the intellective process. The one strives to reproduce the insight, the illumination, the moment of conflict, in all its original flash and drama; the other, to present it after it has been digested—"normalized"—for general use.

This difference can be seen with exceptional clarity in the two poets' management of the couplet. Pope, to be sure, has a virtuosity in the use of this particular medium that was simply not available to poets a century earlier; but this is not the decisive factor. To read in quick succession Donne's fourth satire and Pope's paraphrase of it is to realize that Donne has taken pains to convey the illusion of thought tumbling immediately from the mind, tearing out with it, so to speak, lumps of apparently unpremeditated syntax and haphazard rhyme:

> Well, I may now receive, and die. My sin
> Indeed is great, but yet I have been in

> A purgatory, such as feared hell is
> A recreation to, and scant map of this.

Pope, we discover, has been at equal pains to stress the organization of thought, its articulations into principal and subordinate, prior and posterior, cause and effect; and his opening metaphor is significantly a reference to the stage:

> Well, if it be my time to quit the stage,
> Adieu to all the follies of the age!
> I die in charity with fool and knave,
> Secure of peace at least beyond the grave.
> I've had my Purgatory here betimes,
> And paid for all my satires, all my rhymes.
> The poet's Hell, its tortures, fiends, and flames,
> To this were trifles, toys, and empty names.

Each way of writing, though conditioned in part by the gifts of the man and the age, is essentially an artifice, and each has its triumphs. There is nothing in Pope comparable to Donne's *Anniversaries*; there is nothing in Donne comparable to *Dunciad,* Book IV.

To understand the sense in which Pope's poetry is dramatic, it is helpful, on the other hand, to compare him with the Romantics. Here there are several differences of importance. In the first place, Pope is reticent about revealing his inner self in poetry, as the Romantics are not. There were moments in Pope's life, we know, beset by illness and often by brutal attacks on his deformity, when he could have longed like Keats to fly far above "the weariness, the fever, and the fret,/Here, where men sit and hear each other groan"; but it would have been unthinkable to Pope to make such disclosures in verse. Nor, though he was surely subject to occasional self-pity like other men, could he ever have brought himself to cry out in poetry with Shelley: "I fall upon the thorns of life, I bleed." Pope's afflictions and frustrations, if they enter his poetry at all, must be handled with the humor and self-discipline that we expect of a man who is conscious of a public: "Weak though I am of limb, and short of sight,/Far from a lynx, and not a giant quite. . . ."

Pope's poetry is also dramatic in that he speaks with so many other accents than his own. There is the flatulent inanity of Sir Plume:

> "My Lord, why, what the devil?
> Zounds! damn the lock! 'fore Gad, you must be civil!

> Plague on 't! 'tis past a jest—nay, prithee, pox!
> Give her the hair"—.

There is Papillia, the fashionable cliché-expert: "How charming is a park!"—"Oh, odious, odious trees!" There is the cockney climber, Balaam, into whose description, without direct quotation, Pope fits the idiom that reveals him:

> Sir Balaam now, he lives like other folks,
> He takes his chirping pint, and cracks his jokes.
> My good old Lady catched a cold, and died.

Pope is particularly fond of this device as a way of telescoping the actual motives of a character with the motives which the character likes to believe are his. Thus Cotta, in the *Epistle to Bathurst,* presents his niggardliness to himself as philosophical vegetarianism—"the use of barbarous spits forgot"; choosing to see in his inhospitable English manor a house of spiritual austerities—"some lone Chartreux," and in his penny-pinching habits "no more/Than Brahmins, saints, and sages did before." Just so his spendthrift son sees his prodigality as sacrificial patriotism: " 'Tis George and Liberty that crowns the cup,/And zeal for that great House which eats him up."

Even when Pope speaks with his own idiom in his poems, it is a dramatic idiom, changing markedly from poem to poem in accordance with the theme. The easy ingratiation of the *Epistle to Dr. Arbuthnot* is quite a different thing from the imperious homiletics of the *Essay on Man*; and the ostensibly respectful ironist of the epistle to Augustus is not at all the same man as the animated portraitist of the epistle *On the Characters of Women,* tossing off specimens of his ability as he talks. Furthermore, and this is a point that especially distinguishes Pope from the Romantic poets, we are never safe in identifying the speaker in his poems with the actual Alexander Pope. We may call him Pope for purposes of convenience, but always with the recognition that he reveals himself as an actor in a drama, not as a man confiding in us. The distinction is apparent if we think of Wordsworth's use of the word "young" in a famous passage of the *Prelude* about the early days of the French Revolution: "Bliss was it in that dawn to be alive,/And to be young was very heaven"—and then compare it with the remark put into the mouth of the friend with whom Pope professes to converse in his imitation of the first satire of Horace's second book: "Alas, young

man! your days can ne'er be long." Wordsworth's *young* is determined by conditions outside the poem, something true, in the years
to which the poet refers, of himself in real life. But in real life, when
Pope wrote his imitation, he was all but forty-five; his *young* is true
only of the satiric speaker of the poem, who is, as always, an
assumed identity.

"To the Middle Ages and the Elizabethans," the modern poet
Sidney Keyes once noted in his diary, "Death was the leveler; to the
seventeenth century, a metaphysical problem; to the eighteenth
century, the end of life." This comment, though too sweeping,
points directly at the unruffled acceptance of the human situation
which has already been mentioned as the limitation of eighteenth-
century literature and its strength. If the Augustan age produced
little poetry of the rebellious inner man, it was partly because its
mode was social, and one does not wear the tumults of the soul
before the world; but it was also because the Augustan writer believed profoundly that man is limited, life inexorable. Much of the
deepest feeling in Augustan literature is summed up in Johnson's
powerful lines paraphrasing the proverb, "Go to the ant, thou slug-
gard":

> Amidst the drowsy charms of dull delight,
> Year chases year, with unremitted flight,
> Till Want, now following fraudulent and slow,
> Shall spring to seize thee like an ambushed foe.

Wordsworth, it is useful to remember, called these lines "a hubbub
of words." His disapproval professed to be aimed at Johnson's "poetic diction"; but when one looks at the mood of this passage carefully and then at the mood of Wordsworth's own best work, it is
difficult to believe that Johnson's view of the human predicament,
governed by irremeable laws of decay, want, and folly leading to
eventual defeat, or at best to a sustained cold war between the
human will and the human lot, played no part in the Romantic
poet's distaste. For the strength of the Romantic spirit is transcendental. In the words of a very famous passage from *The Prelude,*

> whether we be young or old,
> Our destiny, our being's heart and home,
> Is with infinitude, and only there;
> With hope it is, hope that can never die,
> Effort, and expectation, and desire,
> And something evermore about to be.

The Romantic spirit inclines to be impatient with the limited Here and Now, restless for the unlimited There and Then. Its gaze is typically away from this sphere of our sorrow, usually on some higher and happier state of being, which it symbolizes in the lark, the nightingale, the daffodil, the Grecian urn, the west wind, the poet's childhood. And the structure of its poems is not infrequently a kind of soaring flight—a curve of increasing psychical approach— to this ideal world, which at last it touches in an ecstasy, followed, as the moment crumbles, by what Browning finely calls "the pain/Of finite hearts that yearn." Augustan poetry has neither this capacity nor this desire. Soaring, like creeping, is for the Augustan poet a mode of motion inappropriate to man, whose place is firmly fixed, and upright, on the earth.

Donne, too, differs from the Augustans in this respect, though he is no less unlike the Romantics. In the typical poem of Donne, a conflict is stated and then by a witty dialectic taken to an apparent resolution, dramatizing not transcendence but defiant conquest of the world, the mind's ability to find or create out of its own ingenui- ties a momentary reconciling view. The view is momentary in that the lovers are still apart at the poem's end ("A Valediction Forbid- ding Mourning"), the sick woman still has her fever ("The Fever"), death is not dead ("Death, Be Not Proud"). But the moment while it lasts becomes the poem, extracted out of time like Mr. Eliot's Chinese jar in "Burnt Norton," a stilled point in a turning world.

The typical Augustan poem realizes something quite remote from this. Here the effort is not to reconcile the conflicting opposites, but to recognize their opposition as part of the settled constitution of things—as in *Windsor Forest* the view of all the hunters is one thing, the view of all the hunted is another, and the poet's sympathy flows to both. The method in this poetry is not that of ingenious thrust and parry, holding a world at bay, but that of poised, and ironic, elucidation of life's conditions. And the spirit behind it is very different from what has been called, in Donne's case, the mystical individualism of the Renaissance. This is a frame of mind that assimilates all experience to the self, amplifying the psyche and the microcosmic world till it swallows up the macrocosm: "What merchant's ships have my sighs drowned?" "She's all states, and all princes, I." "All women shall adore us, and some men." "I, by love's limbeck am the grave/Of all, that's nothing." "Think then, my soul, that Death is but a groom." In Augustan poetry, the ego has been socially conditioned: "Blessed with each talent and each art to please." It does not challenge life, but threads its way through the mighty maze, amplifying not the psyche but the macrocosm to which the psyche must adjust: "Know thy own point: This kind, this due degree/Of blindness, weakness, Heaven bestows on thee." And it therefore finds the decisive standard of behavior in a "path" or "way"—a radical image of the Augustan age, as defiance or challenge is of the Renaissance and soaring is of the Romantic—usually a middle way.

All of this is particularly evident in Pope, from whom indeed the two last quotations above are drawn. Pope was schooled both by his age and his bitter experience as a hunchback in the art of coming to terms with life. "Blessed are those who expect nothing," he was fond of saying, "for they will never be disappointed"; and the punning remark by which he liked to account for his having constructed a grotto beneath the highway running through his grounds carries the same tone of whimsical resignation: "What we cannot overcome, we must undergo."

For Pope's world is a world of controlled endurance. Homer's poetry for this reason struck such responsive chords in him that it is often impossible to tell in reading the English *Iliad* when Pope is translating Homer's outlook and when his own. "To mourn avails not, man was born to bear." "What must be, must be. Bear thy lot." "The happiest taste not happiness sincere." These sound like Homer, but in fact are Pope. Pope's world is also one of relentless transience. A world where "Years following years, steal something every day," where "Estates have wings, and hang in fortune's power," where "locks, curled or uncurled, *will* turn to gray," where language changes and betrays the poet, colors fade and betray the painter; where, even if (which is too much to hope) immortality should attend on human works, "Alas, how little from the grave we claim! Thou but preserv'st a face, and I a name."

But especially, as earlier suggested, Pope's world is a world of limits. Love has limits: even an Eloïsa has finally to acknowledge, "What dust we dote on, when 'tis man we love." Death too has limits; being, as Keyes says, simply the end of life, so much to be taken for granted that it can be dismissed in a parenthesis: "(. . . since life can little more supply/Than just to look about us and to die)," or compared like passing beauty to the passing sun: "When those fair suns shall set, as set they must." Grief itself has limits for the Augustans. They know that, even if some men do better than the friends of the Unfortunate Lady, who "grieve for an hour, . . . then 'mourn' a year," no passion burns forever in so frail a lamp as man; and Swift consciously pays Pope's friendship the highest compliment one man can pay another, when he writes in his *Verses on the Death of Dr. Swift*:

> Poor Pope will grieve a month; and Gay
> A week; and Arbuthnot a day.

This is the kind of statement, the English critic Charles Williams reminds us, that sees life tenderly, yet steadily and whole: "for let us be quite honest and ask for which of our friends we should come anywhere near anything that could be called grieving, for anything like a month? And which of them for us?"

Finally, in Pope's world, ideals are strictly limited to what the human vessel can attain. "An honest man's the noblest work of God," Pope says in one place. "Ah! friend! to dazzle let the vain design," he says in another, "To raise the thought, and touch the heart be thine!" "What then remains but well our power to use,/ And keep good humor still whate'er we lose," he says in a third. And in a fourth, remembering his father's kindly life and painless death: "O grant me thus to live, and thus to die." There is a certain fine excess missing from such ideals. They seem strangely shrunken, strangely modern, when we recall the towering aspirations of Shakespeare's heroes, or Spenser's knight-at-arms, girt with all the twelve Aristotelian virtues. Yet they have the compensatory strength that comes from being unpretentious, from being available to Everyman as well as knights and heroes; and they require an unsensational but continuing heroism of their own. Indeed, Pope's world, for the very reason that it is less "poetic" than some others, assumes a disturbing familiarity as we live with it. In its noonday hubbub, its humdrum practicality, its muted passions that nevertheless gleam like diamonds in the compression of a phrase; in its crowds and chandeliers and coffee spoons; in its Belindas, Balaams, Bentleys, Bubos, doctors, dunces, swindlers, statesmen; in its happy blends of gravity and gaiety, sympathy and anger, imagination and common sense—it may not be the highest world that English poetry offers us, but it is the one we know the best.

On Versification

by Geoffrey Tillotson

I

Pope looked back to Dryden as Dryden had looked back to Waller. For Dryden Waller was the most important technical innovator of the seventeenth century. Certain poets before Waller had hit on the closed couplet accidentally. Shakespeare had produced in Iago's speech on women a string of them. Waller in some of his later work had converted this accidental discovery into a system. So well did he do his work that Dryden, when he began writing, found a measure ready waiting. Dryden's work was twice summarized by Pope. The prose summary is found in Spence:

> I learned versification wholly from Dryden . . . who had improved it much beyond any of our former poets; and would, probably, have brought it to its perfection, had not he been unhappily obliged to write so often in haste.[1]

There was much still to do on the couplet when Pope began to write. Dryden had written it with a knowledge of the compactness of which it was capable, but not always with a realization of that compactness. In some ways he may be said to have helped the measure to revert to a freer form resembling, in rough and ready convenience, the couplets of the Elizabethans.

Dryden avoided the tetrameter (though on occasion he used it superbly) because, as he said, it did not give him "room to turn round in." A poet who looked on metres as spaces for the cycles of a generous body was not the poet to discover the final perfection of the heroic couplet. Dryden found the heroic couplet, as he found the tetrameter, too small to turn round in and enlarged it accord-

"On Versification." From *On the Poetry of Pope,* 2nd ed. by Geoffrey Tillotson (Oxford: The Clarendon Press, 1950), pp. 105–40. Reprinted by permission of the publisher.

[1] p. 281.

ingly. He frequently made it a triplet, especially in his translations, and frequently made the last of the three lines an alexandrine. He does not seem to have been a poet who accommodated an unruly thought to metre by revising the form it had just taken. He was usually more ready to make space for its completion in the line following. Sometimes he will write two triplets on end. Once in the *Aeneid* there are three on end,[2] and in his version of the *Wife of Bath's Tale,* five.[3] The triplet is often in Dryden a mark of slovenliness. On three occasions in his translation of Virgil's second *Georgic* he begins a new sentence with the third line of a triplet simply because he finds a third rime comes conveniently.[4] Triplets have the undesirable effect of introducing an element of stanza among the couplets. When, for instance, the last line of a triplet is, as it often is in Dryden, an alexandrine, he is writing in the stanza form of Rochester's *On Nothing.* Dryden has other abnormalities than triplet or triplet-with-alexandrine, and, from the point of view of "correct" versification, even more serious ones. For instance, *Against the Fear of Death,* a translation from Lucretius, provides such things as two alexandrines on end and even lines of seven feet.

In his dramatic work, and occasionally elsewhere, Dryden had adopted an innovation which Cowley had made in his *Davideis.* Among the more or less strict couplets of this small epic poem, Cowley had introduced the hemistich, or fragmentary line. He has a note on his innovation:

> Though none of the *English Poets,* nor indeed of the ancient
> *Latin,* have imitated *Virgil* in leaving sometimes half-verses (where
> the sense seems to invite a man to that liberty) yet his authority
> alone is sufficient, especially in a thing that looks so naturally and
> gracefully: and I am far from their opinion who think that *Virgil*
> himself intended to have filled up those broken *Hemistiques.*[5]

Unlike Virgil, Cowley uses the hemistich only in direct speech—perhaps this is why he considers that it looks naturally. But it cer-

[2] xi. 925 ff.
[3] 7–21.
[4] ll. 193, 519, 576.
[5] Note 14 to Bk I. Cowley's statement requires the qualification that Ogilby's translation of the *Aeneid* (1649), although a translation into heroic couplets, had preserved Virgil's hemistichs. And Cowley was probably unacquainted with the brief extra-metrical phrases which Marston had inserted among the couplets of his *Scourge of Villanie* (2nd edition 1599). And see note [7, p. 52].

tainly does not look gracefully, since, unlike Virgil, Cowley is writing strictly rimed verse. An unrimed and incomplete line when found in the middle of epic couplets has the effect of boxing the reader's ear. Dryden usually avoids this scrap-line in his nondramatic works—he discusses the point appropriately in his *Dedication of the Aeneis*.[6] In his rimed plays his use of it marks a transitional point between the heroic couplet with complete lines and blank verse. Dryden was justified in making his measure more plastic for the purposes of dramatic speech.[7] Hemistichs may be justified in drama but Dryden's use of them helped to support Cowley's unfortunate authority for their use in non-dramatic poetry. They are frequently used in "lyric" work by the small poets of Dryden's and Tonson's Miscellanies, as, for example, in Henry Cromwell's translation of an elegy from Ovid's *Amores* in the *Miscellany* of 1712:

> The Cow rose slowly from her Consort's Side,
> But when afar the grazing Bull she spy'd,
> Frisk'd to the Herd with an impetuous haste,
> And pleas'd, in new luxuriant Soil, her Taste.
> Oh learn'd Diviner!
> What may this visionary Dream portend,
> If Dreams in any future Truth can end. . . .[8]

Dryden usually justifies his hemistichs. He also justifies his triplets and alexandrines when he is using them for the favourite purpose of onomatopoeia. His triplets and alexandrines are justified when the idea swells or crescendos along with the metre. *Absalom and Achitophel,* for example, contains the couplet:

---

[6] *Essays,* ed. Ker, ii. 230–1.

[7] This was sometimes Shakespeare's practice, though, since Shakespeare's plays are never entirely in couplets, the analogy is not complete. Having adopted the couplet as a device for closing a scene, he seems to have half repented of the precision and to have blurred it by adding a word or two after the rime. *Hamlet* ends with this making and marring of precision:

> *Fortinbras* . . . Take vp the bodies, such a sight as this,
> Becomes the field, but heere showes much amisse.
> Goe bid the souldiers shoote.

The same device is used brilliantly to close *As You Like It,* i. ii.

> *Orlando* . . . Thus must I from the smoake into the smother.
> From tyrant Duke, vnto a tyrant Brother.
> But heauenly *Rosalind.*

[8] *Miscellaneous Poems* . . . , 1712, p. 116. The last instance of the hemistich I have noted comes in *The British Coffee-House* [anon.] (1764).

> Now, free from Earth, thy disencumbred Soul
> Mounts up, and leaves behind the Clouds and Starry Pole.[9]

In his letter to Walsh of 22 October 1706, Pope enunciated the rules he had come to see valuable for the writing of couplets. His fourth rule reads:

> I would also object to the irruption of Alexandrine verses, of twelve syllables, which, I think, should never be allow'd but when some remarkable beauty or propriety . . . atones for the liberty: Mr. Dryden has been too free of these, especially in his latter works. I am of the same opinion as to Triple Rhimes.

In the *Essay on Criticism* he mocked at the alexandrine by comparing it to a wounded snake dragging its slow length along. But its wounded drag need not be offensive—the slowness is often a "remarkable beauty or propriety." The real trouble about the alexandrine, unless it is part of a stanza form as in the *Faerie Queene,* is the incalculableness of its "irruption." The trouble about the alexandrine is that it begins like an ordinary pentameter and the reader is somewhere about the middle of the line before he realizes that the end is an additional foot farther away. This discovery is often delayed because the length of a line in type is accidental and so may or may not represent its length in time. The objection to the alexandrine is really that the snake begins like a normal one and only falls heavily stricken somewhere about its middle joint. The triplet was more predictable. It always advertised its approach in the original editions with a heavy marginal bracket. It seems a law, to use the words which Coleridge applied to Shakespeare's dramatic method, that metre should work by expectation rather than by surprise. Dryden's *Against the Fear of Death* is an irritating poem to read. It begins with a long passage of ordinary couplets, lulling the reader into a sense of metrical security, but then proceeds to toss and turn with alexandrines and heptameters. In his versification, Dryden often took the readiest way, trusting, as he had the right to trust, that his mounting rush of sense and sound could bear down all obstacles. His reader acquiesces since such power is a unique phenomenon, but he cannot escape, in a large measure, that nervous sense of insecurity which it is the duty of versification to tranquilize. Any variations, as Pope knew, should be made responsibly. The reader must feel secure.

[9] i. 850–1.

Pope realized that "remarkable beauty or propriety" might be provided by the alexandrine and triplet. In his early work he tried to secure such effects. He mimics Dryden, at his most worthy, in his translation of Statius—for example:

> Here all their Rage, and ev'n their Murmurs cease,
> And sacred Silence reigns, and universal peace.[10]

> Whence, far below, the Gods at once survey
> The Realms of rising and declining Day,
> And all th'extended Space of Earth, and Air, and Sea.[11]

But as time went on, his standards grew more exclusive. Although the alexandrine and triplet might be justifiable for onomatopoetic reasons, Pope found that the necessary onomatopoeia could be provided for by the strict couplet alone, if enough care were taken. Dryden swelled over into hypermetrics whenever it was easy to do so. Pope has often the same reason but satisfies it without hypermetrics. Pope is relying on the operation of the law which makes difficulties overcome more admirable than difficulties accommodated. Examples come everywhere. One has only to look at the close of the *Dunciad* to see how many Drydenian triplets and alexandrines its pentameter couplets avoid.

In the *Epistle to Augustus* Pope summarizes the history of seventeenth-century versification. His tribute to Dryden takes the form of a recreation of the "darling sin," the triplet-with-alexandrine. (The placing of epithets and the run of the syntax make the mimicry complete.) Pope is thinking of Dryden as an "incorrect" versifier who nevertheless carries off his effect splendidly—but as the conclusion of the passage shows, not always.

> . . . Numbers learn'd to flow.
> Waller was smooth; but Dryden taught to join
> The varying verse,[12] the full-resounding line,
> The long majestic March, and Energy divine.
> Tho' still some traces of our rustic vein
> And splay-foot verse, remain'd, and will remain.
> Late, very late, correctness grew our care,
> When the tir'd Nation breath'd from civil war.
> Exact Racine, and Corneille's noble fire,

[10] ll. 290–1.
[11] ll. 277–9.
[12] Pope is thinking of the Pindarique odes.

> Show'd us that France had something to admire.
> Not but the Tragic spirit was our own,
> And full in Shakespear, fair in Otway shone:
> But Otway fail'd to polish or refine,
> And fluent Shakespear scarce effac'd a line.
> Ev'n copious Dryden wanted, or forgot,
> The last and greatest Art, the Art to blot.[13]

Content apart, Dryden had not advanced the heroic couplet much beyond Waller, except in the matter of onomatopoetic versification. In some ways he had pushed it back. Pope's short history of English versification in the seventeenth century does not state his own position, but implies it.

II

As a boy, Pope was advised by Walsh to be the first "correct" English poet. So far as Walsh, or he, had versification in mind, they meant correctness in writing the heroic couplet.

The couplet was the important measure for these poets principally because of its unpretentious "elegance," a quality essential for anything intended to contribute to the pleasure of a cultured society. (*The Spectator* thought that "the chief Qualification of a good Poet, especially of one who writes Plays" is to be "a very well-bred Man.")[14] Blank verse was suitable for epic or tragedy "where transcendencies are more allowed." The new good poets allowed theoretical supremacy to epic and tragedy—with Aristotle before their eyes they could do no less—but they did their best work in the meaner, more pleasant, and well-bred forms. Pope is always laughing at bad poets who attempt the sublime. The couplet was a measure which did not embarrass the reader, did not make him feel that the poet was giving himself airs. Dryden generally uses the couplet.

> And this unpolish'd, rugged Verse I chose;
> As fittest for Discourse, and nearest prose.[15]

This is in explanation of the verse of the argumentative *Religio Laici.* He chose a more polished style of the couplet for his translations. As early as 1664, in the *Epistle Dedicatory of the Rival Ladies,*

[13] ll. 266 ff.
[14] No. 314.
[15] *Religio Laici,* 453–4.

he argued the supremacy of rimed verse when written, as Waller had
written it, with "easy" art.

III

In attempting correct versification, therefore, the work of Milton,
their revered and immediate predecessor, offered little help. Pope
knew Milton's poems thoroughly and admired them to the point
of echoing them frequently. But the system of blank verse in *Paradise Lost,* or of other verse elsewhere, had little he wished to copy.
Indeed Milton's versification was not considered correct. Even for
so late a critic as Johnson, Milton as a metrist is to be excused on
the ground that he came too early to profit by the improvements of
Dryden—in the same way that Homer is excused by Dryden for coming too early to profit by the Roman poets' discovery of the "turn."
Johnson expressed himself clearly on this point in his *Life of John
Philips*:

> Deformity is easily copied; and whatever there is in Milton which
> the reader wishes away, all that is obsolete, peculiar, or licentious is
> accumulated with great care by Philips. Milton's verse was harmoni-
> ous, in proportion to the general state of our metre in Milton's age,
> and, if he had written after the improvements made by Dryden, it
> is reasonable to believe that he would have admitted a more pleasing
> modulation of numbers into his work. . . .[16]

And even for such an ardent Miltonian as Thomas Warton the
younger, it is the "perspicuous and simple style" of *At a solemn
Music* that he admires.[17] Milton was considered unfortunate in coming too early to write correctly, and Dryden did not scruple to
"versify" some of the blank verse of *Paradise Lost* in his *State of Innocence.* When Pope did write blank verse his master was Rowe.
This may be seen in the surviving lines of his *Brutus* or wherever
he versifies a passage of wrongly alined prose in his edition of
Shakespeare. He told Spence that "Milton's style, in his Paradise
Lost, is not natural; 'tis an exotic style." [18] Pope sees, however, that
its uncouthness is appropriate for parts of the poem:

> As [Milton's] subject lies a good deal out of our world, [his style]
> has a particular propriety in those parts of the poem.

---

[16] *Lives,* ed. G. Birkbeck Hill, i. 318.
[17] See L. C. Martin, *Thomas Warton and the Early Poems of Milton* (1934), 17.
[18] p. 174.

It is because of this that his exotic style can be "borne." [19] Atterbury, who greatly admired Milton, suggested that Pope should "translate" *Samson Agonistes* into correct versification and so provide English poets with a totally correct model for tragedy:

> I hope you won't utterly forget what pass'd in the coach about Samson Agonistes. I shall not press you as to time, but some time or other, I wish you would review, and polish that piece. If upon a new perusal of it . . . you think as I do, that it is written in the very spirit of the Ancients; it deserves your care, and is capable of being improved, with little trouble, into a perfect model and standard of Tragic poetry—always allowing for its being a story taken out of the Bible; which is an objection that at this time of day, I know, is not to be got over.[20]

The correct versification which Atterbury foresaw may have been in heroic couplets, though six years earlier he mentioned having held for thirty years the heresy that blank verse is the superior metre.[21]

IV

The value of correctness in or out of the heroic couplet lies first of all in the effect it has on the reader's attitude. When a reader finds that his poet considers himself responsible for every syllable not simply in this or that poem but in every poem of his entire works, then his alertness is intensified, his curiosity aroused, his trust increased. Here, he sees, is a poet who will set him in a motion which will only change as a dance changes, not as a walk on ice changes. Correctness elicits and does not abuse the reader's confidence. The reader will, however, soon tire if nothing happens to show how strong his confidence is. Once he can trust his poet, he looks to have the steadfastness of his trust proved and deepened by variety of experience. Pope satisfies this expectation in a thousand ways. Pope's practice is to provide expectation rather than surprise. But the expectation is expectation *of* surprise. The reader of Pope anticipates perfect responsibility syllable by syllable, and awaits the changes which will show that the responsibility is being put to advantage. The thousand surprises come and they enchant all the

[19] Id. 200.
[20] Letter of 15 June 1722.
[21] Letter of Dec. 1716.

more because, as certainly as rime in a known stanza, they have been subconsciously anticipated.

V

Some of the principles upon which Pope worked in the heroic couplet were enunciated in letters to Cromwell and Walsh, and most particularly in the letter to Walsh already mentioned. This letter is the fulfilment, as are so many other things in Pope, of a scheme of Dryden's. In the *Dedication to the Aeneis* he wrote:

> I have long had by me the materials of an English *Prosodia,* containing all the mechanical rules of versification, wherein I have treated, with some exactness, of the feet, the quantities, and the pauses.[22]

Pope was also indebted to the excellent preface by Atterbury to the posthumous second part of Waller's *Poems* (1690). Pope's letter to Walsh is written when he is nineteen years old, and it embodies what he had by that time come to realize about English versification from his reading in English and other languages and from his already voluminous practice in writing. The rules were applied in the *Pastorals,* but not so completely in the more difficult poems which followed. The practice, however, fully catches up to the precept by the time these poems appear in the collected *Works* of 1717. Pope writes:

> . . . There are indeed certain Niceties, which, tho' not much observed even by correct versifiers, I cannot but think, deserve to be better regarded.
>
> 1. It is not enough that nothing offends the ear, but a good poet will adapt the very Sounds, as well as Words, to the things he treats of. So that there is (if one may express it so) a Style of Sound. As in describing a gliding stream, the numbers should run easy and flowing; in describing a rough torrent or deluge, sonorous and swelling, and so of the rest. This is evident everywhere in Homer and Virgil, and no where else that I know of, to any observable degree. . . . This, I think, is what very few observe in practice, and is undoubtedly of wonderful force in imprinting the image on the reader: We have one excellent example of it in our language, Mr. Dryden's Ode on St. Cæcilia's day, entitled, *Alexander's Feast.*

---

[22] *Essays,* ed. Ker, ii. 217.

2. Every nice ear must (I believe) have observ'd, that in any smooth English verse of ten syllables, there is naturally a *Pause* at the fourth, fifth, or sixth syllable. It is upon these the ear rests, and upon the judicious change and management of which depends the variety of versification. For example, At the fifth.

Where'er thy navy/spreads her canvas wings,

At the fourth.

Homage to thee/and peace to all she brings.

At the sixth.

Like tracts of leverets/in morning snow.

Now I fancy, that, to preserve an exact Harmony and Variety, the Pause at the 4th or 6th should not be continued above three lines together, without the interposition of another; else it will be apt to weary the ear with one continued tone, at least it does mine: That at the fifth runs quicker, and carries not quite so dead a weight, so tires not so much, tho' it be continued longer.

3. Another nicety is in relation to Expletives, whether words or syllables, which are made use of purely to supply a vacancy: *Do* before verbs plural is absolutely such; and it is not improbable but future refiners may explode *did* and *does* in the same manner, which are almost always used for the sake of rhime. . . .

[For 4 see above, p. 53.]

5. I could equally object to the Repetition of the same Rhimes within four or six lines of each other, as tiresome to the ear thro' their Monotony.

6. Monosyllable Lines, unless very artfully managed, are stiff, or languishing: but may be beautiful to express Melancholy, Slowness, or Labour.

7. To come to the Hiatus, or Gap between two words, which is caus'd by two vowels opening on each other. . . . I think the rule in this case is either to use the Cæsura [by which Pope meant the elision of one of the vowels] or admit the Hiatus, just as the ear is least shock'd by either: For the Cæsura sometimes offends the ear more than the Hiatus itself, and our language is naturally overcharg'd with consonants: As for example; If in the verse,

The old have Int'rest ever in their eye,

we should say, to avoid the Hiatus,

But th'old have Int'rest.

. . . To conclude, I believe the Hiatus should be avoided with more care in poetry than in Oratory; and I would constantly try to prevent it, unless where the cutting it off is more prejudicial to the sound than the Hiatus itself.[23]

Pope's first point is the need for onomatopoeia. In his own work he misses no opportunity where its effects would be appropriate. Pope was following Dryden among the English poets. Dryden had achieved memorable effects of movement, thunder and space, that is, large effects which he could turn round in. Pope has these large effects, but has minute and subtle ones too. The onomatopoetic effects in Pope must be considered as a part of the total elaborate formality of sound, as alternating or coalescing with effects such as balance and inversion. This means that they are not effects erupting from the surface of a poem otherwise careless of formal sound, but effects of equal exactness to those with which they coincide or change places.

Onomatopoeia is a childish effect if it is carried to the extent to which, for instance, Tennyson carried it in the *Idylls*. So ding'd with consonants is a tournament in the *Idylls* that the sounds predominate over the sense. They invite a standard of judgement which is not literary but sonoral. One is made to test the words as an adjudicator at a musical festival would test sound. In his tournaments Tennyson seems to be expecting to produce the actual sounds, rather than to suggest them. The result is that instead of an effect of the deafening clash of real armour against armour, he provides a tintinnabulation which reminds one of the clockwork tournament in Wells Cathedral.

If one neglects Pope's Homer, it would be fair to both Pope and Tennyson to place Tennyson's

> The moan of doves in immemorial elms

beside Pope's

> With all the mournful family of Yews.[24]

In the first place Tennyson is characteristically trying to produce actual sounds, whereas Pope is translating into mournful sound a mournful visual effect. Moreover, in Pope the line, though serious

---

[23] Quoted from Warburton's edition (1753), vii. 49–53.
[24] *Mor. Essays*, iv. To Burlington, 96.

in itself, is intended in its context to have a comic effect. Pope is amused at the changing fashions in gardens:

> Thro' his young Woods how pleas'd Sabinus stray'd,
> Or sat delighted in the thick'ning shade,
> With annual joy the redd'ning shoots to greet,
> Or see the stretching branches long to meet!
> His Son's fine Taste an op'ner Vista loves,
> Foe to the Dryads of his Father's groves;
> One boundless Green, or flourish'd Carpet views,
> With all the mournful family of Yews;
> The thriving plants ignoble broomsticks made,
> Now sweep those Alleys they were born to shade.

The content of Pope's line is more satisfactory than that of Tennyson's, more valuable as poetry than *immemorial elms*. The image of a dove in an elm tree is not so good as the line is musical. Elm trees are whiskery and coarse trees unless seen at a distance, and at a distance the moan of their doves would be inaudible. This happens with the line, if one neglects the music. In practice one cannot neglect the music. It is much too potent. But the result is that the elm trees are not real ones. The line makes one suspend the working of the brain and accept sounds instead. This is a too ready magic, for a great poet. Pope does not allow music to smother sense and his line is the finer because of it. *Mournful family of yews* brings out qualities that are actually there in yews. Pope writes, as Wordsworth counselled, with his eye on the object, and so his ear is kept in its right place, of its right size. Tennyson shuts his eye and extends an ear like a gramophone horn. He shows himself as a Liszt *manqué*, not as an artist in words. There is no need to give examples of Pope's "beautiful" onomatopoetic effects—most of the examples of description in Chapter One would serve to show how far from childish they are. Pope is frequently not so much echoing sound in sound as equating a visual impression with sound. Many of his onomatopoetic effects are comic ones—onomatopoeia was, he saw, a great sharpener of the satiric weapon. And so there come lines like

> And the high dome re-echoes to his nose[25]

> With gun, drum, trumpet, blunderbuss, and thunder[26]

[25] *Rape of the Lock*, v. 86.
[26] *Im. of Hor.* Sat. II. i. To Mr. Fortescue, 26.

> Yet let me flap this bug with gilded wings,
> This painted child of dirt, that stinks and stings[27]

or a hundred examples in the *Dunciad.*

Pope's distinction between *do* before verbs plural and *did* and *does* before verbs singular is due to the conditions of grammar. If a poet wishes to rime the verb "play" with "day" and to use it as a plural of the present tense, the rime is achieved as easily without an expletive as with one. Instead of ending his line with "the boys do play," he can as easily end it with "the young boys play." But if the word which has to have a rime found for it is still "day," and the subject of the convenient rime "play" happens to be singular, then the poet, who is prevented by grammar from "the boy play," can be allowed to write "the boy does play." But Pope came to be numbered among the "future refiners" at the latest by 1717. The many revised poems in the *Works* of this year, as well as the few new poems, mark together a great technical advance. In the edition of the *Rape of the Lock* in this volume there are several verbal changes, four of which affect passages which contain the word *did.*

> *Sol* thro' white Curtains did his Beams display,
>
>   (1712)

becomes

> *Sol* thro' white curtains shot a tim'rous ray,[28]
>
>   (1717)

> Steel did the Labour of the Gods destroy,
> And strike to Dust th'aspiring Tow'rs of *Troy*;
>
>   (1712)

becomes "Steel could . . ." in 1717: ("th'aspiring" had been changed to "th'Imperial" in 1714.)[29]

> 'Twas this, the morning *Omens* did foretel[l];

becomes ". . . seem'd to tell"; in 1717.[30]

> See the poor Remnants of this slighted Hair!
> My hands shall rend what ev'n thy own did spare.
>
>   (1712)

[27] *Epist. to Arbuthnot,* 309–10.
[28] i. 13.
[29] iii. 173–4.
[30] iv. 161.

becomes

> See the poor remnants of these slighted hairs!
> My hands shall rend what ev'n thy rapine spares;
>
> $(1717)^{31}$

These rules drawn up by the young Pope are simple, of course, in comparison with the methods of Pope's mature work. The second rule, for example, shows almost naïvely against the controlled complexity of the couplets in the satires and the *Dunciad*. There are no rules which would adequately cover the later couplets except the philosophic ones which relate difficult matter to style. One or two simplicities, however, may be noted. Pope prefers almost to the point of insistence that the rime word should be monosyllabic. In the *Rape of the Lock* only three couplets have feminine rimes. These feminine rimes are all intended for particular effects. This is universally true of his rimes. The rime-word is therefore almost always stressed.

Shenstone enunciated a subsidiary rule for him:

> Rhymes, in elegant poetry, should consist of syllables that are long in pronunciation; such as *are, ear, ire, ore, your;* in which a nice ear will find more agreeableness than in these *gnat, net, knit, knot, nut.*[32]

Richard Mant considered Dryden responsible for faulty rimes in Thomas Warton the younger:

> He seems to have copied Dryden, perhaps not always judiciously, in one respect; in terminating a verse with a trisyllable, which will hardly bear the accent, where it will then of necessity be, on the last syllable; and in making the verse so formed the leading verse of the couplet. Thus in the Triumph of Isis,

> > Like Greece in science and in liberty,
> > As Athens learn'd, as Lacedæmon free.

> And in Verses to Sir Joshua Reynolds,

> > With arts unknown before to reconcile
> > The willing Graces to the Gothic pile.[33]

Shenstone stated his rule in its strictest form. Pope finds occasion to

---

[31] Id. 167–8.
[32] *On Writing and Books,* maxim XL.
[33] *The Poetical Works of . . . Thomas Warton* (1802), I. cxxxi.

depart from it, but, when he does so, he is conscious of the departure. And the rime on a weak syllable is rare, but does occur:

> Her Priestless Muse forbids the Good to die,
> And opes the Temple of *Eternity*[34]

(though here, it must be remembered, Pope is quoting almost verbatim from *Comus*).

All through his work Pope seems to have preferred a verb for at least one of the rime-words in a couplet. This was a means of attaining a full stress for the rime. A verb at the end of the first line is often followed by its object in the next line. This provided the couplet with bipartite unity instead of with unified duality.

VI

The rules to Walsh touch on but do not go into the most important characteristic of Pope's versification, its skill in effects of balance. (This matter is not, of course, one wholly of versification: it concerns syntax and meaning itself.) Pope's simplest effects of balance may be studied in the *Pastorals,* in which, of all his poems, the versification had been most "laboured" into correctness.[35] The following examples are not to be regarded as "types." It is best, when studying versification, to consider that there is no such thing as a "type" of line. Lines may resemble each other in structure, but each line in poetry should be seen as a unique phenomenon. Pope of course does not "invent" many of the patterns; his poems are remarkable for their combination of so many varieties of the patterns and in their control of that combination.

> (1) The mossy fountains, and the green retreats!
>
> (*Summer,* 72)

This line of virtually four stresses is fairly common, and had been used on several memorable occasions—for example by Sidney:

> A rosie garland, and a wearie head.[36]

Pope's fondness for this kind of line has been noted by Bridges in his *Milton's Prosody*.[37]

---

[34] *Epil. to Sat.* Dial. ii. 234-5
[35] Spence, 312.
[36] *Astrophel and Stella,* xxxix. 11.
[37] Ed. 1901, p. 14.

(2) But often Pope provides an antithesis as well as an echo. For example,

> So sweetly warble, or so smoothly flow   (*Winter*, 4)

where each adverb is so placed as to balance the other with comparison or contrast. Effects of which these are the simplest examples were favourites with Pope. The late seventeenth century may be said to have discovered their fascination. Shakespeare, for example, sometimes went out of his way to avoid the maximum balance. The last eight lines of *King Lear* form four couplets and the last but one of these reads:

> The waight of this sad time we must obey,
> Speake what we feele, not what we ought to say.

The meaning of this line would have been more correctly expressed if the verbs, which are identical in meaning, had been identical in sound. There is no antithesis between *speak* and *say*, the antithesis is between *feel* and *ought*. Shakespeare obscures this by employing two different verbs, each with the meaning of *say*. This is the kind of "elegant variation" which Yeats found to dislike in the prose of Wilde. Pope would have written that line as

> Say what we feel, not what we ought to say.

And this is the natural way the line should run. Shakespeare here avoids making the clauses echo each other as exactly as possible, even though this helps his meaning.

(3) Sometimes there is balance between two unequal parts:

> With Waller's strains, and Granville's moving lays.
> (*Spring*, 46)

This uneven balance tends to draw attention to what causes the unevenness. In this instance, therefore, *moving* has particular force.

(4) This unequal balance is capable of variation, as, for example:

> More bright than noon, yet fresh as early day.
> (*Spring*, 82)

(5) Two Swains, whom Love kept wakeful, and the Muse.
> (*Spring*, 18)

This indicates the ease with which a statement can qualify for treatment in balanced form. There is no antithesis between the swains, although they are two. But their sleep is troubled by two things and these are so used as to make balance possible.

(6) Another instance of unequal balance from the *Pastorals* is

> Fields ever fresh, and groves for ever green,   (*Winter,* 72)

where the latter half is longer and heavier. (Its alliteration is not only heavier and more complete than the *f* and *fr* of the first half, but is also more widely spaced because of the additional *for*.)

(7) So far the examples have been simple balance or parallels. But the line once divided lent itself as easily to inversion as to parallel. There is this line in the *Pastorals*:

> Fresh as the morn, and as the season fair.   (*Spring,* 20)

This example shows an inversion of music but not an inversion of meaning: the half-lines are parallel in meaning but inverted in music.

(8) The following is one example of the many variations possible:

> Feed fairer flocks, or richer fleeces shear,   (*Summer,* 36)

The two verbs are placed at either end of the line and have the same vowel (and that a long one). And there is the further close-knitting provided by the *fl* alliteration of the two nouns.

(9) The principle of inverted echo without antithesis is applied over an entire couplet in:

> Thro' rocks and caves the name of Delia sounds,
> Delia, each cave and echoing rock rebounds.
> (*Autumn,* 49–50)

Rocks . . . caves . . . Delia . . . Delia . . . cave . . . rock. And then the rime with its effect not of inversion but of parallel. Here although the meaning literally concerns echoes (i.e. parallel noises) Pope prefers to invert the music and so clash that inversion against the parallel sense.

(10) This system of balances and inversions can be much more complicated. For example, *January and May* 742–3, reads:

> 'Tis truth I tell, tho' not in phrase refin'd;
> Tho' blunt my tale, yet honest is my mind.

Here there are two major relationships involving minor ones: (*a*)
the first line balances the second; and (*b*) the second line inverts the
first, so that the first half of the first line balances the second half
of the second, and the second half of the first line balances the first
half of the second.

(11) Sometimes the line is balanced about a point deferred until
the end, or until near the end:

> Now leaves the trees, and flow'rs adorn the ground.
>> (*Spring,* 43)

or

> Nor plains at morn, nor groves at noon delight.
>> (*Spring,* 80)

or

> This mourn'd a faithless, that an absent Love.
>> (*Autumn,* 3)

This kind of balance about a deferred pivot gains in importance
when it is found to link itself to a common effect in Pope. As in
Latin poetry, phrases may in themselves seem nonsense and in English also seem ungrammatical, and yet, when read in their context,
be found to catch up between their tightly packed constituents the
additions needed to relate them into sense. For instance, the phrase
"to their improper, Ill" would be a puzzle on its own. In its context
the pause of the comma represents the equivalent of two words
which make sense of it:

> Two principles in human nature reign;
> Self-love, to urge, and Reason, to restrain;
> Nor this a good, nor that a bad we call,
> Each works its end, to move or govern all:
> And to their proper operation still,
> Ascribe all Good; to their improper, Ill.[38]

The reader takes pleasure in supplying for himself the rest of the
construction by an exercise of memory. This is the kind of way he
has to read Latin, though in Latin the case endings make his task
easier. It is possible for Pope to place reliance on this prehensile

[38] *Essay on Man,* ii. 53 ff.

activity with syntax which he has trained his reader to supply. An ambiguity of grammar which would be fairly serious in some authors becomes almost clarity in him. The realization that, in the following couplet, "turns away" is a transitive verb comes readily since the reader is on the watch for such requirements:

> But Britain, changeful as a Child at play,
> Now calls in Princes, and now turns away.[39]

Or

> Celestial Venus haunts Idalia's groves;
> Diana Cynthus, Ceres Hybla loves.   (*Spring*, 65–6)

Or

> Years following years, steal something ev'ry day,
> At last they steal us from ourselves away;
> In one our Frolics, *one Amusements end*,
> In one a Mistress drops, in one a Friend.[40]

VII

Pope's regard for versification which, to speak approximately, began in the cause of music and continued in the cause of meaning, was a major element in his effect and his effectiveness. Without this correctness, his other kinds of correctness would have been insignificant. The musical formality of the *Pastorals* taught the readers of Pope's poetry that here was a poet who weighed every letter of his verse. Like the gnomes with the snuff he was "to ev'ry atom just." After this exhibition, Pope could be certain of having the requisite attention paid to his effects. And, especially in his later, his consummate, work, it was in full knowledge of this preparedness on the part of his readers that Pope played as if magically with his couplets. It has always been acknowledged that Pope's skill with them was magical or devilish and his importance as a poet has sometimes been left at that. His genius has sometimes been regarded as one expressing itself fully in the supersensitive surface of his technique. But the truth is that this triumph in technique is the coun-

---

[39] *Im. of Hor.* Ep. II. i. To Augustus, 155–6.
[40] *Im. of Hor.* Ep. II. ii. 72 ff.

terpart, and no more than that, of a triumph of content. The *Pastorals* draw on a fund of meaning which every poet can draw on without dust or heat. Schoolboys can as readily decorate the pages of their institutional magazines. But the same measure in the satires, burned out of its lacquered placidity and then frozen again into metal,[41] is the medium for a vision of men and things which is as elaborate as intense. So malleable are its twenty syllables that the couplet never stereotypes the vision. It may sometimes help the vision to its sharpness, in the same way that Dryden said rime sometimes helped him to a thought. Pope may sometimes have changed his manner of seeing men when he began to put what he saw into his couplets. One does not know where more praise is owing, for the vision or the verse. Their interaction may well be equal and opposite. By the time the poem has reached the reader there is no indication which pull was the stronger.

With this as preface one can look at some of the effects of the later use of the couplet. Pope has schooled his readers to expect some particular neat effect of balance or antithesis, if not in every line, at least in every couplet. Having set this standard of uniformity in importance, he proceeds to upset it in a hundred ways. He is utilizing to the full the privilege that for the first poet began with metre, the privilege of variety when once uniformity has been established. It would be impossible to cite every example of his skill. The volumes of his collected poems do that. Take this passage from the ending of the *Epistle to Augustus*:

> Not with such majesty, such bold relief,
> The Forms august, of King, or conqu'ring Chief,
> E'er swell'd on marble; as in verse have shin'd
> (In polish'd verse) the Manners and the Mind.
> Oh! could I mount on the Mæonian wing,
> Your Arms, your Actions, your repose to sing!
> What seas you travers'd, and what fields you fought!
> Your Country's peace, how oft, how dearly bought!
> How barb'rous rage subsided at your word,

[41] Cf. Bevil Higgons, *To Mr. Pope* in *Poems on Several Occasions*, 1717 (*Pope's Own Miscellany*, ed. N. Ault, 81):

> Thy wit in vain the feeble Critick gnaws;
> While the hard metal breaks the serpent's jaws.

After Pope, the other satirists of the century seem to wield an axe of wood, however well they have polished and shaped it.

And Nations wonder'd while they dropp'd the sword!
How, when you nodded, o'er the land and deep,
Peace stole her wing, and wrapt the world in sleep;
'Till earth's extremes your mediation own,
And Asia's Tyrants tremble at your Throne—
But Verse, alas! your Majesty disdains;
And I'm not us'd to Panegyric strains;
The Zeal of Fools offends at any time,
But most of all, the Zeal of Fools in rhyme.
Besides, a fate attends on all I write,
That when I aim at praise, they say I bite.
A vile Encomium doubly ridicules:
There's nothing blackens like the ink of fools.
If true, a woeful likeness: and if lies,
'Praise undeserv'd is scandal in disguise':
Well may he blush, who gives it, or receives;
And when I flatter, let my dirty leaves
(Like Journals, Odes, and such forgotten things
As Eusden, Philips, Settle, writ of Kings)
Clothe spice, line trunks, or flutt'ring in a row,
Befringe the rails of Bedlam and Soho.[42]

In this passage the first two couplets form together one unit, divided
after *marble*. The latter part of that unit has to provide weight
enough in its one and a half lines to balance the two and a half
lines of the former part. This balance Pope manages to achieve,
because of the iron emphasis he places on *in verse,* an emphasis reinforced by (*In polish'd verse*). His meaning requires that emphasis
and the couplets are arranged so as to require it, too. This is their
broad outline. One can further note that the second part itself manages to engineer two sets of balance. And the second line of the first
couplet has two pauses each marking the limits of the balanced
phrases. What lies between, i.e., ", of King," is the pivot. Usually
the pivot of a balanced line is a pause or a subdued stress. Here it
is a phrase of two words. That is the account of the line as music.
But as meaning the balance is between this two-word phrase and
the phrase forming the rest of the line as one reads forward. Music
and meaning are here two contraries locked in one embrace. There
are other effects, of alliteration (*m* and *k*) and onomatopoeia (the

[42] *Im. of Hor.* Ep. ii. i. To Augustus, 390 ff.

roundness of *swell'd* and the brightness of *shin'd*). At line six the rising line drops suddenly to bathos,

> Your Arms, your Actions, your repose. . . .

That bathos was all the more complete since the cultivated reader would be thrown off his guard by remembering Pomfret's line in *Cruelty and Lust*:

> Your Sword, your Conduct, and your Cause attend.[43]

Line seven leisurely blows its twin balloons of wonder, while line eight reserves the huge task of bathos to its last two words. *Dearly bought* changes the whole apparent compliment which preceded, and *oft* which had formerly seemed congratulatory strikes in retrospect its own defamatory blow. There is nothing technically important in the next four couplets. In the couplet following,

> The Zeal of Fools offends at any time,
> But most of all, the Zeal of Fools in rhyme.

the balance—as far as music goes—completes itself by the end of the fourth foot of the last line, so that the remnant, *in rhyme*, which completes the balance of meaning, breaks like a shot from a gun. The last but two of the couplets is broken in half. Its first line finishing off what has been progressing through the last five couplets, its second line beginning, as if from zero, the rise which proceeds like the perpendicular mounting of an aeroplane to a point marked by *trunks* from which summit begins the descent into silence. It is difficult to see what Wordsworth meant when he described Pope's couplets as "too timidly balanced." [44]

The above passage may be taken as an ordinary sample of Pope's couplets in the satires. There is no end to his variety. He can break them into small fragments:

> Shut, shut the door, good John! fatigu'd, I said,
> Tie up the knocker, say I'm sick, I'm dead.
> The Dog-star rages! nay 'tis past a doubt,
> All Bedlam, or Parnassus, is let out. . . .[45]

[43] *Poems*, ed. 1736, 69.
[44] Letter to Dyce, May 1830.
[45] *Ep. to Arbuthnot*, 1 ff.

Or this dialogue of barks:

> *F.* . . . Spare then the Person, and expose the Vice.
> *P.* How, Sir? not damn the Sharper, but the Dice?
> Come on then, Satire! gen'ral, unconfin'd,
> Spread thy broad wing, and souse on all the kind.
> Ye Statesmen, Priests, of one Religion all!
> Ye Tradesmen vile, in Army, Court, or Hall,
> Ye Rev'rend Atheists—*F.* Scandal! name them! Who?
>   *P.* Why that's the thing you bid me not to do.
> Who starv'd a Sister, who foreswore a Debt,
> I never nam'd; the Town's enquiring yet.
> The pois'ning Dame—*F.* You mean—*P.* I don't.—
>   *F.* You do!
> *P.* See, now I keep the Secret, and not you! [46]

Or this, in which the antithesis straddles over two and a half lines, the pivotal point taking up the odd half line in the middle:

> If, when the more you drink, the more you crave,
> You tell the Doctor; when the more you have,
> The more you want; why not with equal ease
> Confess as well your Folly, as Disease? [47]

Pope sometimes varies the structure of the couplet by placing a normal line partly in the first half of the couplet and partly in the second. For example

> In vain, in vain—the all-composing Hour
> Resistless falls: the Muse obeys the Pow'r.[48]

Here "In vain, in vain, the Muse obeys the Pow'r" and "the all-composing Hour resistless falls" are normal lines. But their normality is complicated, since the first one has its two component parts severed by the placing of a complete pentameter between them, and the second is broken into unequal sections by coming up against the rime-word. Pope used balance and inversion when he wanted them. He used a less geometrical line when he wanted that:

> Eyes the calm Sun-set of thy various Day[49]

> Lull with Amelia's liquid name the Nine[50]

---

[46] *Epil. to Sat.* Dial. ii. 12 ff.
[47] *Im. of Hor.* Ep. ii. 2. 212 ff.
[48] *Dunc.* iv. 627–8.
[49] *Epistle to Robert, Earl of Oxford*, 38.
[50] *Im. of Hor.* Sat. ii. i. To Mr. Fortescue, 31.

> Coffee, (which makes the politician wise,
> And see thro' all things with his half-shut eyes)[51]

> And Shadwell nods the Poppy on his brows[52]

> And universal Darkness buries All.[53]

The undecorated smoothness of such lines is all the smoother for the reader's release from the pointed style either of the immediate or the general context. Pope, like Milton, found such lines were demanded by the architecture of the paragraph.

In the *Essay on Criticism* and much more in the *Essay on Man* Pope is using what amounts almost to a different kind of heroic couplet. The couplets of the *Essay on Man* bound on feathered heels. Pope is seldom so easy to read as Dryden, whose verses are sometimes too glib. But he attains something of Dryden's speed in this poem. The following is a fair sample:

> Whate'er the Passion, knowledge, fame, or pelf,
> Not one will change his neighbour with himself.
> The learn'd is happy nature to explore,
> The fool is happy that he knows no more;
> The rich is happy in the plenty giv'n,
> The poor contents him with the care of Heav'n.
> See the blind beggar dance, the cripple sing,
> The sot a hero, lunatic a king;
> The starving chemist in his golden views
> Supremely blest, the poet in his Muse.[54]

The concluding invocation to Bolingbroke adapts this style to as light a lyric as Pope ever shows:

> Come then, my Friend! my Genius! come along;
> Oh master of the poet, and the song!
> And while the Muse now stoops, or now ascends,
> To Man's low passions, or their glorious ends,
> Teach me, like thee, in various nature wise,
> To fall with dignity, with temper rise;
> Form'd by thy converse, happily to steer
> From grave to gay, from lively to severe;

---

[51] *Rape of the Lock,* iii. 117–18.
[52] *Dunc.* iii. 22.
[53] Id. iv. 656.
[54] ii. 261 ff.

> Correct with spirit, eloquent with ease,
> Intent to reason, or polite to please. . . .[55]

As befits a conclusion it then develops a more weighty rhythm.

VIII

No poet has confined himself as strictly as Pope did to a confined metre and yet managed so often to astonish the reader with the unpredictable. Some of the examples given above are sufficient to show that Pope's greatest triumph in the couplet lies in his making it dramatic. He can make it sound like actual passionate speech. The Elizabethan dramatists left the couplet for blank verse when they wanted to get similar effects. But Pope's sense of the capacities of the couplet forbade such a transition. And in consequence of his realization of that sense, the reader is excited by the mere distance between these new couplets and Waller's, between the *Imitations of Horace* and *Windsor Forest*. So stately, decorative, courtly a metre is now embodying the accents of normal speech. The complex art is so perfect that it is hidden. The lines read themselves.

> Pretty! in amber to observe the forms
> Of hairs, or straws, or dirt, or grubs, or worms!
> The things, we know, are neither rich nor rare,
> But wonder how the devil they got there.[56]

> Why am I ask'd what next shall see the light?
> Heav'ns! was I born for nothing but to write? [57]

> I lose my patience, and I own it too,
> When works are censur'd, not as bad but new.[58]

> Tho' still some traces of our rustic vein
> And splay-foot verse, remain'd, and will remain.[59]

> But after all, what would you have me do?
> When out of twenty I can please not two.[60]

[55] iv. 373 ff.
[56] *Ep. to Arbuthnot*, 169–72.
[57] Id. 271–2.
[58] *Im. of Hor.* Ep. ii. i. To Augustus, 115–16.
[59] Id. 270–1.
[60] *Im. of Hor.* Ep. ii. ii. 80–1.

> F. Why then so few commended?
>   P. Not so fierce!
> Find you the Virtue, and I'll find the Verse.[61]
>
> Yes, I am proud; I must be proud to see
> Men not afraid of God, afraid of me.[62]

With these effects goes that of the long word with a single stress. To begin with, Pope used these words for their gravity. Donne had realized the ponderous value of such words: for instance in the famous

> we are swallowed up, irreparably, irrevocably, irrecoverably, irre-mediably.[63]

In pronouncing words of this kind the reader compensates for the vague pother of weak accents by trebly reinforcing the strong accents. Pope uses them first as Donne did:

> Full in the midst proud Fame's imperial seat,
> With jewels blaz'd, magnificently great.[64]
>
> . . . the God's Array
> Refulgent, flash'd intolerable Day.[65]

Later Pope came to see the value of these words for producing variously graded effects of contempt:

> With scornful mien, and various toss of air,
> Fantastic, vain, and insolently fair.[66]
>
> Alive, ridiculous, and dead, forgot! [67]

It becomes one of the favourite weapons of the *Dunciad.*

> Cibberian forehead, and Cibberian brain.[68]
>
> Cibberian forehead, or Cimmerian gloom.[69]

---

[61] *Epil. to Sat.* Dial. ii. 104–5.
[62] Id. 208–9.
[63] Sermon LXVI.
[64] *Temple of Fame,* 249–50.
[65] *Iliad,* viii. 53–4. Cf. Dryden, *Knight's Tale,* iii. 81.
[66] *The Looking Glass,* 1–2.
[67] *Mor. Ess.* ii. *Of the Characters of Women,* 248.
[68] *Dunciad,* i. 218.
[69] Id. iv. 532.

To where Fleet-ditch with disemboguing streams
Rolls the large tribute of dead dogs to Thames.[70]

Not so bold Arnall; with a weight of skull,
Furious he drives, precipitately dull.[71]

a skull,
Of solid proof, impenetrably dull.[72]

A friend in glee, ridiculously grim.[73]

[70] Id. ii. 271–2.
[71] Id. 315–16.
[72] Id. iii. 25–6.
[73] Id. 154.

Rhetoric and Poems

by *William K. Wimsatt, Jr.*

. . . οἷον εἰ καὶ τὰ ὀνόματα μεταφορὰ εἴη καὶ
μεταφορὰ τοιαδὶ καὶ ἀντίθεσις καὶ παρίσωσις.

—Rhetoric, III, xi

When we seek to confront two such elusive entities as a theory of poems and poems themselves and to determine relations between these two, I think there is much to be said for placing them first, tentatively, in their most generic and noncommittal relation. There is much to be said for the conjunctional form of title commonly given to the academic paper: X *and* Y, Shakespeare *and* Hall's Chronicle, Theory *and* Poems. I for one find it convenient to distinguish five main types of relation between theory and poems, all five of which are frequently to be observed in critical and historical studies, though often more or less confused.

I.   There is for one thing the kind of relation between theory and poems with which we are concerned when our interest is chiefly in the theory itself, that is, when we try to describe and assess a given theory as objectively as we can with reference to whatever general norms for poems and hence for theory we possess. Is the classical theory of imitation in any sense a good or fruitful theory of poems? Or the classical theory of poems? Or the classical theory of ornament and system of rhetoric? Or do these deserve to be completely demolished, as in the Crocean history of Aesthetic? Is Matthew Arnold's view of the high seriousness and critical function of poems the right view? Or, does it, as Tate and others have argued, deliver poems into the hands of science and morals? My purpose at the moment is not to maintain the importance of such questions, but merely to note their occurrence.

II. It may at times be difficult to distinguish between such a general evaluative interest in theory and what I consider a second kind of interest, that with which we approach a theorist, especially a technical or rhetorical theorist and his cousins of the trivium, the grammarian and logician, for the purpose of borrowing tools which we shall put to the partly unpredictable uses of our own analysis: *fable,* or *character,* or *metaphor* from Aristotle, *antithesis* or *parallel* from the rhetoricians, *sentences,* for that matter, and *nouns* and *verbs* from the grammarians. To do this may imply that we think a theorist a good theorist of poems, and yet I believe it may come short of that, in so far as concepts themselves may come short of integrated or achieved theory, and also in so far as this borrowing extends readily, and perhaps most profitably, to the less literary philosophers, the grammarian and logician.

To look in the historical direction, I should say that when we take up the more generic concepts of rhetoric, grammar, and logic, we ought to be on our guard against imputing to them special connections with the poems of any specific period—as would happen if one were to note the Aristotelian "categories" in Renaissance logic and read in them an influence on the imagery of Drayton or Donne. Richards in his *Philosophy of Rhetoric* has found the concept of the morpheme as defined by Bloomfield a useful one for explaining certain powers of words. But it would be somewhat wide of the mark to learn that Auden had read either Richards or Bloomfield and from that go on to discover such elements as morphemes in Auden's poems. The idea of the circulation of the blood was expounded by Harvey in 1616, but we do not conceive that it was about that time that blood began to circulate in the human body.

III. A third relation between theory and poems is that which obtains when a given theory does have a specific, historical relation to a poem, but has this in virtue of the special fact that it appears in the poem as part of the poem's meaning or content. One will recall numerous instances in the history of English poetry: Chaucer's burlesque of Geoffrey of Vinsauf in the mock heroic of the cock and the fox, Stephen Hawes' celebration of "golden" words in his *Pastime of Pleasure,* the Horatian arts of poetry (especially that of Pope), Mark Akenside's *Pleasures of the Imagination,* Wordsworth's *Prelude,* and Shelley's *Ode to the West Wind* (where the sparks from the unextinguished priestly hearth mingle with the sparks of "inextinguishable thought" which appear twice in his prose *Defense of Poetry*). This relation between theory and poems is that which for the most part obtains in historical studies of the neutrally observational type—but often with some implication that the relation established is of a more formal, or actually theoretical, sort.

IV.   A fourth relation between theory and poems which I believe it worth while to distinguish is again a specific historical relation, that which obtains when in a given era a theory helps to determine poems not as subject matter but as an influence or cause why they are written in a certain way. Perhaps the most important thing to note about this relation is that (like number III) it does not require that the theory as theory be an adequate account of the poems. The classic theory concerning imitation of models, for instance, had a close bearing on the Augustan vogue of translations, paraphrases, and "imitations." Yet a theory of models is never really a literary theory, only a practical rule of inspiration. And the classic theory in particular seemed almost unconscious of the paramount factor of parody, or allusiveness, which worked in the most lively Augustan instances. Again, the massive theory of epic which prevailed in that day might be taken as a partial cause of Blackmore's *Prince Arthur* or, in jocular reversal, of *The Rape of the Lock*, or *The Dunciad*. But there are no successfully serious epics with which the theory can be compared. During the same period, the doctrine *Ut pictura poesis* may have joined with empirical views of imagination to determine the subject matter of some poems; it may have been responsible for certain instances of the pictorial fallacy or opaqueness in word painting; but, as Lessing was partly to show, the analogy between words and marble or paint is of limited service for analyzing the positive qualities of verbal art.

V.   A fifth relation between theory and poems, that which will be the final focus of our argument, is that which obtains when in any historical era we can discern a specific affinity between theory as such and poems; that is, when what the theory says seems to be a specially appropriate description of what the poems are. Such a relation may of course coincide with the causal relation which we have just considered. There may be instances of a close causal connection between theory and poems and at the same time a high degree of validity for the theory as theory. A successful poet may be shown to have read a certain theory with profit, or he may even, though this

I believe is rare, succeed in uttering a theory which explains his own poems. But these are matters for another sort of inquiry. It is only by keeping clear of such intentionalistic complications that we can focus upon the literary and critical issue: that is, the degree of resemblance between the theory and the poems or the adequacy of the theory to describe the poems.

To show a real correspondence between the theory of an era and the poems of the era would be, I take it, one of the most proper concerns of the student of criticism in its historical aspect, and to show that the theory gave an adequate account of the poems would be his masterpiece. Such an achievement, we ought at the same time to note, would be a special challenge to the student of either theory or poems who was interested in universal definitions or norms. Poems in different eras, it is assumed, will be to some extent different. But theory deals with universals. It is more disconcerting to find the theory of successive ages different than to find the poems different. No matter how well we, with our historical desires, succeed in localizing the theory or assimilating it to the poems of its own age, we can still see that the theory itself aims at the universal. If the poems and the theory vary in step with each other, then I suppose a great appearance of support is offered to historical relativism —unless indeed one's dialectic rises to reconciling certain valid special theories of poetry, say the metaphysical theory of wit and the romantic theory of imagination, in a more inclusive harmony. Or unless one is brave enough to decide in a given case that both poems and theory are bad—as Yvor Winters has not scrupled to say the poems of Poe are bad because they perfectly illustrate Poe's theory, a deliquescent version of romantic imagination.

Not every theory found in a given age is equally relevant to describing the poems of that age. There are not only bad theories which have no special bearing on any kind of poems, but another and more important kind, those of such general significance (if not complete truth) that they transcend a special application to the poems of their age. Such, for example, I should call the neoclassic doctrine that poetry reveals the generic or universal. Despite the game of omber and the all too specific and solid Dunces, the doctrine of the universal is if correctly interpreted a valid doctrine, and furthermore it is itself universal, that is, neither more nor less true of good neoclassic poems than of good poems in any other mode. Or the related doctrine that "Style is the dress of thought" [1] —true poetry is "nature to advantage dressed." This would appear to be the Augustan version of a paradox which literary criticism has so far by no means solved. Today we speak of art signs as iconic or as calling attention to their own excellence, or we speak of poetry as intensely realized meaning, or as dramatized meaning, or perhaps as structure of meaning. Poetic meaning still seems to contain other meanings and to make use of them, but seems not to be tested in the end by the same norms. The doctrine that style is the dress of thought is as much our concern as it was Pope's, and, whatever its degree of truth, it applies no more specially to Augustan poems than to any other kind. [2]

In somewhat the same way I believe we should have to discuss the whole classical theory of imitation and the antitheses deriving from the theory and flourishing in Pope's time, between art and nature, between invention and imitation of models, between wit and judgment, between genius and the rules. Or perhaps some of these theoretical formulas do show a special relation to the poems of the age, though one which will make acceptable sense to us only after a certain adjustment. One such example seems to me of importance here as a partial frame of reference for the more specific rhetorical ideas which I wish to discuss. I have in mind the Augustan concept of "correctness," which, distinguished from greatness or "genius," sometimes took the form of an ideal, as in the well known advice of Walsh to Pope: that there had been *great* English poets, but no great poet who was *correct;* but sometimes also was conceived as a fault or limitation, as in Addison's *Spectators,* Nos. 160 and 291, where the untrammeled productions of ancient Genius are preferred to the scrupulous nicety or correctness of the moderns. As Sir Joshua Reynolds was later to phrase it: "So far, indeed, is the presence of genius from implying an absence of faults, that they are considered by many as its inseparable companions." [3] The paradox was still

---

[1] Samuel Wesley, *Epistle to a Friend* (London, 1700), 15.

[2] We have long ago been equipped by Professor Lowes with a theory of Convention and Revolt which provides for the appearance of poetic diction in every poetic generation. If then we have a theory equal to discriminating between good and bad poetic diction within a given age (I am not sure that we have), I do not see that it can apply any more to the age of Pope than to that of Wordsworth or that of Eliot.

[3] *Eleventh Discourse,* second paragraph.

vital in the next century, when Ruskin preferred the *imperfections,*
that is, the irregularities, of Gothic architecture to the *perfection,*
that is the regularity, of geometric ornaments in Greek architecture.
This bizarre critical tradition seems to arise from the capacity of the
term *correctness* to be taken not only (1) as a general term of value
(certainly what is "correct" is right and good), but (2) as a more
specially descriptive term, meaning something like symmetry and
something like restraint and precision. It is in the latter sense of
course that we shall have to take it if we apply it to Augustan poems
—if we wish to say that Pope followed the advice of Walsh and
became a *correct* poet. The other sense will hardly go with the
liberal and usually accepted view that Shakespeare's verse and
rhetoric fit what Shakespeare is saying, just as Pope's fit what Pope
is saying. In the final sense of poetic value, each kind of good poetry
is correct.

II

It is under the head of correctness in its limited sense that the
most precise resemblances between neoclassic theory and neoclassic
poems seem to be available—I mean in the rhetoric of the closed
couplet. Perhaps it is not too much to say that the resemblance between theory and poems which obtains here is one of the most precise in the history of literature and criticism—that the hexameter
couplets of Boileau and Racine and the pentameters of Dryden and
Pope represent the maximum fulfillment of a classic technical
theory. Yet the relation between theory and poems which obtains
even here is not, as we shall see, strictly a synchronous one.

The year 1935 gave us two highly competent studies, one by Professor Williamson, concerning the history of English couplet theory
from Puttenham in 1589 to Edward Bysshe in 1702; and one by Miss
Wallerstein, concerning the practice of English couplet writers,
from the poems of Grimald in Tottel's *Miscellany* to Denham's lines
on the Thames in 1655. Professors Williamson and Wallerstein, writing from these different directions, theory and poems, produced
notably harmonious accounts of couplet rhetoric: the sententious
closure, the balanced lines and half-lines, the antithesis and inversion, the strict metric and accordingly slight but telling variations,
the constantly close and tensile union of what are called musical
with logical and rhetorical effects. The dates embraced in the works

of these two writers may, however, invite the reflection that so far
as the couplets of Alexander Pope (at the English neoclassic zenith)
conform to a theory of rhetoric, it is to a theory which had reached
its full development a generation or two earlier. For a good account
in English of the figures of speech and thought to be found in Pope's
verse one will perhaps go even as far back as Puttenham's *Arte of
English Poesie.* In Puttenham one will find too the main metrical
rules and even the important emphasis on the caesura. Edward
Bysshe's *Art of English Poetry,* which may plausibly be taken as
representative of what had happened to English poetics by the time
Pope was a youth, says nothing at all of the figures, though it carries the metrics to a far greater degree of rigidity than Puttenham
and includes the now famous dictionary of rhymes. The classical
figures of speech and thought, joined with poetics during the Middle
Ages, had by Bysshe's time been reseparated from poetics and confined again in the treatises on prose rhetoric—such as that of
Thomas Blount, *The Academie of Eloquence* (1654) or that of John
Smith, *The Mysterie of Rhetorique Unvail'd* (1657).[4] Puttenham's
Arte of 1589, though it is only one of many English accounts of
rhetorical figures up to Pope's day, remains the most lively and in-
formative and the most precisely focused upon poems.[5]

Pope himself in Chapters X and XI of *Peri Bathous* wrote a comic
treatment of "Tropes and Figures" (including "The Antithesis, or
See-Saw"), and he once observed to Spence that the "stiffness of
style" in Wycherley's plays was "occasioned by his always studying
for antithesis." But neither in his *Essay on Criticism,* nor in his
remarks to Spence, nor in his letters, even the elaborate letter on
versification to Walsh, has Pope anything substantial to say about
the system of artful figures which later critics have considered characteristic of his couplets. Pope talks of the metrical "niceties," of
suiting the sound to the sense, of caesura, of expletives, and of
hiatus, or of avoiding extravagance in diction. The rhetorical sinews
of the kind of verse in which he was the champion—the essential
patterns where Waller's strength and Denham's sweetness joined,
where Dryden had achieved the long resounding march and energy

---

[4] Smith's *Mysterie* was apparently the reigning popular rhetoric of the age,
reaching a tenth edition in 1721.
[5] It was known by Ben Jonson and perhaps by Drayton, and was copied by
the mid-century metrical theorist of Poole's *Parnassus*—perhaps John Dryden.
George Williamson, "The Rhetorical Pattern of Neo-Classical Wit," in *Modern
Philology,* XXXIII (1935), 59–60.

divine[6]—these perhaps had been learned so well by Pope as a boy that he could forget them. "It was our family priest," he told Spence, "who taught me the figures, accidence, and first part of grammar." In later life perhaps the figures were assumed by Pope under the general head of "correctness." At any rate he seems to have been able to take them for granted.

Among the hundred odd figures, "auricular," "sensable," and "sententious," presented by Puttenham, there are certain ones, a rather large number if all subdivisions of the main types are counted, which would seem to be fundamental to the logic of the formally ordered verbal style. Thus, *"Parison, or the figure of even [clauses]," "Omoioteleton, or the figure of like-loose [like endings],"* and *"Anaphora, or the figure of report"* (that is, repetition of a word at the beginning of successive clauses) are the figures in Puttenham which refer to formal parallels and which under one set of terms or another are a constant part of the rhetorical tradition from Puttenham back to Aristotle. Contrast or antithesis is the natural accompaniment of parallel. This appears in Puttenham as *"Antitheton, or the quarreller, otherwise called the overthwart or rencounter."* Wherever there is a parallel, there is a distinction, and wherever a distinction, the possibility of a paradox, an antithesis, or at least a modulation. Thus, to illustrate now from the verse of Pope:

> Who sees with equal eye, as God of all,
> A hero perish, or a sparrow fall.

> Favours to none, to all she smiles extends;
> Oft she rejects, but never once offends.

> Survey the WHOLE, nor seek slight faults to find
> Where nature moves, and rapture warms the mind.

This brings us, still quite naturally, to a third group of figures, those distinguished by Puttenham as *"Zeugma, or the single supply"* and *"Sillepsis, or the double supply."* Zeugma is further distinguished by Puttenham into *Prozeugma* (or the Ringleader), *Mezozeugma* (or the Middlemarcher), and *Hypozeugma* (or the Rerewarder), accordingly as the zeugma, or yoking word, occurs at the beginning, the middle, or the end of a total construction. He treats zeugma among the figures "merely *auricular* in that they reach no furder than the

---

[6] "I learned versification wholly from Dryden's works." Joseph Spence, *Anecdotes*, S. W. Singer, ed. (London, 1820), 212.

eare," and among figures "that work by defect," that is, by the absence of "some little portion of speech." He does not say anything about the relation of zeugma to parallel. But we might observe that zeugma or ellipsis[7] is almost the inevitable effect of a tightened and precise economy of parallel. If A, B, C and X, B, Z are presented, then A, B, C and X, Z is an easy result; or if A, B and X, B, then A, B and X—in the more usual case, the parallel of two elements. Thus, in Pope's verse:

> *Who* could not win the mistress, wooed the maid. (Prozeugma)
>
> And now a bubble *burst,* and now a world. (Mezozeugma)
>
> Where nature moves, and rapture warms the *mind*
> (Hypozeugma)

And, to note a special and significant kind of zeugma that occurs in Pope's verse, such examples as these:

> Or lose her heart, or necklace, at a ball.
>
> Or stain her honour or her new brocade.

This is metaphor. I mention it here not simply to list the figure of metaphor among Pope's accomplishments. Puttenham also duly lists "*Metaphora,* or the figure of transport." But here it seems to me curious, and worth noting, though it is not noted by Puttenham, that a series of several logical steps, distinction, parallel, then simplification or canceling a common element, has led us to metaphor, something that has often, and notably by some in Pope's day, been considered the very essence of the irrational or merely imaginative in poetry. Let us carry our series to its conclusion, returning to Puttenham for help. Consider the figure of "*Sillepsis,* or the double supply," which occurs according to Puttenham when a verb is used either with a double grammatical congruity, or in a double sense.[8] The latter may be thus illustrated from Pope's verse.

> Here thou, great Anna! whom three realms obey,
> Dost sometimes counsel take—and sometimes tea.

---

[7] The terms "ellipsis," "zeugma," and "syllepsis" have been used variously by English writers. See *O.E.D.* under "zeugma"; John Smith, *Mysterie of Rhetorique,* 1657, under "zeugma"; H. W. Fowler, *Modern English Usage,* under "ellipsis" and "technical terms: zeugma." It is sufficient for our purpose to follow Puttenham.

[8] Cp. Pope, *Peri Bathous,* chap. X, on "The Paranomasia, or Pun," "where a Word, like the tongue of a jackdaw, speaks twice as much by being split."

> With earnest eyes, and round unthinking face,
> He first the snuff-box opened, then the case.

Worse and worse. We have now descended from logical parallel and ellipsis, through metaphor, into pun. In short, by starting with what might have been thought the most logical and prosaic aspects of Pope's verse (both *Antitheton* and *Parison* were mentioned by Puttenham as figures specially related to prose), and by moving through a few shades of meaning we have arrived at the very things which the modern critic Empson noticed first in looking for the shiftiness or ambiguity of this kind of verse. We may note too, as we pass, that the distinction between the two figures last described, the metaphoric zeugma and the punning syllepsis, is not always easy. Take the couplet preceding that about counsel and tea:

> Here Britain's statesmen oft the fall foredoom
> Of foreign Tyrants and of Nymphs at home.

It depends on how technically and specifically we are accustomed to think of a "fall" from virtue, whether we take "the fall of tyrants and of nymphs" as metaphor or pun.

But now I should like to backtrack into an area of rhetoric different from antitheses and parallels, though joining them or branching off from them, in Puttenham's *Arte,* under the figure *Anaphora,* the word or phrase repeated at the beginning of successive clauses. Puttenham supplies a large battery of figures in this area: "counter-turns," "redoubles," "eccho sounds," "swifte repeates," "rebounds," and "counterchanges," among which the pick is *"Traductio,* or the tranlacer." This, says Puttenham, "is when ye turne and tranlace a word into many sundrie shapes as the Tailor doth his garment, and after that sort do play with him in your dittie." The principle of these figures is that a word or root is repeated in various syntactic positions, and sometimes in various forms, with a consequent shifting, version, turning, or translacing of the sense. These are the figures which Dryden in 1693 calls "turns, both on the words and on the thought," and which, despite a report by Dryden to the contrary, are nowhere better illustrated than in Milton's *Paradise Lost.* The turn is one of the main sinews of the sense variously drawn out from line to line. "So Man . . . Shall . . . die, And dying rise, and rising with him raise His Brethren, ransomed with his own dear life." Toward the end of the seventeenth century this kind of wordplay had fallen into comparative disfavor.[9] We need not be surprised that in Pope's verse it is less heavily underscored.

> Yet graceful ease, and sweetness void of pride,
> Might hide her faults, if Belles had faults to hide.

> Jilts ruled the state, and statesmen farces writ,
> Nay wits had pensions, and young lords had wit.

These are lighter turns than Milton's—and at the same time wittier turns. By a different route we have arrived at somewhat the same terminus as when we pursued the forms of logical parallel, that is, at something like illogical pun—a difference being that whereas before we found the single word of two meanings, we find now two or more words of similar sound and one or another kind of play between their meanings.

In the couplet rhetoric which we have been examining, the abstract logic of parallel and antithesis is complicated and offset, then, by the turn and by the metaphoric zeugma and the punning syllepsis. It is complicated also by one other element of alogical counterpattern—the most important by far and, I believe, the apex of all the rhetorical phenomena which we have been considering—that is, rhyme. "Symphonie" or "cadence," says Puttenham, meaning rhyme, is "all the sweetnesse and cunning in our vulgar poesie." And here we have too, as it happens, a theoretical statement by the master of practice. Pope told Spence:

> I have nothing to say for rhyme but that I doubt whether a poem can support itself without it in our language, unless it be stiffened with such strange words as are likely to destroy our language itself. The high style that is affected so much in blank verse would not have been borne even in Milton had not his subject turned so much on such strange, out-of-the-world things as it does.

Rhyme, in this offhand statement, seems to be something like a stiffening or support of verse, rather than the commonly conceived music. Puttenham remarks that the Greeks and Latins "used a manner of speech, by clauses of like termination, which they called *homoioteleuton*," a thing somewhat like vernacular rhyme, yet different. The difference between *rhyme* and *homoeoteleuton* is, in

---

[9] Butler in his often quoted character of *A Quibbler* had predicted its decline. Dryden's enthusiasm was waning in his Dedication of the *Aeneis* and Preface to the *Fables*.

fact, one of the most profound of rhetorical differences. For *ho-moeoteleuton,* the repetition of inflected endings (morphemes) to support logical parallels of statement, is that which added to parallel and antithesis makes the rhetoric of pointed prose. But rhyme, the use of alogical or accidental sound resemblances between different morphemes, is that which added to parallel and antithesis makes the rhetoric of the pointed couplet. As the turn was the characteristic stiffener of classical Latin verse and of its English counterpart the blank verse of Milton, so rhyme was the characteristic stiffener of vernacular verse and especially of the couplet.

> Whatever Nature has in worth denied
> She gives in large recruits of needful Pride.

The music of the rhyme is mental; it consists in an odd, almost magic, relation of phonetic likeness which encourages us to perceive and believe in a meaning otherwise asserted by the words of the couplet. The nonparallel or chiastic[10] chime (worth*1*-denied,*2* gives*2'*-Pride*1'*) is the phonetic expression of the unhappy receptivity of the mental void. The principle is well illustrated in a few of Pope's proper-name rhymes, where we may note an affinity for a certain old-fashioned and childish form of riddle to be found in the pages of *The Farmer's Almanac.* Why is A like B? Because the name of A or of something connected with A means B or something connected with B. Why is a dog dressed warmer in summer than in winter? Because in winter he wears a fur coat, and in summer he wears a fur coat and pants. Why is a certain poet a dangerous influence upon married women? Because his name sounds like something.

> Poor Cornus sees his frantic wife elope,
> And curses Wit, and Poetry, and Pope.

Why is a certain scholar a graceless figure? Because his name shows it.

> Yet ne'er one sprig of laurel graced these ribalds,
> From slashing *Bentley* down to pidling *Tibbalds.*

Here the words *sprig* and *pidling* play a part too in proving what it means to have a name like that. *Paronomasia,* "*Prosonomasia,* or the Nicknamer," is Puttenham's name for this figure. "As, *Tiberius*

---

[10] The figure of *Antimetavole* found in Puttenham is a combination of chiasmus and the turn.

the Emperor, because he was a great drinker of wine, they called him by way of derision to his owne name, *Caldius Biberius Nero,* in steade of *Claudius Tiberius Nero."* But Puttenham, I admit, does not connect this figure with the "symphonie" or "tunable consente" called rhyme.

Poetry, it would appear, is not an affair of pure ideas—where X or Y could by agreement be substituted for any given word—nor strictly speaking is it an affair of sound as such or verbal music. Poetry is both sense and sound, and not by parallel or addition, but by a kind of union—which may be heard in onomatopoeia and expressive rhythm and in various modes of suggestion, extension, and secret verbal functioning. Of these the pun and its cousin the rhyme are but the most extravagant instances. Poetry exploits the *facts* of language, that words *do* mean so and so and acquire a kind of prerogative to do this.

English critics of the Renaissance, among them Milton and latterly even Dryden, were inclined to be hard on rhyme, calling it a jingling bondage, rude, beggarly, and Gothic. (Even Puttenham remarks that rhyme was brought into Greek and Latin by "barbarous souldiers out of the Campe.") The Earl of Roscommon in polished couplets recited the bardic and monkish history of rhyme and hailed the glorious day when the British Muse should put on the rhymeless majesty of Rome and Athens. Critics of Pope's day—Dennis, Felton, and Gildon—took the same cue and called rhyme "soft," "effeminate," "emasculating." [11] At the same time, as we have seen, the basic figures of parallel and antithesis originated as prose figures and by their nature tended to abstraction, order, and regular lines. Other factors too in the latter half of the seventeenth century—the scientific mistrust of inventive imagination, the plain style of scientists and pulpit orators, a refined and moderate way of talking adopted by society—are sometimes supposed to have helped in making the Augustan couplet poems the nearest things to prose poems in our language. Dryden and Pope, we remember Arnold said, are "classics of our prose." This of course we do not fully believe any more. Yet I suggest that we are confronted by an extremely curious and challenging situation in the heroic couplet of Pope: where a verse basically ordered by the rational rules of parallel and antithesis and showing at least a certain characteristic restraint of imagination, as

[11] *Critical Works of John Dennis,* E. N. Hooker, ed. (Baltimore, 1939), I, 297, 375–79, 430, 499–500.

contrasted say with metaphysical verse, at the same time is found to rely so heavily for "support" or "stiffening"—to use again the terms of Pope—on so barbarous and Gothic a device as rhyme.

In tracing the parallel between Puttenham and Pope we have observed perhaps the maximum degree of resemblance that obtains between the poems of Pope and any contemporary or nearly contemporary set of poetic rules. At the same time we have scarcely been able to refrain at each step from noting the incompleteness of Puttenham when compared to the fullness of the poetic actuality, even at the level specifically cited from Puttenham, the rhetorical. How far, we may now return and ask, does Puttenham or does any other rhetorician take us either in stating the main principles of couplet rhetoric or in exploring them? The answer, I believe, is: Not far. Puttenham can list and to some extent describe our figures of speech for us. He does little to show their interrelation or total significance. We can improve on Puttenham by going back to antiquity, where in the third book of Aristotle's *Rhetoric* we find a chapter (XI) saying that the smartest expressions consist in a concurrence of antithesis, parallel, metaphor, and "metaphor of a special kind"— by the last of which it would appear that Aristotle means "homonym." All this may seem to relegate the rhetorical theory of Pope's age or that of earlier ages to the status described under the second heading at the start of this paper: rhetorical, grammatical, or logical theory upon which we draw merely for tools that we shall turn to the uses of our own analysis. Perhaps this is what happens. I do not know the remedy—unless in the interests of Puttenham and his fellows, we are to cut our criticism off from all that subsequent linguistics and rhetoric and our own insight may tell us.

"Rules," said Sir William Temple and was paraphrased by Sir Thomas Pope Blount in his *De Re Poetica* of 1694, "at best are capable only to prevent the making of *bad Verses,* but never able to make men *good Poets.*" This might have been interpreted in Pope's day and by Pope himself according to the well known doctrine of the *je-ne-sais-quoi,* the "grace beyond the reach of art," the Longinian concession to genius and the element of the unpredictable in art. It ought to be interpreted by us in the further sense that the rules of a given age never contain even all that can be subsequently formulated about the poems of the age and hence are never able to prescribe our interpretation or limit our understanding of the poems. Poems, if not always prior to theory—in the case of the couplet they seem not to be—are certainly always more concrete than theory.

III

What I have just said is the logical climax and completion of my argument. What I shall say now, briefly, may be taken as a kind of tailpiece. In the part of this essay where I made a brief survey of rhetorical theory in Pope's age and the preceding, I suppressed one curious facet of that history, for the purpose of introducing it at this point. It is a noteworthy fact that some of the most penetrating technical remarks made by critics during the age of Pope were made by those who disapproved of the devices they were describing. One will no doubt recall Addison's *Spectator* No. 62, where he mentions doggerel rhymes and puns as instances of that "mixt Wit" which consists "partly in the Resemblance of Ideas, and partly in the Resemblance of Words." Addison also promises to tell us something, on another day, about the "wit" of antithesis. Far more spectacular are some of the analyses made by Pope's preromantic enemy John Dennis. "Rime," says Dennis in a Miltonic demonstration prefixed to one of his own blank verse poems, "is the same thing in Relation to Harmony that a Pun is in Relation to Wit. . . . Rime may not so absurdly be said to be the Pun of Harmony." [12] And so far as puns proper and ambiguity are concerned, Empson was not the first to detect their presence in the poetry of Pope.

Nay wits had pensions, and young lords had wit.

"Here," says Dennis, "in the compass of one poor line are two devilish Bobs for the Court. But 'tis no easy matter to tell which way the latter squinting Reflection looks." [13] Cleanth Brooks has noticed the indecent pun upon the word "die" in the Fifth Canto of *The Rape of the Lock*. It is not to be supposed that this had been overlooked by Dennis. "That is to say," observes Dennis, *"He wish'd for nothing more than to fight with her, because he desired nothing more than to lie with her.* Now what sensible Meaning can this have?" Puns, says Dennis, are everywhere in *The Rape of the Lock*. "Puns bear the same Proportion to *Thought,* that *Bubbles* hold to *Bodies,* and may justly be compared to those gaudy Bladders which

[12] *Preface to Britannia Triumphans,* 1704 (*Works,* I, 376–77).
[13] *Reflections on an Essay upon Criticism,* 1711 (*Works,* I, 413).

Children make with Soap." Nor is it to be supposed that Dennis
had overlooked the kind of pun hinted by Puttenham in the figures
of syllepsis and zeugma. "A Receipt for dry Joking," says Dennis.
"For by placing something important in the Beginning of a Period,
and making something very trifling to follow it, he seems to take
pains to bring *something* into a Conjunction Copulative with *nothing,* in order to beget *nothing.*" [14] Perhaps it is needless to add that
Dennis chooses for illustration of this formula the same examples
which I have quoted in my own admiring analysis—those about
staining her honor or her new brocade, and taking counsel and tea.
At a certain level, Dennis saw very well what Pope was up to. Not
an innuendo got past him. This, however, was not the kind of poetry
which Dennis prescribed. These were not the rules he would write.
We are confronted in our final exhibit with a relation between
theory and poems which we have up to now scarcely canvassed. In
this version of the critic's role there is a marked correlation not between poems and contemporary poetics but actually between poems
and contemporary antipoetics.

[14] *Remarks on the Rape of the Lock,* 1728 (*Works,* II, 347–49).

The Case of Miss Arabella Fermor

by Cleanth Brooks

Aldous Huxley's lovers, "quietly sweating, palm to palm," may
be conveniently taken to mark the nadir of Petrarchianism. The
mistress is no longer a goddess—not even by courtesy. She is a con-
geries of biological processes and her too evident mortality is pro-
claimed at every pore. But if we seem to reach, with Huxley's lines,
the end of something, it is well to see what it is that has come to an
end. It is not the end of a naïve illusion.

The Elizabethans, even those who were immersed in the best tradition of Petrarchianism, did not have to wait upon the advent of
modern science to find out that women perspired. They were thoroughly aware that woman was a biological organism, but their
recognition of this fact did not prevent them from asserting, on occasion, that she was a goddess, nevertheless. John Donne, for instance, frequently has it both ways: indeed, some of the difficulty
which the modern reader has with his poems may reside in the fact
that he sometimes has it both ways in the same poem. What is
relevant to our purposes here is not the occurrence of a line like
"Such are the sweat drops of my Mistres breast" in one of the satiric
"elegies," but the occurrence of lines like

> Our hands were firmely cimented
> With a fast balme, which thence did spring

in a poem like "The Ecstasy"! The passage quoted, one may argue,
glances at the very phenomenon which Huxley so amiably describes;
but Donne has transmuted it into something else.

But if Donne could have it both ways, most of us, in this latter

"The Case of Miss Arabella Fermor." From *The Well Wrought Urn*, by
Cleanth Brooks (New York: Harcourt Brace Jovanovich, Inc., 1947), pp. 80–104.
Reprinted by permission of Harcourt Brace Jovanovich, Inc., and Dennis Dobson
Ltd.

day, cannot. We are disciplined in the tradition of either-or, and lack the mental agility—to say nothing of the maturity of attitude —which would allow us to indulge in the finer distinctions and the more subtle reservations permitted by the tradition of both-and. Flesh *or* spirit, merely a doxy or purely a goddess (or alternately, one and then the other), is more easily managed in our poetry, and probably, for that matter, in our private lives. But the greater poems of our tradition are more ambitious in this matter: as a consequence, they come perhaps nearer the truth than we do with our ordinary hand-to-mouth insights. In saying this, however, one need by no means confine himself to the poetry of Donne. If we are not too much blinded by our doctrine of either-or, we shall be able to see that there are many poems in the English tradition which demonstrate a thorough awareness of the problem and which manage, at their appropriate levels, the same kinds of synthesis of attitudes which we associate characteristically with Donne.

Take Pope's *Rape of the Lock,* for instance. Is Belinda a goddess, or is she merely a frivolous tease? Pope himself was, we may be sure, thoroughly aware of the problem. His friend Swift penetrated the secrets of the lady's dressing room with what results we know. Belinda's dressing table, of course, is bathed in a very different atmosphere; yet it may be significant that Pope is willing to allow us to observe his heroine at her dressing table at all. The poet definitely means to give us scenes from the greenroom, and views from the wings, as well as a presentation "in character" on the lighted stage.

Pope, of course, did not write *The Rape of the Lock* because he was obsessed with the problem of Belinda's divinity. He shows, indeed, that he was interested in a great many things: in various kinds of social satire, in a playful treatment of the epic manner, in deflating some of the more vapid clichés that filled the love poetry of the period, and in a dozen other things. But we are familiar with Pope's interest in the mock-epic as we are not familiar with his interest in the problem of woman as goddess; and moreover, the rather lurid conventional picture of Pope as the "wicked wasp of Twickenham" —the particular variant of the either-or theory as applied to Pope— encourages us to take the poem as a dainty but rather obvious satire. There is some justification, therefore, for emphasizing aspects of the poem which have received little attention in the past, and perhaps for neglecting other aspects of the poems which critics have already treated in luminous detail.

One further point should be made: if Pope in this account of the poem turns out to be something of a symbolist poet, and perhaps even something of what we call, in our clumsy phrase, a "metaphysical poet" as well, we need not be alarmed. It matters very little whether or not we twist some of the categories which the literary historian jealously (and perhaps properly) guards. It matters a great deal that we understand Pope's poem in its full richness and complexity. It would be an amusing irony (and one not wholly undeserved) if we retorted upon Pope some of the brittleness and inelasticity which we feel that Pope was inclined to impose upon the more fluid and illogical poetry which preceded him. But the real victims of the maneuver, if it blinded us to his poem, would be ourselves.

Pope's own friends were sometimes guilty of oversimplifying and reducing his poem by trying to make it accord with a narrow and pedantic logic. For example, Bishop Warburton, Pope's friend and editor, finds an error in the famous passage in which Belinda and her maid are represented as priestesses invoking the goddess of beauty. Warburton feels forced to comment as follows: "There is a small inaccuracy in these lines. He first makes his Heroine the chief Priestess, then the Goddess herself." The lines in question run as follows:

> First, rob'd in White, the Nymph intent adores
> With Head uncover'd, the *Cosmetic* Pow'rs.
> A heav'nly Image in the Glass appears,
> To that she bends, to that her Eyes she rears. . . .

It is true that Pope goes on to imply that Belinda is the chief priestess (by calling her maid the "inferior Priestess"), and that, a few lines later, he has the maid deck the goddess (Belinda) "with the glitt'ring Spoil." But surely Warburton ought not to have missed the point: Belinda, in worshiping at the shrine of beauty, quite naturally worships herself. Whose else is the "heav'nly Image" which appears in the mirror to which she raises her eyes? The violation of logic involved is intended and is thoroughly justified. Belinda *is* a goddess, but she puts on her divinity at her dressing table; and, such is the paradox of beauty-worship, she can be both the sincere devotee and the divinity herself. We shall certainly require more sensitive instruments than Bishop Warburton's logic if we are to become aware of some of the nicest effects in the poem.

But to continue with the dressing-table scene:

> The Fair each moment rises in her Charms,
> Repairs her Smiles, awakens ev'ry Grace,
> And calls forth all the Wonders of her Face;
> Sees by Degrees a purer Blush arise,
> And keener Lightnings quicken in her Eyes.

It is the experience which the cosmetic advertisers take at a level of dead seriousness, and obviously Pope is amused to have it taken seriously. And yet, is there not more here than the obvious humor? Belinda is, after all, an artist, and who should be more sympathetic with the problems of the conscious artist than Pope himself? In our own time, William Butler Yeats, a less finicky poet than Pope, could address a "young beauty" as "dear fellow artist."

In particular, consider the "purer Blush." Why purer? One must not laugh too easily at the purity of the blush which Belinda is engaged in painting upon her face. After all, may we not regard it as a blush "recollected in tranquility," and therefore a more ideal blush than the spontaneous actual blush which shame or hauteur on an actual occasion might bring? If we merely read "purer" as ironic for its opposite, "impurer"—that is, unspontaneous and therefore unmaidenly—we shall miss not only the more delightful aspects of the humor, but we shall miss also Pope's concern for the real problem. Which is, after all, the more maidenly blush? That will depend, obviously, upon what one considers the essential nature of maidens to be; and Belinda, we ought to be reminded, is not the less real nor the less feminine because she fails to resemble Whittier's robust heroine, Maude Muller.

One is tempted to insist upon these ambiguities and complexities of attitude, not with any idea of overturning the orthodox reading of Pope's irony, but rather to make sure that we do not conceive it to be more brittle and thin than it actually is. This fact, at least, should be plain: regardless of what we may make of the "purer Blush," it is true that Belinda's dressing table does glow with a special radiance and charm, and that Pope, though amused by the vanity which it represents, is at the same time thoroughly alive to a beauty which it actually possesses.

There is a further reason for feeling that we shall not err in taking the niceties of Pope's descriptions quite seriously. One notices that even the metaphors by which Pope characterizes Belinda are not casual bits of decoration, used for a moment, and then forgotten. They run throughout the poem as if they were motifs. For instance, at her dressing table Belinda is not only a priestess of "the Sacred Rites of Pride," but she is also compared to a warrior arming for the fray. Later in the poem she is the warrior once more at the card table in her conquest of the two "adventrous Knights"; and again, at the end of the poem, she emerges as the heroic conqueror in the epic encounter of the beaux and belles.

To take another example, Belinda, early in the poem, is compared to the sun. Pope suggests that the sun recognizes in Belinda a rival, and fears her:

> *Sol* thro' white Curtains shot a tim'rous Ray,
> And op'd those Eyes that must eclipse the Day.

But the sun's fear of Belinda has not been introduced merely in order to give the poet an opportunity to mock at the polite cliché. The sun comparison appears again at the beginning of Canto II:

> Not with more Glories, in th' Etherial Plain,
> The Sun first rises o'er the purpled Main,
> Than issuing forth, the Rival of his Beams
> Lanch'd on the Bosom of the silver *Thames.*

Belinda is like the sun, not only because of her bright eyes, and not only because she dominates her special world ("But ev'ry Eye was fix'd on her alone"). She is like the sun in another regard:

> Bright as the Sun, her Eyes the Gazers strike,
> And, like the Sun, they shine on all alike.

Is this general munificence on the part of Belinda a fault or a virtue? Is she shallow and flirtatious, giving her favors freely to all; or, does she distribute her largesse impartially like a great prince? Or, is she simply the well-bred belle who knows that she cannot play favorites if she wishes to be popular? The sun comparison is able to carry all these meanings, and therefore goes past any momentary jest. Granting that it may be overingenious to argue that Belinda in Canto IV (the gloomy Cave of Spleen) represents the sun in eclipse, still the sun comparison does appear once more in the poem, and quite explicitly. As the poem closes, Pope addresses Belinda thus:

> When those fair Suns shall sett, as sett they must,
> And all those Tresses shall be laid in Dust;
> *This Lock,* the Muse shall consecrate to Fame,
> And mid'st the stars inscribe *Belinda's* Name!

Here, one notices that the poet, if he is forced to concede that Belinda's eyes are only metaphorical suns after all, still promises that the ravished lock shall have a celestial eternity, adding, like the planet Venus, "new Glory to the shining Sphere!" And here Pope, we may be sure, is not merely playful in his metaphor. Belinda's name has been inscribed in the only heaven in which a poet would care to inscribe it. If the skeptic still has any doubts about Pope's taking Belinda very seriously, there should be no difficulty in convincing him that Pope took his own work very seriously indeed.

We began by raising the question of Belinda's status as a goddess. It ought to be quite clear that Pope's attitude toward Belinda is not exhausted in laughing away her claims to divinity. The attitude is much more complicated than that. Belinda's charm is not viewed uncritically, but the charm is real: it can survive the poet's knowledge of how much art and artifice have gone into making up the charm. The attitude is not wholly unrelated to that of Mirabell toward Millamant in Congreve's *The Way of the World*. Mirabell knows that his mistress has her faults, but as he philosophically remarks: ". . . I like her with all her faults; nay, like her for her faults. Her follies are so natural, or so artful, that they become her. . . . She once used me with that insolence, that in revenge I took her to pieces, sifted her, and separated her failings; I studied 'em, and got 'em by rote. . . . They are now grown as familiar to me as my own frailties; and in all probability, in a little time longer, I shall like 'em as well." The relation of author to creation can be more philosophical still: and though Pope's attitude toward his heroine has a large element of amused patronage in it, I find no contempt. Rather, Pope finds Belinda charming, and expects us to feel her charm.

To pursue the matter of attitude further still, what, after all, is Pope's attitude toward the iridescent little myth of the sylphs which he has provided to symbolize the polite conventions which govern the conduct of maidens? We miss the whole point if we dismiss the sylphs as merely "supernatural machinery." In general, we may say that the myth represents a qualification of the poet's prevailingly naturalistic interpretation. More specifically, it represents his attempt to do justice to the intricacies of the feminine mind. For, in spite of Pope's amusement at the irrationality of that mind, Pope acknowledges its beauty and its power.

In making this acknowledgement, he is a good realist—a better realist, indeed, than he appears when he tries to parade the fashionable ideas of the Age of Reason as in his "Essay on Man." He is good enough realist to know that although men in their "Learned Pride" may say that it is Honor which protects the chastity of maids, actually it is nothing of the sort: the belles are not kept chaste by any mere abstraction. It is the sylphs, the sylphs with their interest in fashion notes and their knowledge of the feminine heart:

> With varying Vanities, from ev'ry Part,
> They shift the moving Toyshop of their Heart;
> Where Wigs with Wigs, with Sword-knots Sword-knots strive,
> Beaus banish Beaus, and Coaches Coaches drive.

Yet the myth of the sylphs is no mere decoration to this essentially cynical generalization. The sylphs do represent the supernatural, though the supernatural reduced, of course, to its flimsiest proportions. The poet has been very careful here. Even Belinda is not made to take their existence too seriously. As for the poet, he very modestly recuses himself from rendering any judgment at all by ranging himself on the side of "Learned Pride":

> Some secret Truths from Learned Pride conceal'd,
> To Maids alone and Children are reveal'd:
> What tho' no Credit doubting Wits may give?
> The Fair and Innocent shall still believe.

In the old wives' tale or the child's fairy story may lurk an item of truth, after all. Consider the passage carefully.

"Fair" and "Innocent" balance "Maids" and "Children." Yet they act further to color the whole passage. Is "fair" used merely as a synonym for "maids"—e.g., as in "the fair"? Or, is it that beauty is easily flattered? The doctrine which Ariel urges Belinda to accept is certainly flattering: "Hear and believe! thy own Importance know/ . . . unnumber'd Spirits round thee fly. . . ." Is "innocent" to be taken to mean "guiltless," or does it mean "naïve," perhaps even "credulous"? And how do "fair" and "innocent" influence each other? Do the fair believe in the sylphs because they are still children? (Ariel, one remembers, begins by saying: "If e'er one Vision touch'd thy *infant* Thought . . .") Pope is here exploiting that whole complex of associations which surround "innocence" and connect it on the one hand with more than worldly wisdom and, on the other, with simple gullibility.

Pope, as we now know, was clearly unjust in suggesting that Addison's advice against adding the machinery of the sylphs was prompted by any desire to prevent the improvement of the poem. Addison's caution was "safe" and natural under the circumstances. But we can better understand Pope's pique if we come to understand how important the machinery was to become in the final version of the poem. For it is Pope's treatment of the sylphs which allows him to develop, with the most delicate modulation, his whole attitude toward Belinda and the special world which she graces. It is precisely the poet's handling of the supernatural—the level at which he is willing to entertain it—the amused qualifications which he demands of it—that makes it possible for him to state his attitude with full complexity.

The sylphs are, as Ariel himself suggests, "honor," though honor rendered concrete and as it actually functions, not honor as a dry abstraction. The sylphs' concern for good taste allows little range for critical perspective or a sense of proportion. To Ariel it will really be a dire disaster whether it is her honor or her new brocade that Belinda stains. To stain her honor will certainly constitute a breach of good taste—whatever else it may be—and that for Ariel is enough. Indeed, it is enough for the rather artificial world of manners with which Pope is concerned.

The myth of the sylphs is, thus, of the utmost utility to Pope: it allows him to show his awareness of the absurdities of a point of view which, nevertheless, is charming, delightful, and filled with a real poetry. Most important of all, the myth allows him to suggest that the charm, in part at least, springs from the very absurdity. The two elements can hardly be separated in Belinda; in her guardian, Ariel, they cannot be separated at all.

In this connection, it is well to raise specifically the question of Pope's attitude toward the "rape" itself. We certainly underestimate the poem if we rest complacently in the view that Pope is merely laughing at a tempest in a teapot. There is such laughter, to be sure, and late in the poem, Pope expresses his own judgment of the situation, employing Clarissa as his mouthpiece. But the tempest, ridiculous though it is when seen in perspective, is a real enough tempest and related to very real issues. Indeed, Pope is able to reduce the incident to its true importance, precisely because he recognizes clearly its hidden significance. And nowhere is Pope more careful to take into account all the many sides of the situation than just here in the loss of the lock itself.

For one thing, Pope is entirely too clear-sighted to allow that the charming Belinda is merely the innocent victim of a rude assault. Why has she cherished the lock at all? In part at least, "to the Destruction of Mankind," though mankind, of course, in keeping with the convention, wishes so to be destroyed. Pope suggests that the Baron may even be the victim rather than the aggressor—it is a moot question whether he has seized the lock or been ensnared by it. Pope does this very skillfully, but with great emphasis:

> Love in these Labyrinths his Slaves detains,
> And mighty Hearts are held in slender Chains.
> With hairy Sprindges we the Birds betray,
> Slight Lines of Hair surprize the Finny Prey,
> Fair Tresses Man's Imperial Race insnare,
> And Beauty draws us with a single Hair.

Indeed, at the end of the poem, the poet addresses his heroine not as victim but as a "murderer":

> For, after all the Murders of your Eye,
> When, after Millions slain, your self shall die. . . .

After all, does not Belinda want the Baron (and young men in general) to covet the lock? She certainly does not want to retain possession of the lock forever. The poet naturally sympathizes with Belinda's pique at the way in which the Baron obtains the lock. He must, in the war of the sexes, coax her into letting him have it. Force is clearly unfair, though blandishment is fair. If she is an able warrior, she will consent to the young man's taking the lock, though the lock still attached to her head—and on the proper terms, honorable marriage. If she is a weak opponent, she will yield the lock, and herself, without any stipulation of terms, and will thus become a ruined maid indeed. Pope has absolutely no illusions about what the game is, and is certainly not to be shocked by any naturalistic interpretation of the elaborate and courtly conventions under which Belinda fulfills her natural function of finding a mate.

On the other hand, this is not at all to say that Pope is anxious to do away with the courtly conventions as a pious fraud. He is not the romantic anarchist who would abolish all conventions because they are artificial. The conventions not only have a regularizing function: they have their own charm. Like the rules of the card game in which Belinda triumphs, they may at points be arbitrary; but they make the game possible, and with it, the poetry and pageantry involved in it, in which Pope very clearly delights.

The card game itself, of course, is another symbol of the war of the sexes. Belinda must defeat the men; she must avoid that debacle in which

> The *Knave* of *Diamonds* tries his wily Arts,
> And wins (oh shameful Chance!) the *Queen* of *Hearts*.

She must certainly avoid at every cost becoming a ruined maid. In the game as played, there is a moment in which she is "Just in the Jaws of Ruin, and *Codille*," and gets a thrill of delicious excitement at being in so precarious a position.

If the reader objects that the last comment suggests a too obviously sexual interpretation of the card game, one must hasten to point out that a pervasive sexual symbolism informs, not only the description of the card game, but almost everything else in the poem, though here, again, our tradition of either-or may cause us to miss what Pope is doing. We are not forced to take the poem as either sly bawdy *or* as delightful fantasy. But if we are to see what Pope actually makes of his problem, we shall have to be alive to the sexual implications which are in the poem.

They are perfectly evident—even in the title itself; and the poem begins with an address to the Muse in which the sexual implications are underscored:

> Say what strange Motive, Goddess! cou'd compel
> A well-bred Lord t'assault a gentle *Belle?*
> Oh say what stranger Cause, yet unexplor'd,
> Cou'd make a gentle *Belle* reject a *Lord?*

True, we can take *assault* and *reject* in their more general meanings, not in their specific Latin senses, but the specific meanings are there just beneath the surface. Indeed, it is hard to believe, on the evidence of the poem as a whole, that Pope would have been in the least surprised by Sir James Frazer's later commentaries on the ubiquity of hair as a fertility symbol. In the same way, one finds it hard to believe, after some of the material in the "Cave of Spleen" section ("And Maids turn'd Bottels, call aloud for Corks"), that Pope would have been too much startled by the theories of Sigmund Freud.

The sexual implications become quite specific after the "rape" has occurred. Thalestris, in inciting Belinda to take action against the Baron, cries:

> Gods! shall the Ravisher display your Hair,
> While the Fops envy, and the Ladies stare!

Even if we take *ravisher* in its most general sense, still the sexual symbolism lurks just behind Thalestris' words. Else why should honor be involved as it is? Why should the Baron desire the lock, and why should Belinda object so violently, not as to an act of simple rudeness, but to losing "honor" and becoming a "degraded Toast"? The sexual element is involved at least to the extent that Belinda feels that she cannot afford to suffer the Baron, without protest, to take such a "liberty."

But a deeper sexual importance is symbolized by the whole incident. Belinda's anguished exclamation—

> Oh hadst thou, Cruel! been content to seize
> Hairs less in sight, or any Hairs but these!

carries on, unconsciously, the sexual suggestion. The lines indicate, primarily, of course, Belinda's exasperation at the ruining of her coiffure. The principal ironic effect, therefore, is one of bathos: her angry concern for the prominence of the lock deflates a little her protests about honor. (Something of the bathos carries over to the sexual parallel: it is hinted, perhaps, that the worst thing about a real rape for the belle would be that it could not be concealed.) But though Belinda's vehemence gives rise to these ironies, the exclamation itself is dramatically appropriate; and Belinda would doubtless have blushed to have her emphasis on "any" interpreted literally and rudely. In her anger, she is obviously unconscious of the *faux pas.* But the fops whose admiring and envious comments on the exposed trophy Thalestris can predict—"Already hear the horrid things they say"—would be thoroughly alive to the unconscious *double entendre.* Pope's friend, Matthew Prior, wrote a naughty poem in which the same *double entendre* occurs. Pope himself, we may be sure, was perfectly aware of it.

In commenting on Pope's attitude toward the rape, we have suggested by implication his attitude toward chastity. Chastity is one of Belinda's most becoming garments. It gives her her retinue of airy guardians. As a proper maiden, she will keep from staining it just as she will keep from staining her new brocade. Its very fragility is part of its charm, and Pope becomes something of a symbolist poet in suggesting this. Three times in the poem he refers to the breaking of a frail china jar, once in connection with the loss of chastity, twice in connection with the loss of "honor" suffered by Belinda in the "rape" of the lock:

> Whether the Nymph shall break *Diana's* Law,
> Or some frail *China* Jar receive a Flaw. . . .

> Or when rich *China* Vessels, fal'n from high,
> In glittring Dust and painted Fragments lie!

> Thrice from my trembling hands the *Patch-box* fell;
> The tott'ring *China* shook without a Wind. . . .

Pope does not say, but he suggests, that chastity is, like the fine porcelain, something brittle, precious, useless, and easily broken. In the same way, he has hinted that honor (for which the sylphs, in part, stand) is something pretty, airy, fluid, and not really believed in. The devoted sylph who interposes his "body" between the lock and the closing shears is clipped in two, but honor suffers little damage:

> Fate urg'd the Sheers, and cut the *Sylph* in twain,
> (But Airy Substance soon unites again).

It would be easy here to turn Pope into a cynic; but to try to do this is to miss the point. Pope does not hold chastity to be of no account. He definitely expects Belinda to be chaste; but, as a good humanist, he evidently regards virginity as essentially a negative virtue, and its possession, a temporary state. He is very far from associating it with any magic virtue as Milton does in his *Comus*. The only magic which he will allow it is a kind of charm—a *je-ne-sais-quoi* such as the sylphs possess.

Actually, we probably distort Pope's views by putting the question in terms which require an explicit judgment at all. Pope accepts in the poem the necessity for the belle to be chaste just as he accepts the necessity for her to be gracious and attractive. But in accepting this, he is thoroughly alive to the cant frequently talked about woman's honor, and most of all, he is ironically, though quietly, resolute in putting first things first. This, I take it, is the whole point of Clarissa's speech. When Clarissa says:

> Since painted, or not painted, all shall fade,
> And she who scorns a Man, must die a Maid,

we need not assume with Leslie Stephen that Pope is expressing a smug masculine superiority, with the implication that, for a woman, spinsterhood is the worst of all possible ills. (There is actually no reason for supposing that Pope thought it so.) The real point is that, for Belinda, perpetual spinsterhood *is* the worst of all possible ills. In her own terms, it would be a disaster to retain her locks forever—locks turned to gray, though still curled with a pathetic hopefulness, unclaimed and unpossessed by any man. Belinda does not want *that;* and it is thus a violation of good sense to lose sight of the fact that the cherished lock is finally only a means to an end—one weapon to be used by the warrior in the battle, and not the strongest weapon at that.

Clarissa is, of course, promptly called a prude, and the battle begins at once in perfect disregard of the "good sense" that she has spoken. Pope is too fine an artist to have it happen otherwise. Belinda *has* been sorely vexed—and she, moreover, remains charming, even as an Amazon. After all, what the poet has said earlier is sincerely meant:

> If to her share some Female Errors fall,
> Look on her Face, and you'll forget 'em all.

Though Pope obviously agrees with Clarrisa, he is neither surprised nor particularly displeased with his heroine for flying in the face of Clarissa's advice.

The battle of the sexes which ensues parodies at some points the combat in the great epic which Milton fashioned on the rape of the apple. But the absurdity of a battle in which the contestants cannot be killed is a flaw in Milton's great poem, whereas Pope turns it to beautiful account in his. In *Paradise Lost,* the great archangels single each other out for combat in the best Homeric style. But when Michael's sword cleaves the side of Lucifer, the most that Milton can do with the incident is to observe that Lucifer feels pain, for his premises force him to hurry on to admit that

> . . . th'Ethereal substance clos'd
> Not long divisible. . . .

Lucifer is soon back in the fight, completely hale and formidable as ever. We have already seen how delightfully Pope converts this cabbage into a rose in the incident in which the sylph, in a desperate defense of the lock, is clipped in two by the shears.

The absurdity of a war fought by invulnerable opponents gives an air of unreality to the whole of Milton's episode. There is a bickering over rules. Satan and his followers cheat by inventing gunpowder. The hosts under Michael retort by throwing the celestial hills at the enemy; and the Almighty, to put a stop to the shameful rumpus, has the Son throw the troublemakers out. But if the fight were really serious, a fight to the death, why does the heavenly host not throw the hills in the first place? Or, why does not the Almighty cast out the rebels without waiting for the three days of inconclusive fighting to elapse? The prevailing atmosphere of a game—a game played by good little boys and by unmannerly little ruffians, a game presided over by the stern schoolmaster—haunts the whole episode. The advantage is wholly with Pope here. By frankly recognizing that the contest between his beaux and belles is a game, he makes for his basic intention.

The suspicion that Pope in this episode is glancing at Milton is corroborated somewhat by Pope's general use of his celestial machinery. The supernatural guardians in *The Rape of the Lock* are made much of, but their effectiveness is hardly commensurate with their zeal. The affinities of the poem on this point are again with *Paradise Lost,* not with the *Iliad.* In Milton's poem, the angels are carefully stationed to guard Adam and Eve in their earthly home, but their protection proves, in the event, to be singularly ineffectual. They cannot prevent Satan from finding his way to the earth; and though they soar over the Garden, their "radiant Files,/Daz'ling the Moon," they never strike a blow. Even when they discover Satan, and prepare to engage him in combat, God, at the last moment, prevents the fight. Indeed, for all their numbers and for all their dazzling splendor, they succeed in determining events not at all. They can merely, in the case of Raphael, give the human pair advice and warning. Milton, though he loved to call their resonant names, and evidently tried to provide them with a realistic function, was apparently so fearful lest he divert attention from Adam's own freely made decision that he succeeds in giving them nothing to do.

If this limitation constitutes another ironical defect, perhaps, in Milton's great epic, it fits Pope's purposes beautifully. For, as we have seen, Pope's supernatural machinery is as airy as gossamer, and the fact that Ariel can do no more than Raphael, advise and warn

—for all his display of zeal—makes again for Pope's basic intention. The issues in Pope's poem are matters of taste, matters of "good sense," and the sylphs do not violate the human limitations of this world which Pope has elected to describe and in terms of which judgments are to be made. Matters of morality—still less, the ultimate sanctions of morality—are never raised.

One more of the numerous parallels between *The Rape of the Lock* and *Paradise Lost* ought to be mentioned here, even though it may well be one of which Pope was unconscious. After the Fall has taken place, Michael is sent to prepare Adam for his expulsion from the happy garden. The damage has been done, the apple has been plucked and eaten, the human pair must prepare to go out into the "real" world, the "fallen" world of our ordinary human experience. Yet, Michael promises that Adam can create within his own breast "A Paradise . . . happier farr." Clarissa's advice to Belinda makes the same point. For better or worse, the lock has been lost. That fact must be accepted. In suggesting Belinda's best course under the circumstances, Clarissa raises quite explicitly Belinda's status as a divinity:

> Say, why are Beauties prais'd and honour'd most . . .
> Why Angels call'd, and Angel-like ador'd?

The divine element cannot reside in mere beauty alone, painted cheeks, bright eyes, curled locks. All human beauty is tainted with mortality: true "angelhood" resides in a quality of mind, and therefore can survive the loss of mere mortal beauty—can survive the loss of the lock, even the destruction of its beauty by the shears of time. The general parallel between the two speeches is almost complete. Belinda's true divinity, like Adam's happier paradise, is to be found within her. Pope, like Milton, can thus rationalize the matter in terms which allow him to dismiss the supernatural machinery and yet maintain the presence of a qualified supernatural in the midst of a stern and rational world in which no longer one may expect "God or Angel Guest/With Man, as with his Friend, familiar us'd/ To sit indulgent"—an altered world in which Belinda will expect no more intimate communications from Ariel, and where she, like Adam and Eve, must rely on an inner virtue for advice and protection.

Indeed, one is tempted to complete the parallel by suggesting that Belinda is, at this point, like Adam, being prepared to leave her

happy garden world of innocence and maidenly delight for a harsher
world, the world of human society as it is and with the poetic
illusions removed.

   To return to the battle between the beaux and belles: here Pope
beautifully unifies the various motifs of the poem. The real nature
of the conventions of polite society, the heroic pretensions of that
society as mirrored in the epic, the flattering clichés which society
conventionally employs—all come in for a genial ragging. Indeed,
the clichés of the ardent lover become the focal point of concentration. For the clichés, if they make the contention absurd and pom-
pous, do indicate, by coming alive on another level, the true, if unconscious, nature of the struggle.

> No common Weapons in their Hands are found,
> Like Gods they fight, nor dread a mortal Wound.

"Like Gods they fight" should mean, in the epic framework, "with
superhuman energy and valor." And "nor dread a mortal Wound"
logically completes "Like Gods they fight"—until a yet sterner logic
asserts itself and deflates the epic pomp. A fight in which the opponents cannot be killed is only a sham fight. Yet, this second meaning
is very rich after all, and draws "Like Gods they fight" into its own
orbit of meanings: there may be an extra zest in the fighting because
it *is* an elaborate game. One can make godlike gestures because one
has the invulnerability of a god. The contest is godlike, after all,
because it is raised above the dust and turmoil of real issues. Like
an elaborate dance, it symbolizes real issues but can find room for a
grace and poetry which in a more earnest struggle are lost.

   I have said earlier that Pope, by recognizing the real issues involved, is able to render his mock-epic battle meaningful. For the
beaux of Hampton Court, though in truth they do not need to dread
a mortal wound, can, and are prepared to, die. We must remember
that "to die" had at this period, as one of its submeanings, to experience the consummation of the sexual act. Pope's invulnerable beaux
rush bravely forward to achieve such a death; for the war of the
sexes, when fought seriously and to the death, ends in such an act.

   The elegant battleground resounds with the cries of those who
die "in *Metaphor*, and . . . in *Song*." In some cases, little more is
implied than a teasing of the popular clichés about bearing a "living Death," or being burnt alive in Cupid's flames. But few will
question the sexual implications of "die" in the passage in which
Belinda overcomes the Baron:

> Nor fear'd the Chief th'unequal Fight to try,
> Who sought no more than on his Foe to die. . . .
> "Boast not my Fall" (he cry'd) "insulting Foe!
> Thou by some other shalt be laid as low. . . ."

The point is not that Pope is here leering at bawdy meaning. In the full context of the poem, they are not bawdy at all—or, perhaps we put the matter more accurately if we say that Pope's *total* attitude, as reflected in the poem, is able to absorb and digest into itself the incidental bawdy of which Pope's friends, and obviously Pope himself, were conscious. The crucial point is that Pope's interpretation of Belinda's divinity does not need to flinch from bawdy interpretations. The further meanings suggested by the naughty *double entendres* are not merely snickering jibes which contradict the surface meaning: rather those further meanings constitute the qualifying background against which Belinda's divinity is asserted. Pope's testimony to Belinda's charm is not glib; it is not thin and one-sided. It is qualified by, though not destroyed by, a recognition of all the factors involved—even of those factors which seem superficially to negate it. The touch is light, to be sure; but the poem is not flimsy, not mere froth. The tone is ironical, but the irony is not that of a narrow and acerb satire; rather it is an irony which accords with a wise recognition of the total situation. The "form" of the poem is, therefore, much more than the precise regard for a set of rules and conventions mechanically apprehended. It is, finally, the delicate balance and reconciliation of a host of partial interpretations and attitudes.

It was observed earlier that Pope is able to reduce the "rape" to its true insignificance because he recognizes, as his characters do not, its real significance. Pope knows that the rape has in it more of compliment than of insult, though he naturally hardly expects Belinda to interpret it thus. He does not question her indignation, but he does suggest that it is, perhaps, a more complex response than Belinda realizes. Pope knows too how artificial the social conventions really are and he is thoroughly cognizant of the economic and biological necessities which underlie them—which the conventions sometimes seem to mask and sometimes to adorn. He is therefore not forced to choose between regarding them as either a hypocritical disguise or as a poetic and graceful adornment. Knowing their true nature, he can view this outrage of the conventions with a wise and amused tolerance, and can set it in its proper perspective.

Here the functional aspect of Pope's choice of the epic framework becomes plain. The detachment, the amused patronage, the note of aloof and impartial judgment—all demand that the incident be viewed with a large measure of aesthetic distance. Whatever incidental fun Pope may have had with the epic conventions, his choice of the mock-epic fits beautifully his general problem of scaling down the rape to its proper insignificance. The scene is reduced and the characters become small and manageable figures whose actions can always be plotted against a larger background.

How large that background is has not always been noticed. Belinda's world is plainly a charming, artificial world; but Pope is not afraid to let in a glimpse of the real world which lies all about it:

> Mean while declining from the Noon of Day,
> The Sun obliquely shoots his burning Ray;
> The hungry Judges soon the Sentence sign,
> And Wretches hang that Jury-men may Dine;
> The Merchant from th'*Exchange* returns in Peace,
> And the long Labours of the *Toilette* cease—
> *Belinda* now. . . .

It is a world in which business goes on and criminals are hanged for all that Belinda is preparing to sit down to ombre. This momentary glimpse of the world of serious affairs, of the world of business and law, of the world of casualness and cruelty, is not introduced merely to shrivel the high concerns of polite society into ironical insignificance, though its effect, of course, is to mock at the seriousness with which the world of fashion takes its affairs. Nor is the ironical clash which is introduced by the passage uncalculated and unintentional: it is not that Pope himself is unconsciously callous—without sympathy for the "wretches." The truth is that Pope's own perspective is so scaled, his totality of view so honest, that he can afford to embellish his little drama as lovingly as he likes without for a moment losing sight of its final triviality. A lesser poet would either have feared to introduce an echo of the "real" world lest the effect prove to be too discordant, or would have insisted on the discord and moralized, too heavily and bitterly, the contrast between the gay and the serious. Pope's tact is perfect. The passage is an instance of the complexity of tone which the poem possesses.

The Cistern and the Fountain:
Art and Reality in Pope

by Irvin Ehrenpreis

Few of Pope's works pretend to exhibit throughout the sort of design which his couplets and his verse paragraphs possess. I wish now to argue that the second "Moral Essay," *An Epistle to a Lady, Of the Characters of Women*, has just this virtue in addition to its others. *To a Lady* is a finished masterpiece such as Pope rarely created. Parts of it have received famous praise from Professor Empson, Dr. Leavis, and Lytton Strachey.[1] Yet little attention has fallen, I think, on the elaborated form of the whole poem. So I should like to consider this in terms of the arrangement of parts and pattern of images, and then to ask how it depends on allusions to reality. Through comparisons with similar poems both by Pope and by Edward Young, I hope to show that the achievement is remarkable.

The *Epistle to a Lady* can be divided into three parts: the first two hundred lines are a group of portraits of women, mostly sinners; the next fifty lines are a didactic analysis of their sins; and the final forty lines are a eulogy addressed to a Lady listener, easily identifiable as Martha Blount. Portraits, analysis, eulogy—among these the connection seems obvious. The concentrated praise in lines 249 to 292 balances the distributed attacks in lines 1 to 198, and the analysis in lines 199 to 248 forms a bridge between the two. The

"The Cistern and the Fountain: Art and Reality in Pope" (editor's title) by Irvin Ehrenpreis. From *Studies in Criticism and Aesthetics, 1660–1800: Essays in Honor of Samuel Holt Monk*, ed. Howard Anderson and John S. Shea (Minneapolis: University of Minnesota Press, 1967), pp. 158–70. Copyright © 1967 by the University of Minnesota. Printed originally as "The Cistern and the Fountain: Art and Reality in Pope and Gray." Reprinted by permission of the publisher.

[1] Empson in *Seven Types of Ambiguity,* Leavis in *Revaluation,* Strachey in *Pope.*

virtues Mrs. Blount owns—modesty, tenderness, fidelity—are conspicuously those the sinners lack; and their vices—vanity, avarice,
ambition, lust—have no place in her character.

The structure of the first section will easily be seen to have a
formal order. Thus in the series of portraits we find several kinds
of rising lines. For one thing, the poet surveys his sinners roughly
in order of size: a couplet or two on each of the first few names; four
couplets on Silia; six on Calypso; eight on Narcissa; nine on Philomede; seven on Flavia; eighteen on Atossa; and twelve on Cloe,
with some very brief profiles interspersed. In the *Epistle to Bathurst*,
Pope had used the same rough order of size: one couplet on Cole-
pepper, eight on Blunt, twenty-two on Sir Balaam, and so forth; the
principle seems ordinary enough. But in the *Epistle to a Lady* Pope
combines it with another, which Professor Elder Olson has noticed
in the *Epistle to Dr. Arbuthnot*.[2] There, as the speech progresses,
the satire sharpens: the portrait of Atticus is more severe than the
ridicule of fools at the beginning, and the portrait of Sporus is more
severe than that of Atticus. So in the *Epistle to a Lady*, Atossa's portrait is the climax of violence as well as the climax in length; Philomede's is milder; Narcissa's, still milder. But, as it happens, the sinners are also arranged in degrees of reality. Out of the first six, five
seem fictitious: i.e., the poem does not invite us to search for an
original. But Sappho, the next, can only refer to Lady Mary Wortley
Montagu. Four additional pseudonyms—Philomede, Flavia, Atossa,
and Cloe—have been associated with the second Duchess of Marlborough, the Duchess of Montagu, the Duchess of Buckinghamshire,
and the Countess of Suffolk. Finally, the Queen is actually named,
as is the Duchess of Queensberry (who does not, however, count as
a sinner).[3] From the pseudonymous and fictitious, therefore, through
the pseudonymous but recognizable, Pope moves to proper public
names; and from a countess and an earl's daughter, through duchesses, he rises to the Queen. Admitting many irregularities and in-
terruptions, we may say that he moves roughly through degrees of
reality and degrees of rank. In other words, as Pope gets further
along in the poem, and strengthens his grip on the audience, he
grows bolder.

There is a further meaning to Pope's order. Those women who

---

[2] "Rhetoric and the Appreciation of Pope," *MP*, XXXVII (1939), 13–35.
[3] For these identifications see F. W. Bateson's edition of Pope's *Epistles to
Several Persons* (III, pt. ii, Twickenham ed.).

can be identified are peeresses or royalty, in contrast to the humble station of Mrs. Blount. Such targets of course give weight to the poem, just as an imperial dramatis personae gives weight to tragedy. They are courtiers, natural focuses of national concern. Lady Irwin had remarked of the *Epistle to Bathurst,* "As the objects of [Pope's] satire are low, people will be less offended, for who cares for [Peter] Waters, Charters, or Ward." [4] One never feels that the figures of *An Epistle to a Lady* are too inconsequential to be worth reading about. As we approach the peak of society, however, we approach the peak of corruption: the poet evokes an urgency suggesting a national crisis.

Young has two satires on women which deeply influenced Pope's work—numbers five and six of *The Universal Passion,* which are commonly judged to be the most satisfactory poems in that book. Yet Young completely misses Pope's effect of urgency because not only does he assign no particular ranks to his group of criminals but he also singles out royalty as the example of virtue:

> 'Midst empire's charms, how *Carolina's* heart
> Glows with the love of *virtue, and of art?* [5]

But Pope, from the long sequence of portraits, swings us up through the passage of didactic analysis into the final eulogy of Mrs. Blount; and there he shifts his point of view; for he addresses the poem to the good woman and holds up the vicious to her examination. Their corrupted natures are described in the third person; her virtuous self, in the second. They are spoken about; she is present, to be saluted directly. The effect gives to goodness, in its limited space, an immediacy and a substance which evil, though intensely realized and extended over hundreds of lines, has lacked. On this drawn-out moral contrast the poem is built. Like the coils of a long spring, the vicious characters are stretched at length and then let go to provide rebounding impetus for the final panegyric.

The moral implications of this relationship bear out the formal order. The Lady is both the positive climax of the entire poem and the justification of the satire. Obviously, Pope wishes to compliment Martha Blount. But in an age when sincerity was the most imitative form of flattery, and in a poem which singled out panegyric as the

[4] Letter of January 18, 1733/4, in Historical Manuscript Commission, *XV Report, Appendix,* pt. vi, p. 97.

[5] Young, *Universal Passion,* satire VI, p. 155.

most suspect kind of literature, he had to exert himself to give force to his praise. By employing most of his lines in condemnation of dangerous women, he adds distinction to the solitary approval bestowed upon Mrs. Blount. Conversely, by loudly recognizing virtue as it appears in a unique specimen, he gives energy to his dispraise of vice. Years earlier, in the *Epistle to Burlington,* Pope had followed the same method; but there the attack on Timon is so much longer than the neighboring eulogy of Burlington, and so far more brilliant, that it submerges the latter. In both cases, however, Pope is especially convincing because as a normal thing he places an envoi or apostrophe, addressed to a primary reader, at the end of a long poem. Since this person is conventionally given his proper name, as the subject of a public tribute, the anonymous Lady inherits such authenticity. Here Pope is in a sense merely expanding and heightening the envoi so that it becomes the positive climax of his poem.

The apotheosis of Mrs. Blount also helps Pope meet a demand normally attached to the production of satire. By what right, a reader naturally wonders, does any author take it upon himself to expose so many faults in others? Most satirists answer by making explicit their moral principles and thereby establishing their own integrity. Thus in *An Epistle to Dr. Arbuthnot,* Pope displays the poet himself as *integer vitae scelerisque purus,* to balance the ignobility of his enemies. This makes sense rhetorically, but the inevitable suggestion of vanity weakens his power as a satirist. In the *Epistle to a Lady* he works less directly but places himself more effectively under the banner of righteousness; for here he embodies virtue in another person and then aligns himself with her. To incarnate his positive values, he invokes not a set of propositions but the concrete description of Martha Blount. Where he does have a long generalizing, didactic passage—and that is to bridge the great series of vicious women and the final portrait of his heroine—he is not expounding virtue but analyzing evil. By establishing his friend as his standard, Pope not only makes his ideal vivid; he also gives us implicit assurance of his own moral elevation. Since she appears as goodness itself, and he makes himself out to be her wholesale and accepted admirer, Mrs. Blount has the effect of a supreme character witness for him, and thereby encourages us to accept his denunciation of the world. Although Pope had employed a similar method at the close of the *Epistle to Burlington,* the tie between the earl and the poet is too thin, and the effect correspondingly weak.

If the formal order of parts thus reveals extraordinary internal coherence directed to a significant rhetorical purpose, the pattern of imagery in the *Epistle* supplies some fascinating reinforcement of that impression. We must remember that *To a Lady* presents a dramatic situation in which the readers overhear the poet as he talks to a woman friend about some paintings. The pair are strolling through a gallery or around a studio hung with portraits and sketches of ladies. As they stop before the various pictures or studies, the poet delivers remarks on the subjects. At the end of the tour and the end of the poem, he turns to his friend and pronounces an encomium contrasting her with the persons whose character he has just unmasked.

It was a traditional literary device, as Professor Jean Hagstrum has shown, to use a gallery of painted portraits as the imagined scene of a disquisition upon moral types.[6] Pierre Lemoyne had employed it in his *Peintures Morales* (1645). Farquhar staged the idea in the *Beaux' Stratagem,* and Addison supplies an instance in a *Spectator* paper (no. 83). Professor Hagstrum also reminds us of the convention of satire formulated as instructions given to a painter. This was established by the Italian, Businello, in his serious panegyric, *Il Trionfo Veneziano,* where the poet does not describe scenes directly but tells an artist how to represent them. Waller, one of Pope's acknowledged masters, naturalized the device to England when he composed a eulogy upon the Duke of York's heroism during a naval battle; here again the poet tells an artist how to bring out the value of the scenes, and Waller entitled his work *Instructions to a Painter.* The formula was soon copied by satirists as a means of pinpointing the corruptions of Charles II's court. Although most of these bitter, libelous pieces seem ephemeral, at least two are by Andrew Marvell.[7] Pope is only tangentially instructing a painter, and his scheme is far more peripheral than either Waller's or Marvell's. However, the tradition was familiar to him; and for the reader who remembers the Restoration poems, the overtone is there:

[6] For my discussion of the metaphors drawn from painting I am indebted to Jean H. Hagstrum's *The Sister Arts: The Tradition of Literary Pictorialism and English Poetry from Dryden to Gray* (Chicago, 1958), pp. 236–40, and to Robert J. Allen's "Pope and the Sister Arts" in *Pope and His Contemporaries: Essays Presented to George Sherburn,* ed. James A. Clifford and Louis A. Landa (Oxford, 1949), pp. 78–88.

[7] See H. M. Margoliouth's discussion in his edition of Marvell's *Poems and Letters* (Oxford, 1927), I, 268–70, 289.

> Chuse a firm Cloud, before it fall, and in it
> Catch, ere she change, the Cynthia of this minute.
> . . . .
> Some wand'ring touches, some reflected light,
> Some flying stroke alone can hit 'em right.
>
> (ll. 19–20, 153–54)

All this is figurative, of course; for we normally treat the Lady of the poem as a transparent screen between the poet and ourselves; we treat the poem as a monologue; and we treat the allusions to painting as metaphors. However, I should like to indicate what the figurative setting contributes to the design and rhetoric of the poem. Young, like Pope, states his theme in terms of painting, and he makes casual use of plastic similes:

> What picture's yonder loosen'd from its frame?
> Or is't *Asturia*? that affected dame? [8]

But he never hints at more, or connects the separate similes to a general scheme. Pope, however, explores the symbolic value of treating sinners this way; and he puts his meaning explicitly at the opening of the attack. In his substitution of paintings for persons he implies the vices of vanity, deceit, and—above all—fickleness:

> How many Pictures of one Nymph we view,
> All how unlike each other, all how true!   (ll. 5–6)

Pope contrasts the corrupted women's dependence upon visible charms with the Lady's reliance on virtue within. The theme is a commonplace: Juba's praise of Marcia in *Cato*, Swift's praise of Biddy Floyd, Welsted's epilogue to Steele's *Conscious Lovers*, all sing the same tune, exalting not the visible but the moral, intellectual, and domestic resources of the ideal woman; yet in Pope's poem the implicit contrast, point for point, with the tangibilities of the villainous women who have just been observed, produces a marvelous ironical transformation of the adjectives associated with them— "art," "pride," etc.—when these are applied to Mrs. Blount:

> Reserve with Frankness, Art with Truth ally'd,
> Courage with Softness, Modesty with Pride,
> Fix'd Principles, with Fancy ever new.   (ll. 277–79)

Young publishes similar aphorisms: "Your strongest charms are native innocence"; "Be kind and virtuous, you'll be blest and wise."

---

[8] Young, *Universal Passion*, satire VI, p. 141.

But he confuses his arguments by also praising good women for appearances—for physical beauty and elegant clothes; he never ties the moral contrast to a pervasive metaphor; and his flattery of the highest-born compels him to shun opportunities for irony.

While Pope's objects of satire are present only as paintings, his Lady appears as a living being. The two-dimensional portraits therefore enhance one's sense of positive climax, because it is only after passing over these dozen surfaces that we meet the rounded heroine. To Pope's remark that we distinguish such females by their color— "black, brown, or fair"—Professor Hagstrum applies the principle, accepted by Pope's generation of connoisseurs, that line is more real and stable than color, that color is more changeable and therefore like women.[9] The same motif occurs in the *Essay on Criticism,* where the "faithful pencil" is opposed to "treacherous colours," and where the true lines of sound judgment are contrasted with the deceitful colors of false learning:

> But as the slightest Sketch, if justly trac'd,
> Is by ill *Colouring* but the more disgrac'd,
> So by *false Learning* is *good Sense* defac'd.   (ll. 23–25)

The motif appears again in the lines on Cynthia in the *Epistle to a Lady*:

> Come then, the colours and the ground prepare!
> Dip in the Rainbow, trick her off in air.   (ll. 17–18)

And later in the poem it is employed more generally:

> Pictures like these, dear Madam, to design,
> Asks no firm hand, and no unerring line.   (ll. 151–52)

Pope even suggests that simple or unmixed (i.e., "equal") colors will not suit the problem; for only blended paints, implicitly less pure than the unmixed, can represent woman's evanescence and superficiality:

> For how should equal Colours do the knack?
> Chameleons who can paint in white and black?
>   (ll. 155–56)

Within the paintings Pope makes further refinements. The pseudonymous women pose generally in costume or disguise, and not as

⁹ Hagstrum, *Sister Arts,* pp. 236–40.

themselves; and the costume is often of a mythological rather than historical figure: false names, false dress, false models. Or the sinners pose ironically as saints—Mary Magdalen, Cecilia. To such tokens of deception is linked the ancient contrast between naked truth and overdressed vice.

> Artists! who can paint or write,
> To draw the Naked is your true delight.
> That Robe of Quality so struts and swells,
> None see what Parts of Nature it conceals.   (ll. 187–90)

Professor Hagstrum reminds us of Titian's *Sacred and Profane Love,* in which sacred love is naked and profane love clothed.[10] It is also obviously symbolic that the same woman should adopt contradictory roles in different paintings. The very syntax of such descriptions presses ambiguity upon us:

> Arcadia's Countess, here, in ermin'd pride,
> Is there, Pastora by a fountain side.   (ll. 7–8)

The couplet seems deliberately paradoxical. Although she comes from Arcadia and should therefore be a shepherdess, she poses for one picture in the robes of a peeress; on the contrary, although her husband is presumably Earl of Pembroke and a great courtier, she disguises herself in the pendant picture as a country lass.

Finally, the metaphor of painting is borne out in the use of color imagery to contrast the Lady and the sinners. Gray and silver belong to her; red and gold to them; her scene is shaded; theirs is dazzling; she evokes the quiet moon, they the beaming sun. Since the Lady happens to be a spinster, the lunar tones appropriately suggest Diana and chastity.

If one were simply adhering to the principle of self-contained art, this point might well be the stopping place of criticism. The internal structure of Pope's poem has been, however hastily (I have not even mentioned the brilliant versification of the couplets leading up to the introduction of Mrs. Blount), set forth; his superiority to a rival (and mentor) has been indicated. Yet the power of the *Epistle* is obviously too great for one to feel right about leaving it so soon: the poem overflows, reaching beyond literature into reality. It is in the very structure of the *Epistle* that the overflowing occurs

[10] *Ibid.*

most beautifully, but the effect is evident as well in humbler ways that may be noticed first. There is, for example, a historical truth in the imagined situation. Pope had early experience of pictures like those he describes; he took painting lessons from Jervas; he was accustomed to thinking of poetry in pictorial terms; and he was accustomed to hearing an artist discuss painting in literary terms.[11] Though for him pictorial art was divided, in the curious categories of his age, between portraits and history painting, it was of portraits that he had the most experience; all his own efforts were in that category. He had, as it happens, seen pictures of some of the women to whom he alludes in the poem; he had himself copied one—the Duchess of Montagu—on canvas; and he had commissioned and owned at least two—Mrs. Blount herself and Lady Mary.[12] Since Mrs. Blount spent much time in his house, therefore, the setting of the poem is remarkably close to reality. Of course, Pope shields himself by the use of misleading details. To smother rumors and to protect the maiden Lady of his poem, he gives her a husband and a daughter; yet we all know she is drawn from the spinster Martha Blount.

As it was originally printed, the poem suffered enormous excisions, the most sensational characters being prudently omitted until Pope felt secure enough to face the consequences of releasing them —or else so near death that no consequence could touch him.[13] He would hardly have held back from publication the magnificent lines on Philomedé, Atossa, Cloe, and Caroline if they were not allusions to the second Duchess of Marlborough, the Duchess of Buckinghamshire, the Countess of Suffolk, and the Queen. Sappho has universally been taken as a lampoon on Lady Mary Wortley Montagu. Arcadia's Countess is probably Margaret, first wife of the eighth earl of Pembroke. This employment of recognizable people and events is one persuasive ground of Pope's satirical appeal. Poetically, he keeps hinting, "These things have really happened." He does not mean that every name alludes to an existing person, or that every

---

[11] On Pope's interest in painting and his connection with Jervas, see George Sherburn, *The Early Career of Alexander Pope* (Oxford, 1934). For the correspondence between Jervas and Pope, see the first volume of Sherburn's edition of Pope's *Correspondence* (Oxford, 1956). I refer particularly to *The Early Career,* pp. 69 and 102–3; the *Correspondence,* I, 189, 239, 315, 332.

[12] See Mr. Bateson's note to I, 107; Pope's *Correspondence,* I, 189, and II, 21–22; and Pope's *Minor Poems,* Twickenham ed., VI, ed. John Butt, 211–12.

[13] Bateson, ed., *Epistles to Several Persons,* pp. ix–xvi, 40–44.

rumored scandal is true as represented. But since he claims that his insights are worth our attention, he must assume the wisdom of experience. By implying that he has observed at first hand the profusion of cases displayed in his argument, he encourages the reader to take him seriously. As a corollary, if the reader is to trust the obvious fables, he must recognize some facts. Just as Pope's didactic propositions shade from overt conventionalities to covert audacities, so his factual allusions shade from parables to direct reporting. The truisms serve to win the reader's faith so that he will respect the individual judgments; the facts season the legends so that the reader may credit the author as both an experienced and a faithful historian.

A more special effect is also felt because one never can be certain whether the poet has created an example or witnessed it. Once the reader thinks he can correctly name a pseudonymous character, he is bound to keep searching for new clues; and this search adds to Pope's late satires a vibrancy which deepens and strengthens their rhetoric. Young, in his satires, both sacrifices this special effect and weakens his general argument by dropping clues to a subject's name only when he is praising the person. His topical allusions are, as a careful scholar remarks, "not malicious," and individuals, if pointed out at all, are "generally mentioned in flattering terms." [14] Our curiosity is therefore dampened rather than aroused, and we infer that evil has less power than good.

The most brilliant allusion to reality, and the last effect I shall analyze in the poem, is central to the structure. This occurs at the negative climax and peripety, as Pope is completing and abandoning his collection of sinners; and it shows how a rhetorical order can be determined by facts external to a literary work. With the sequence of Atossa, Cloe, the Queen, and the Duchess of Queensberry, Pope seems to plot his path so as to reveal the sharpest contrast between the vicious and the good. He almost certainly intended the Duchess of Buckinghamshire to be recognized in Atossa. Katherine Darnley, Duchess of Buckinghamshire and Normandy, was the illegitimate daughter of James II. All her life, she exhibited a paranoid pride in her ancestry; she had a long feud with her husband's bastards, became famous for her megalomania, and ended up insane by any definition. "Cloe" almost certainly points to Henrietta Howard, Countess of Suffolk. She was at the same time both lady-in-waiting

---

[14] Charlotte E. Crawford, "What Was Pope's Debt to Edward Young?" *ELH*, XIII (September 1946), 161.

to the Queen and *maîtresse en titre* to the King. But although, as Prince of Wales, he had indeed made love to her, she was now superannuated, overweight, and deaf. It was years since he had shown her much tenderness. At court she endured the contemptuous protection of the Queen, who did not wish her to be replaced by a less manageable instrument. The Countess of Suffolk was Pope's neighbor and friend.

Of course, the lines on Caroline are cautious. Pope discusses neither the Queen nor a painting of her. Instead, he ridicules the stereotype which always seems to be substituted for a description when a painter or author must represent the majesty of Britain. There is a parallel passage in Pope's version of Horace's *Satires*, II. i, addressed to Fortescue (ll. 21–32). No scholar seems to have observed that in both places the poet was probably alluding to Young's tinny tributes, in his satires, to the Queen and her eldest daughter.[15] It is such cliché praises and cliché poses that Pope pretends to be attacking, rather than the royal person. Because of these screens of nonsense, he says, one cannot look to the throne for a model of virtue.

As an alternative, however, he suggests, of all people, an avowed enemy of the court, whose title has a pun on "queen." Catherine Douglas, Duchess of Queensberry, was celebrated not only for her beauty and wit. She had bestowed the most liberal patronage on Pope's friend, Gay; and recently she had withdrawn from court because of a furious quarrel with the royal household over her grace's aggressive support of Gay's opera *Polly*. Nevertheless, says Pope, this duchess is too modest to act as a cynosure. He will therefore pass on to the general fact that humble persons are easier to see truly than the great; and the humble, therefore, will better provide us with examples. "If Queensberry to strip there's no compelling,/'Tis from a handmaid we must take a Helen" (ll. 193–94).

In giving us a king's bastard, followed by a king's mistress, followed by the same king's queen, to whom the same mistress was lady-in-waiting, followed by a Duchess of Queensberry who had thrown over the whole court, I think Pope must be sounding a fanfare of innuendoes to draw attention to his theme and to announce

[15] Young, *Universal Passion*, satire V, p. 113; satire VI, pp. 155–56. Cf. Crawford, "Pope's Debt," p. 167. The ridicule of the stereotype-maker is also found in the *Epistle to Cobham*, ll. 87–92. The end of *To Augustus* is, I suppose, the last refinement of the theme.

his heroine.[16] Yet it is only by going outside the poem, to external facts, that we can establish the meaning of this sequence. We have touched the point of the social pyramid and found it the pinnacle of evil as well as of rank: the greatest vanity, the greatest lust, and the greatest power appear together; and since it is here alone that Pope uses proper names, we may also say this marks his most direct appeal to reality.[17]

Applying to Young the test that Pope meets so easily, one produces quite different results; for at several points Young may be described as defeated by reality. As a comprehensive principle the argument to which he tries to relate all the instances of vice or frivolity in his satires seems unpleasantly shallow: namely, that a desire for fame of one sort or another is the common source of foolish and vicious actions. Young may perhaps have flattered himself that he had a proposition to prove—and consequently more intellectual coherence than Pope in the *Epistle*—but the proposition is so weak and unconvincing as to disgrace its asserter. Even if it should be regarded not as a supposed truth but merely as a structural device, it fails, because many of the most effective passages in the poems cannot be related to the central theme—the denunciation of patron-hunters:

> Who'd be a *crutch* to prop a rotten peer;
> Or living *pendant,* dangling at his ear.[18]

The failure of the poems to cohere as a general argument would seem less offensive if Young allowed subordinate pleadings to move consistently with themselves. But repeatedly when he claims to fight for one doctrine, he wears the uniform of another. In his own person, for example, he reproaches venal authors and bemoans the willingness of poets to sacrifice truth to profit. Yet in the dedications, compliments, and apostrophes which intermit the satire, his quivering eagerness for mercenary advancement appears so openly that no reader can observe the reproaches without sneering. Furthermore, the portraits that seem to excite the poet's greatest energy do not

---

[16] The reference in l. 198 to "honest Mah'met," a servant to George II, seems intended to strengthen the innuendoes.

[17] Cf. Mr. Bateson's comment, p. xlviii, on the accuracy of the poem. Pope's allusions to Martha Blount in his letters, and the contrast he draws between her and Lady Suffolk, are remarkably close to his language in the poem; see his *Correspondence*, III, 349, 434–35, 450, and IV, 187.

[18] Young, *Universal Passion,* satire IV, p. 71.

exhibit threats to a real order of morality but reveal mere freaks or triflers, such as Brabantio, who is proud of a reputation for absent-mindedness.[19] Normally, one has little sense that the characters are drawn from living people; they are too often governed by meaningless whimsies, and Young too willingly abandons the facts of human nature to satisfy his love of paradox—as in the character of Philander, who secretly loves his own charming wife but publicly keeps a mistress to avoid an unfashionable reputation.[20] Young's supreme blunder, in a work supposed to advance virtue and ridicule vice, is to choose his objects of admiration from the irregular circles of political power. Several of his eulogies would, with no other change, become ironical insults if set in the frame of some lines by Pope. The fawning praise of Dodington, whom sober historians compare to a jackal, the exaltation of a pawn like Compton—"the *crown's* asserter, and the *people's* friend"![21]—imply a contempt for the reality of British public life that vitiates Young's attack upon corrupt politicians.[22] As a final and wholly appropriate streamer to trail after his wobbling car, Young consecrates his closing "satire" to the climactic and wildly indecorous flattery of Walpole and the King.

[19] *Ibid.*, satire III, p. 49.
[20] *Ibid.*, satire III, pp. 54–55.
[21] *Ibid.*, satire IV, p. 63.
[22] *Ibid.*, satire III, pp. 56–60.

Pope and Dulness

by Emrys Jones

I

The strangeness of Pope's *Dunciad* is a quality that often gets lost from sight. During the last few decades criticism has worked so devotedly to assimilate the poem and make it more generally accessible, that, inevitably perhaps, we may now have reached the point of distorting it out of its original oddity. The *Dunciad* is both a work of art and something else: it is, or was, a historical event, a part of literary and social history, an episode in the life of Pope as well as in those of his enemies. And its textual complications—the different versions it went through—present unwieldy problems to editor and critic alike, which add to the difficulty of seeing clearly what it is. When the *Dunciad* is mentioned do we think of one, or more than one, poem? And do we include the elaborate editorial apparatus supplied by Pope, or do we suppress it, as being inessential? Is it in fact necessary to understand Pope's references to his now often totally obscure contemporaries? The *Dunciad* is so deeply immersed in history—the final version contains references or allusions to about two hundred actual persons—that its status as poetry is problematical, and has perhaps always seemed so.

In so far as the poem has been read at all, and it has surely never been widely read, the real critical effort has been to find in it some coherent meaning independent of its dead personalities. In the nineteenth century one tendency was to see the poem so much in terms of Pope's private character, to see it so confinedly within the context of his war with Grub-street, that it was impossible to take seriously any of its supra-personal, cultural pretensions. In this period the *Dunciad* was, so to speak, under-generalized. In recent years, on

"Pope and Dulness," by Emrys Jones. From *A Chatterton Lecture On An English Poet* (London: The British Academy, 1968), pp. 231–63. Reprinted by permission of the British Academy.

the contrary, a prevalent temptation—or so it seems to me—has been to over-generalize it, or to generalize it in a dubiously valuable way. I am thinking of the current tendency to praise the poem for taking a stand against barbarism on behalf of civilization, and to argue that, since such cultural issues are always with us, Pope has given expression to a permanent dilemma. The *Dunciad* may then be compared—indeed has been—with Arnold's *Culture and Anarchy*. The implication is that we read Pope as we might read a cultural or educational treatise, with a view to finding some guidance for practical activity. There is of course something to be said for this approach, for there is a genuine Arnoldian side to the *Dunciad* which comes out especially in the fourth Book, and no doubt general issues such as these may legitimately arise from a discussion of the poem. But it may be doubted whether they are the reasons why we read the poem in the first place, or, more important, why those of us who enjoy the poem return to it.

To say so much is certainly not to be ungrateful for such a scrupulous and thorough work of scholarship as Aubrey Williams's *Pope's Dunciad: A Study of its Meaning* (1955), despite some reservations one might feel about the limited sense in which "meaning" is being used here. In their study of Pope's "meaning" Aubrey Williams and those who share his approach confine their attention to Pope's deliberate artistry, his conscious intentions so far as these can be ascertained; and for their purpose they are quite right to do so. They emphasize the intellectual qualities of the *Dunciad* and those parts of it which comprise statement or allegory or approximate to either. And in such a treatment the great fourth Book rightly gets preeminent attention. And yet it is possible to read the *Dunciad* again and to feel that there is something else to say, that such accounts of the poem's "meaning" do not wholly tell us what it feels like to read, and that the first three Books especially have a good deal in them which seems to elude such treatment.

The *Dunciad* on the page is a formidable *object*, dense, opaque, intransigently and uncompromisingly itself. Its apparatus of prefatory material, voluminous annotation, and after-pieces helps to create something like a spatial sense of the area occupied by the central object, the poetic text. One can indeed contemplate it as something with real physical dimensions. Just as the Lilliputians one day found the sleeping man-giant Gulliver within their kingdom, so Pope's contemporaries can be imagined as discovering this strange offensive object, lying in a public place like an enemy weapon or a ponderous missile: essentially not a set of abstract verbal statements but a thing, to be walked around and examined, interpreted, and possibly dealt with. Certainly the *Dunciad* when printed simply as a poetic text, without its surrounding paraphernalia, is not quite itself; it has lost something of its solid three-dimensional presence. This impression that the *Dunciad* makes of being a thing, an object, is important to our sense of a quality with which I shall be particularly concerned here: its energy. When we read the poem we can, I think, sometimes feel that there is great energy and vitality in it, that Pope transmits formidable waves of power which affect us emotionally and psychologically, and that this aspect of the poem's impact—its emotional and psychological effect—is not really accounted for in those descriptions of the *Dunciad* which seem to have now become widely accepted. Works of satire can often seem more emotionally straightforward, the sources of their power less mysterious than they really are. And when, as in the *Dunciad,* the verse is crammed with the names of actual persons and with references to real events, the poetic end-product may all seem a triumph of the controlled will—and of nothing else.

If Pope were in complete control of his material, it would be easier than it is to speak of the unity of the *Dunciad.* For critics still debate whether it is one poem in four Books, or two in three and one. Ian Jack concludes that Pope shows "a fundamental uncertainty about the subject of the poem, a fatal indefiniteness of purpose." [1] He has been challenged by H. H. Erskine-Hill,[2] who finds a satisfying unity of purpose in the final four-Book version; but although his argument is a highly interesting one he does not, to my mind, altogether dispose of Ian Jack's original objections. But whatever one thinks about this question, there can be no doubt that the poem did go through several stages after its first appearance in print, that Pope did change his intentions to some extent, and that this happened with no other of his major poems with the exception of that other mock-heroic *The Rape of the Lock.* Uncertainty of purpose—if that is what it is—is not the same thing as mysteriousness, but these external considerations might be borne in mind when

---

[1] *Augustan Satire* (1952), 134.
[2] "The 'New World' of Pope's *Dunciad,*" *Renaissance and Modern Studies,* vi (1962); reprinted in *Essential Articles for the Study of Alexander Pope,* ed. Maynard Mack (1964).

one tries to account for the *Dunciad*'s strange power. Pope himself may not have been clear what it was he wanted to do.

Like some other great works of its age, like *A Tale of a Tub* and *Clarissa,* the *Dunciad* seems to engage us on more than one level. The first level one might describe as a level of deliberate artistry: the poet works in terms of play of wit, purposeful allegory, triumphantly pointed writing, in all of which we are made aware of the pressure of a highly critical and aggressive mind. But on another level the poetry works more mysteriously and obscurely: one seems to see *past* the personal names and topical allusions to a large fantasy-world, an imaginative realm which is infused with a powerful sense of gratification and indulgence. The first level is primarily stimulating to the mind, while the second works affectively in altogether more obscure ways. It is indeed relevant here to recall Johnson's remark about the "unnatural delight" which the poet of the *Dunciad* took in "ideas physically impure"—a notion to which I shall return.

It seems altogether too simple to think of Pope as a defender of cultural standards confronting an army of midget barbarians. It might be nearer the truth to regard the *Dunciad* as having something of the quality of a *psychomachia,* to see Pope as dramatizing, or trying to reduce to order, his own feelings, which were possibly more divided and mixed than he was willing or able to acknowledge. In what follows I shall be using several approaches to justify the feeling that the poem is often more deeply ambiguous than Pope's overt purposes suggest; and I use several routes because there are different ways of explaining and describing this state of affairs.

II

I shall begin by observing that the Scriblerus Club has a markedly retrospective, even somewhat archaic, character for the reign of Queen Anne. In an age much given to club activity this one stands out for certain qualities which recall nothing so much as the circle of More and Erasmus: not only literary cultivation and critical stringency but an almost conspiratorial intimacy and high spirits. The admiration in which Swift held More and the reverence which Pope more than once expressed for Erasmus are too well known to need insisting on: *Gulliver's Travels* is, of course, an example of

Utopian fiction, while in one or two respects (which I shall return
to) Pope's Praise of Dulness, the *Dunciad*, recalls *The Praise of Folly*
(and was dedicated to Swift just as *The Praise of Folly* was to More).
But more generally the later seventeenth and early eighteenth centuries seem to have been much engaged in taking stock of the early
and middle sixteenth century, the age of the New Learning and the
Reformation. Bishop Burnet wrote a great *History of the Reforma-*
tion and translated the *Utopia*; during Pope's lifetime *The Praise of*
Folly was available in two new versions, Samuel Knight's *Life of*
Erasmus appeared in 1726, and Nathan Bailey's standard translation
of the *Colloquies* in 1733, while a few years earlier (1703–6) the
editio princeps of Erasmus's collected works had been published at
Leyden. Montaigne was newly translated by Cotton in 1685, and the
great Urquhart–Motteux translation of Rabelais—an important
event for Augustan literature—was finally completed in 1708. The
Epistolae Obscurorum Virorum were not translated, but were reprinted in 1710, dedicated to Steele. And Pope himself edited a selec-
tion of Latin poetry of the Italian Renaissance. Indeed when Pope
wrote the first *Dunciad* in the 1720s, he was not (as readers fresh to
the poem often suppose) simply scoring off his enemies by adapting
a few of the incidents in Virgil, Milton, and others to the degraded
setting of contemporary Grub-street—although he did of course do
this. But he was also fusing together certain other traditional kinds
of writing, some of which had previously been associated with prose.
Pope's concern to preserve the names of men who would, most of
them, otherwise have been forgotten is comparable with the intention of the authors of the prose *Epistolae Obscurorum Virorum*
(1515, 1517). And their satirical interest in obscure men in turn
gains definition from such a work as Petrarch's *De Viris Illustribus*,
with its characteristic Renaissance concern with true fame. Petrarch,
who stands on the threshold of the Renaissance, seems to have invented the concept of the Dark Ages: at the end of his epic poem
Africa—the first Renaissance neo-classical epic—he affirmed the
hope that the dark age in which he was fated to live would not last
for ever: posterity would emerge again into a radiance like that of
antiquity.[3] Pope, at the end of the Renaissance, closes the cycle: his

---

[3] See Theodor E. Mommsen, "Petrarch's Conception of the Dark Ages," *Specu-*
lum, xvii (1942), 226–42; quoted by Erwin Panofsky, *Renaissance and Renascences*
in Western Art (Stockholm, 1960), 10.

poem ushers in an age of darkness more profound than any envisaged by Petrarch:

And Universal Darkness buries All.

The connections of the Augustan satirists, including Pope, with the early and high Renaissance probably deserve more attention than they have yet received.[4]

More precisely, it is becoming increasingly clear[5] that the *Dunciad* owes something to a literary tradition whose chief classical exponent was Lucian. In the sixteenth century Lucian was particularly associated with More and Erasmus, who both translated some of his satires and whose *Utopia* and *Praise of Folly* were in part Lucianic in inspiration; and the same is true of the *Epistolae Obscurorum Virorum* and Rabelais's *Gargantua* (except that in them Erasmus's own influence is also important). These Christian humanist works have all caught something of the Lucianic flavour: an elusive scepticism, a vein of cool, ironical fantasy, and an irreverent critical spirit, which has often been attacked as merely reductive and irresponsible.[6] (Especially useful to More and Rabelais was Lucian's way of describing the manners of fabulous peoples, so as to produce an unsettling sense of relativity.) The Lucianic mode might be epitomized as a serio-comic style, in which the extent to which the writer is in jest or earnest is often left deliberately unclear.

There is one direct connection between this serio-comic tradition and the *Dunciad*. During the Renaissance a classical *genre* was revived which was not especially Lucianic, although Lucian did contribute to it. This *genre* has been given the name *adoxography:* the rhetorical praise or defence of things of doubtful value. The writing of such perverse or paradoxical *encomia* had been a recognized rhetorical exercise in antiquity, and was enthusiastically taken up again in the Renaissance. A bulky collection of such writings, in Latin, appeared in Hanover in 1619, and was followed by other editions; it was edited by Caspar Dornavius and called *Amphithea-*

---

[4] For example, the third of Oldham's *Satires upon the Jesuits* was modelled on George Buchanan's Latin satire against the Franciscans, *Franciscanus*. See *Poems on Affairs of State*, ii, 1678–81, 44, ed. Elias F. Mengel, Jr. (Yale, 1965).

[5] See Aubrey Williams and H. H. Erskine-Hill, op. cit.

[6] The use made of Lucian by Erasmus and More is fully discussed in H. A. Mason's *Humanism and Poetry in the Early Tudor Period* (1959).

trum Sapientiae Socraticae Joco-Seriae.[7] It includes elaborate
rhetorical praises of such things as hair (and baldness), gout, deaf-
ness, poverty, fleas, lice, and so on; Erasmus's *Praise of Folly* is included, since that work belongs to this *genre;* so is Lucian's *Encomium of the Fly.*[8] There are, interestingly, several poems in praise
of Nothing—interesting because they form precursors of Rochester's
famous poem *Upon Nothing,* which is itself probably an important
formative influence on the *Dunciad.*[9] (Pope's imitation of it, *Upon
Silence,* comes into the same *genre;* and, as is well known, Pope
helped to improve Wycherley's "adoxographical" poem *A Panegyric
of Dulness.*) Also included in this collection are several works of a
rather different nature, which treat indecent or "scatological" subjects.[10] Considerable verbal ingenuity is lavished on these scurrilous
nugae, and one is strongly reminded of some of the effects of mock-
heroic: the treatment is ludicrously verbalistic, the tone earnest, the
style solemnly elevated and necessarily much given to circumlocu-
tion. What further anticipates Swift and Pope—and among Pope's
poems the *Dunciad* in particular—is the combination of scholastic
method with gross and indecent subjects. The result is a manner or
tone which might be called a learned puerility.

I remarked that the *Dunciad* can be seen as Pope's Praise of Dulness, a work which, at however great a remove, owes something to
The Praise of Folly. Mr. Erskine-Hill has convincingly described
Pope's ambiguity of response towards the "world" of Dulness created
in the *Dunciad,* and has related Pope's Goddess Dulness to Erasmus's
Folly. Structurally, too, *The Praise of Folly* may have helped Pope
to organize his poem. Erasmus's Folly is presented as a kind of universal principle: every one is in some sense a fool, and Erasmus's
ironical understanding of the multiple applications of *folly* as he

---

[7] See A. S. Pease, "Things without Honor," *Classical Philology,* xxi (1926), 27–
42; quoted by Charles Osborne McDonald, *The Rhetoric of Tragedy* (Massachu-
setts, 1966), pp. 89 ff.

[8] Pope's insect-winged Sylphs perhaps owe something to Lucian's Fly. Lucian's
Podagra (Gout) formed the basis of a poem, *The Triumphs of the Gout,* by
Pope's contemporary Gilbert West.

[9] V. de Sola Pinto suggested a connection between the two poems in "John
Wilmot, Earl of Rochester and the Right Veine of Satire," *Essays and Studies,*
1953. Dornavius's collection includes Passerat's *Nihil,* which was quoted in full
(apparently from memory) by Johnson in his *Life of Rochester.*

[10] Such things as *Podicis encomium, Latrinae querela,* and *Stercoris encomium,*
and several pages each under the titles *Problemata de Crepitu Ventris* and *De
Peditu Eiusque Speciebus.*

uses it allows him to embark on a survey of mankind from which no walk of life is exempt. Between Erasmus and Pope came Rochester, whose poem *Upon Nothing,* for all its brevity, is similarly all-inclusive or potentially so, since every one and everything contains the principle of "nothingness." Like Erasmus's Folly and Rochester's Nothing, Pope's Dulness is a fundamental principle of being, and the phrase "great Negative" which Rochester applied to Nothing could equally be applied to Dulness. The concept of Dulness becomes for Pope a structural device which makes possible a certain kind of poem: its inclusiveness allows him to treat a wide variety of subjects so that in the *Dunciad* he managed to write a poem which impinges on much more than its subject would seem to promise. F. R. Leavis's phrase, "a packed heterogeneity," which occurs in his essay on the *Dunciad,* very aptly characterizes it.[11] In one of Pope's prefatory pieces to the *Dunciad* he says: "And the third book, if well consider'd, seemeth to embrace the whole world." *The Praise of Folly* also embraces the whole world, and like the *Dunciad* it could be indefinitely extended: the structure is a capacious hold-all. The author does put an end to it, but it is possible to imagine it given repeated additional material, as Pope found with his poem. In this respect—its tendency to accumulate additional material—the *Dunciad* foreshadows two other works which share a relation to the Lucianic Rabelaisian tradition: Sterne's *Tristram Shandy* and Byron's *Don Juan.* Neither is finished, and in theory both could be (and in a sense were) extended for as long as the author lived. In the case of *A Tale of a Tub* and the *Dunciad,* part of their power seems to derive from the appeal, inherent in the subject-matter, of formlessness: both authors are overtly hostile to the chaotic threat embodied in their subject, but both betray a strong interest, indeed fascination, in it. In this they are interestingly different from Sterne and Byron, who are frankly delighted by the rule of accident, the unpredictable flow of things, which is perceived as the principle of Nature, the inexhaustible source of organic form. The attitudes of Swift and Pope are more divided: hostile on the face of it, but in their over-all treatment of the subject more equivocal.

The point I want to stress is this. The traditions and *genres* of writing which I have just been referring to were of a kind to exert a two-sided influence. They could be liberating, but they could also

---

[11] "The *Dunciad,*" in *The Common Pursuit* (1952), p. 95.

be unstabilizing; they could help a writer to realize his creative impulse, but they might do so at the expense of his rational equilibrium. His powers of judgment might be compromised by a spirit of reckless, possibly generous, irresponsibility.

III

A comparable influence, liberating but in some ways unsettling, might be ascribed to the mock-heroic kind itself, to which of course the *Dunciad* belongs—if it belongs to anything.

It is in the first place remarkable that some of the best imaginative writing from the Restoration to about 1730 is mock-heroic or burlesque or in some way parodic in form. The mock-heroic has been very fully discussed in terms of its literary conventions, its comic use of epical situations, characters, diction, and so on, but the secret of its fascination remains not wholly accounted for. These mocking parodic forms had been available to English writers since the sixteenth century, but they have usually taken a very subsidiary place in the literary scene. But in the later seventeenth and early eighteenth centuries they seem to move to the centre of things: they attract writers of power. The result is such works as *Mac Flecknoe, A Tale of a Tub, The Battle of the Books, Gulliver's Travels,* and *The Beggar's Opera,* as well as, on a lower level, Cotton's *Virgil Travestie* and his versifications of Lucian, and such burlesque plays as Buckingham's *Rehearsal,* Gay's *What D'you Call It,* and some of Fielding's farces. Certainly no other period in English history shows such a predilection for these forms. Why were so many of the best writers of the time drawn to mock-heroic and burlesque? No doubt it is useless to look for a single comprehensive answer, but a partial explanation may be sought by considering the time, the age, itself.

The period from the Restoration to Pope's death was one whose prevailing ethos was avowedly hostile to some of the traditional uses of the poetic imagination. It disapproved of the romantic and fabulous, and saw little reason for the existence of fiction. "The rejection and contempt of fiction is rational and manly": the author is Dr. Johnson, writing in 1780,[12] but the attitude was common, even prevalent, during Pope's lifetime. The literary world into which the young Pope grew up was, it seems fair to say, relatively poor in imaginative opportunities. The poets writing immediately

[12] *The Life of Addison.*

before Pope were without fables and without myths, except those taken in an etiolated form from classical antiquity; they seemed content with verses that made little demand on the imaginative life of their readers. It is suggestive that in his final collection of poems, *Fables Ancient and Modern* (1700), Dryden drew away from contemporary manners and affairs with versions of Ovid, Boccaccio, and Chaucer: the fabulous and romantic are readmitted through translation and imitation. Otherwise the literary scene as Pope must have viewed it as a young man was, at its best, lucidly and modestly sensible; but in feeling and imagination it was undeniably somewhat impoverished. What characterizes the literature of the Restoration is a brightly lit, somewhat dry clarity, a dogmatic simplicity; it is above everything the expression of an aggressively alert rational consciousness.

Something of this imaginative depletion can be observed in the structure of single poems. If we leave Milton aside, the poetry of the Restoration with most life in it suffers from a certain formal laxity: there is brilliance of detail but often a shambling structure. Parts are added to parts in a merely additive way, with often little concern for the whole: poems go on and on and then they stop. The poets often seem too close to actual social life, as if the poetic imagination had surrendered so much of its autonomous realm that they were reduced to a merely journalistic role; their longer poems seem to lack "inside." At one time Milton thought of Dryden as "a good rimist, but no poet." And T. S. Eliot's words still seem true of much of Dryden's verse: "Dryden's words . . . are precise, they state immensely, but their suggestiveness is often nothing."

In such a period the mock-heroic and burlesque forms seem to minister to a need for complexity. The mock-heroic, for example, gave the poet the possibility of making an "extended metaphor," a powerful instrument for poetic thought—as opposed to thought of more rationally discursive kinds. It allowed him entry into an imaginative space in which his mythopœic faculties could be freed to get to work. And yet, while offering him a means of escape from a poetry of statement, from a superficially truthful treatment of the world around him, it at the same time seemed to guarantee his status as a sensible adult person—as a "wit"—since what arouses laughter in the mock-heroic is precisely a perception of the ludicrous incongruities between the heroic fabulous world of epic and the unheroic, non-fabulous world of contemporary society. Presumably

few people nowadays think that the essence of mock-heroic is really
mockery of the heroic, but neither is simply the reverse true: mockery, by means of the heroic, of the unheroic contemporary world.
It would be truer to say that the mock-heroic poet—at his best, at
any rate—discovers a relationship of tension between the two realms,
certainly including mockery of the unheroic present, but not by
any means confined to that. It might be nearer the full truth to think
of him as setting out to exploit the relationship between the two
realms, but ending up by calling a new realm, a new world, into
being.[13] And this new realm does not correspond either to the coherent imagined world of classical epic or to the actual world in
which the poet and his readers live and which it is ostensibly the
poet's intention to satirize. It is to some extent self-subsistent, intrin-
sically delightful, like the worlds of pastoral and romance. In
various ways it gratifies an appetite, perhaps all the more satisfying
for doing so without the readers' conscious awareness. And in any
case, mock-heroic, with its multiple layers of integument, its inherent obliquity, was temperamentally suited to a man like Pope,
who "hardly drank tea without a stratagem."

Before coming to the *Dunciad* I should like to glance at Pope's
first great success in mock-heroic, *The Rape of the Lock*. It takes
"fine ladies" as its main satirical subject, and the terms in which the
satire works are explained in Ariel's long speech in the first canto.
Since the sylphs are the airy essences of "fine ladies," Ariel's object
is to impress such young ladies as Belinda with a sense of their own
importance and to confirm them in their dishevelled scale of values:

> Some secret Truths from Learned Pride conceal'd,
> To Maids alone and Children are reveal'd:
> What tho' no Credit doubting Wits may give?
> The Fair and Innocent shall still believe.

Pope characteristically blurs his moral terms, so that his own position as a man of good sense is represented by the ironical phrases
"Learned Pride" and "doubting Wits," whereas the empty-headed
young girls have access to "secret Truths": they are "Fair and Innocent," they shall have faith. Such faith abhors any tincture of good
sense, for fine ladies are characterized by an absence of good sense.
They are preoccupied with their own appearance, with the outward
forms of society, and—it is suggested—with *amours*. "Melting

---

[13] This is the argument of H. H. Erskine-Hill.

Maids" are not held in check by anything corresponding to sound moral principles; they are checked only by something as insubstantial, or as unreal, as their "Sylph." Mere female caprice or whim prevents a young girl from surrendering her honour to the importunity of rakes. Pope is working on a double standard: as readers of the poem we enjoy the fiction of the sylphs, but the satire can only work if we are also men and women of good sense who do not confuse fiction with fact—so that we do not "believe in" the sylphs any more than we "believe in" fairies. Judged from this sensible point of view, the sylphs are nothing, thin air. So in answer to Ariel's question, "What guards the purity of melting Maids?" our sensible answer is "Nothing": if a young lady rejects a man's improper proposal it is simply because—she doesn't want to accept it: she is restrained by her "Sylph." For the principles of female conduct are not rational: they are, as Ariel says, "mystic mazes," and sometimes mere giddy inconstancy will happen to keep a young lady chaste.

> When *Florio* speaks, what Virgin could withstand,
> If gentle *Damon* did not squeeze her Hand?
> With varying Vanities, from ev'ry Part,
> They shift the moving Toyshop of their Heart. . . .

and so to the conclusive irony:

> This erring Mortals Levity may call,
> Oh blind to Truth! the *Sylphs* contrive it all.

What is the nature of Pope's poetic interest in "fine ladies" in *The Rape of the Lock?* From the standpoint of men of good sense —the "doubting Wits" of Ariel's speech—such women are silly, vain, and ignorant. They are of course badly educated: they may be able to read and write a little, but their letters, ludicrously phrased and spelt, will only move a gentleman to condescending amusement. (As Gulliver found with the Lilliputians: "Their manner of writing is very peculiar, being neither from the left to the right, like the Europeans; nor from the right to the left, like the Arabians; nor from up to down, like the Chinese; but aslant, from one corner of the paper to the other, like ladies in England.") This at least is how women, or many of them, often appeared in *The Tatler* and *The Spectator*—and how they appeared to Pope to the extent that he was a satirist. However, simply because women were less rational than men, they were also, from another point of view, more imaginative because more fanciful than their male superiors. They were more credulous, more superstitious, more given to absurd notions. For if gentlemen, or "wits," were creatures of modern enlightenment, women could be regarded as belonging to the fabulous dark ages. Accordingly what women, or women of this kind, provided for a poet like Pope, a poet working in a *milieu* of somewhat narrow and dogmatic rationalism, was a means of entry to a delightful world of folly and bad sense. For although Pope as a satirist pokes fun at them, he is yet as a poet clearly fascinated by them. Women are closer than men to the fantastic and fabulous world of older poetry, such as that of *A Midsummer Night's Dream,* and it is precisely the "fantastic" nature of women that allows Pope to create his fantastic, fairylike beings, the sylphs. *The Rape of the Lock* is full of the small objects and appurtenances of the feminine world which arouse Pope's aesthetic interest: such things as "white curtains," combs, puffs, fans, and so on. This world of the feminine sensibility is one which offers a challenge to the larger world of the masculine reason. The man of good sense might laugh at it, but he could not destroy it; and to some extent he had to recognize an alternative system of values.

The subject I have been keeping in mind is the more general one of the imaginative appeal of mock-heroic, and what I have just said about the poetic attraction of the feminine world applies also, with certain modifications, to the attraction of the *low.* The age in which Pope lived seems to have been markedly aware of the high and the low in life as in literature. The high level of polite letters, indeed the contemporary cult of politeness, and the genteel social tone of the Augustan heroic couplet seem to have coexisted with a strong awareness of what they left out below. That is to say, in this period of somewhat exaggerated politeness, correctness, rationalism, there existed a correspondingly strong interest in the low, the little, the trivial, the mean, the squalid, and the indecent —to the extent of giving all these things expression in imaginative writing. The structure of mock-heroic and burlesque forms provided a means of getting at this kind of material and thus gratifying a desire which might otherwise have been hard to reconcile with the poet's and his readers' dignity as sensible and adult men and women. For all Pope's and Swift's different intentions, one can discern something distinctly similar in Pope's sylph-attended young ladies and Swift's Lilliputians: Pope's young ladies have something

of the aesthetic fascination of children's dolls, while the Lilliputians
—as when the army parades on Gulliver's handkerchief—call to
mind in a rather similar way the nursery world of toy soldiers; they
are both enchantingly *below* our own level. *The Rape of the Lock*
and Gulliver's Voyage to Lilliput are undoubtedly remarkable creative efforts: in Pope's case his poem for a good many of his readers
(and not necessarily the undiscerning many) has represented the climax of his fictive powers: it has an achieved roundness, a plenitude,
and an affectionate warmth, for the absence of which nothing in his
later poems compensates. And yet in both works—this is a matter I
shall take up later—the creative impulse seems close to something
childish or childlike in the minds of their authors.

IV

It is easy enough to see how Pope came to value the *little* in the
form it took in his earlier mock-heroic poem: the feminine and the
absurd. More problematical is the use he makes of the *low,* especially in the form it takes in the *Dunciad*: the gross and the obscene.
I want to consider mainly the first three books, which are mock-
heroic in a way in which the fourth is not. Each of these books treats
a different aspect of Dulness as Pope imagined it, and does so
through an appropriate action or setting. The result is to create in
each book one or two large composite images which—such is the
interest with which Pope invests them—are exciting, or disturbing,
or even exhilarating, to contemplate. However, as I suggested earlier,
we can be said to contemplate these images only obliquely, since
what engages the foreground of our attention is the luxuriantly pro-
fuse detail of the poem's verbal activity. Our minds are stimulated
and energized by a ceaseless flow of wit, word-play, allusion, and so
on, which exercise a control over us almost hypnotic—and particularly important is the arresting use of proper names. Obliquely,
however, we are made aware of these larger images, and it is these
that I want very tentatively to investigate.

Book One presents the Grub-street poet in his setting: Grub-
street, a night town of poverty, hunger, mercenary writers, and
urban squalor. As usual Pope is at his happiest as a poet when dealing with a body of material which had been frequently used before:
he can then treat it allusively, confident that his readers will be
familiar with the *kind* of material he is alluding to. Pope came at

the end of forty or fifty years of an Augustan tradition which had
taken the topic of bad mercenary poets as itself a poetic subject; the
result was some poetry of a startling intensity. Pope could of course
take for granted the most famous of Grub-street poems, Dryden's
Mac Flecknoe; he would certainly have known, even if some of his
readers might not, Oldham's *Satyr Concerning Poetry* and Swift's
Progress of Poetry; while Juvenal's Third Satire, which Oldham
had imitated, and which Pope quoted in one of his notes to the
Dunciad, supplied the authoritative classical version of the "Cave
of Poverty and Poetry." Oldham's imitation of part of the Juvenal
includes the following:

> The movables of *P——ge* were a Bed   [Pordage]
> For him and 's Wife, a Piss-pot by its side,
> A looking-glass upon the Cupboards Head,
> A Comb-case, Candlestick and Pewter-spoon,
> For want of Plate, with Desk to write upon:
> A Box without a Lid serv'd to contain
> Few Authors, which made up his *Vatican*:
> And there his own immortal Works were laid,
> On which the barbarous Mice for hunger prey'd. . . .

Some lines from Oldham's *Satyr upon a Printer* contain more Grub-
street imagery, and end with a horrifying simile:

> May'st thou ne'er rise to History, but what
> Poor Grubstreet Penny Chronicles relate,
> Memoirs of *Tyburn* and the mournful State
> Of Cut-Purses in *Holborn's* Cavalcade,
> Till thou thy self be the same Subject made.
> Compell'd by Want, may'st thou print Popery,
> For which, be the Carts Arse and Pillory,
> Turnips, and rotten Eggs thy Destiny.
> Maul'd worse than *Reading, Christian,* or *Cellier,*
> Till thou, daub'd o'er with loathsome filth, appear
> Like Brat of some vile Drab in Privy found,
> Which there has lain three Months in Ordure drown'd.

Images such as those of the hack writer's garret, the bookseller's stall
or post—

> The meanest Felons who thro' *Holborn* go,
> More eyes and looks than twenty Poets draw:
> If this be all, go have thy posted Name

> Fix'd up with Bills of Quack, and publick Sham;
> To be the stop of gaping Prentices,
> And read by reeling Drunkards, when they piss. . . .[14]

—the whole underworld of prostitute, thief, and gamester merge in Pope's mind with such images as the following (from an ironical dispraise of learning):

> Let *Bodley* now in its own ruins lie,
> By th'common Hangman burnt for Heresie.
> Avoid the nasty *learned* dust, 'twill breed
> More Plagues than ever Jakes or Dunghill did.
> The want of Dulness will the World undo,
> This learning makes us mad and Rebels too.[15]

The *Dunciad*'s original connection with Theobald, the restorer of Shakespeare, entailed admitting into the poem the dulness of learning—the world of silent libraries, unread tomes, the brains of scholars laden with unusable *data*—and mixing it with the socially different *milieu* of Grub-street. Indeed in the person of Theobald, as far as Pope was concerned, the two worlds were actually united: he was a learned emendator, treading in Bentley's footsteps, but he also wrote pantomime *libretti* to keep himself alive.

This is the world which Pope so allusively and economically re-creates in the first Book of the *Dunciad*. The question arises: why does this Grub-street imagery arouse such an intense response? The Grub-street mythology, which fuses together the concerns of "high," polite literature with material poverty and every sort of personal deprivation, produced—one may conjecture—a peculiar thrill in Pope and his contemporaries, one which may still be felt, to some extent, by a reader of his poetry. (A single line in the *Epistle to Arbuthnot*—"Lull'd by soft Zephyrs thro' the broken Pane"—brilliantly evokes the whole of this mythology.) No doubt merely to glimpse such misery, degradation, and squalor produced a fascinated shudder in some readers. But in Pope's handling there is more to it than that. The condition of Grub-street's inhabitants was, above all, one of deprivation: a state of physical need combined

[14] From Oldham's *Satyr Concerning Poetry*. Quotations from Oldham are from the 1710 edition.
[15] From an elegy on Oldham by T. Wood, dated 1684, in *Remains of Oldham*, 1710. Pope uses the phrase "learned dust" in *Dunciad*, iii. 186, a parallel not noted by Sutherland.

with a state of mental vacuity. We may consider the two constituents separately.

Pope exposed himself to a good deal of adverse criticism, on moral and humanitarian grounds, for taking poverty as a subject for satire. He defended himself in various ways: by citing the authority of Juvenal, or, more often, by claiming that what he was attacking was the *pride* of dull writers who had only their own lack of self-knowledge or their dishonesty to blame for landing themselves in a condition which might otherwise be pitiable. But these high-minded professions of Pope do not wholly carry conviction: one may at least feel that there must have been more to it than that. The literary treatment of poverty in Pope and his predecessors seems to have something in common with the harsh comic treatment of hunger or even starvation which is a common feature of Spanish literature of the sixteenth and seventeenth centuries—the constant stress on pangs of hunger, bellies emptily rumbling, and so on, which we find in Spanish drama and picaresque fiction. Oldham, Pope, and the others find the subject funny, but also—it seems—in some way interesting and stimulating.

One of the aspects of the Grub-street setting which they give marked attention to is that of ludicrous physical discomfort: the material conditions of life press with a harsh and unwelcome force on the hack writer's consciousness; the unlovely objects which furnish his garret loom large in his vision of the world—and the fact that they do so is given mirthful emphasis for us because the Grub-street hack is, after all, attempting to write *poetry* in this setting: he is "Lull'd by soft Zephyrs thro' the broken Pane," or as Oldham put it:

> And there his own immortal Works were laid,
> On which the barbarous Mice for hunger prey'd.

What the Grub-street setting does is to force into violent antithesis the notions of body and mind by showing the etherially spirited poet of tradition yoked to a clumsy machine of a body which constantly craves to be fed, clothed, warmed, and cleaned. Such a poet drags out a doleful existence—which we are invited to find funny— in a world of unsympathetic *objects,* an environment totally hostile to and unsuggestive of mental and literary activity. The traditional garret setting seems to make the writing of poetry—any poetry— absurd; it derides it. And as it derides it, it calls in question the necessity of its existence, by insisting on the primacy of matter, mere things, mere bodies. The Grub-street myth is primarily a Restoration creation: it has some classical prototypes, but it makes its full appearance in English poetry in the satires of Marvell, Rochester, Oldham, and others, and it may be that its strong appeal is to be related to the rise of the new philosophy with its strong bias against the poetic and the imaginative. Such poets as Oldham may have seen in the reduced condition of the Grub-street poet as they imagined him, a grotesque reflection of the impoverishment of themselves. And so the peculiarly radical nature of the challenge put to the poet by the Grub-street myth was one to arouse powerful and mixed feelings: an intense curiosity (possibly unconscious of its own motive), intense mirth, and perhaps a vague feeling of alarm. There seems at times something almost hysterical in the violent response of such a poet as Oldham.

But there is another side to the subject. Poverty reduced the hack poet to a man struggling for survival amidst unfriendly objects; and one way in which Pope and his predecessors exploit the Grub-street theme is to insist on the gross materiality of *poems,* to focus attention on the poem not as a mental artefact but as so many pages of solid paper, something that can be eaten by mice, burnt for fuel, used for "wrapping Drugs and Wares" (Oldham), lining trunks (Pope), or, as Oldham put it, addressing the hack poet:

> Then who'll not laugh to see th' immortal Name
> To vile *Mundungus* made a Martyr flame?
> And all thy deathless Monuments of Wit,
> Wipe Porters Tails, or mount in Paper-kite? [16]

Both Oldham and Rochester degrade poetry further even than this by zestfully comparing it to excrement—a peculiarly Restoration conceit. Of course the satirical target in such passages is ostensibly *bad* poetry, but the satirical strategy is such as to involve good poetry —poetry of whatever quality—along with it. In the *Dunciad* Pope too uses this theme, but with less intensity than the Restoration satirists. The action of Book One takes place, we may say, in the

[16] There was a strong element of realism in this topic. Cf. an observation by T. J. B. Spencer: "The demand for waste paper, for a variety of domestic and other uses, has, until comparatively recent times, been heavy and continuous and urgent and far in excess of the supply. The consequences for English literature have been serious." ("Shakespeare *v.* The Rest: The Old Controversy," *Shakespeare Survey,* xiv (1961), 81.)

archetypal Grub-street night, with Cibber writing in his garret sur-
rounded by the fragments of his literary efforts:

> Round him much Embryo, much Abortion lay,
> Much future Ode, and abdicated Play;
> Nonsense precipitate, like running Lead,
> That slipp'd thro' Cracks and Zigzags of the Head. . . .

and later, in despair, he addresses some of his literary works (his
"better and more christian progeny") before consigning them to the
flames:

> Ye shall not beg, like gratis-given Bland,
> Sent with a Pass, and vagrant thro' the land;
> Not sail, with Ward, to Ape-and-monkey climes,
> Where vile Mundungus trucks for viler rhymes;
> Not sulphur-tipt, emblaze an Ale-house fire;
> Not wrap up Oranges, to pelt your Sire!

—the last line one of Pope's brilliant effects of agile concentration.
Poems ("papers of verses") had frequently been made to wrap food-
stuffs in satires before Pope, but to make them wrap oranges for
theatre audiences to use as missiles is a new refinement. Pope uses
the theme of the materiality of literary works with much less emotional involvement than his Restoration forebears, but the topic
still has enough life in it to arouse him to considerable artistic excitement. His treatment of Cibber here is less ferocious than Oldham
would have made it, but more elaborate and ingenious. And Pope's
verse is of course rhetorically orchestrated, shaped, and climaxed in
a fashion beyond Oldham's reach.

This aspect of the Grub-street setting has to do with the hack
poet's physical need, his uncomfortable awareness of his physical
environment. The other aspect I mentioned concerned the poet's
own *mental* poverty. To some extent what I have said of the materiality of poetry has already touched on this. For the bad poet's
mental vacuity, his mental dulness, is imagined in terms of solid
inert matter, heaviness, retarding friction, torpor, and so on, in a
manner learnt from Dryden's example in *Mac Flecknoe*. The whole
topic has been admirably treated by D. W. Jefferson.[17] Like Dryden,
Pope is keenly stimulated by images of solidity and inertness—he
has a remarkably sensitive insight into insensitivity.

[17] "Aspects of Dryden's Imagery," *Essays in Criticism*, iv (1954), 20–41.

I am suggesting that images such as these of the sordid and the grossly material are as exciting to Pope as they are repulsive. The deprived social underworld of Grub-street presented a challenge and stimulus to a poet who was placed in a position of social comfort and even superiority; as did the spectacle of insensitivity to a mind acutely sensitive. In both, the poet of consciousness and wit can be said to be contemplating a form of the mindless. A further related aspect of Pope's treatment of Dulness might be called the challenge of the unconscious to a mind keenly conscious, perhaps even over-confidently so. This is an area of my subject about which I want to remain tentative, and which I will approach somewhat obliquely.

There is in the further dim recesses of the *Dunciad* a region of Dulness, created for us by hints and allusions, which is an important element in the imaginative impact of the poem. It is there in Cibber's address to his literary offspring:

> O! pass more innocent, in infant state,
> To the mild limbo of our Father Tate:
> Or peaceably forgot, at once be blest,
> In Shadwell's bosom with eternal rest!

as well as in single lines like that describing the poets of Grub-street:

> Sleepless themselves, to give their readers sleep

or the dunce's "Gothic Library," where

> high above, more solid learning shone,
> The Classics of an Age that heard of none.

This is an elusive region, but recognizable to anyone familiar with the poem: a vast dim hinterland of book-writing, book-reading, and book-learning, not so much a dream of learning as a nightmare of dead knowledge. This striking fantasy seems essentially a late-Renaissance phenomenon, something peculiar to a period not too far removed from the first age of print to have altogether lost its sense of the power and objectivity of printed books, but so late in the era of humanism that its sense of the closing of a cycle was very strong.[18] Milton had said that "books are not absolutely dead things," and that a good book was "the precious life blood of a

---

[18] Marshall McLuhan ends *The Gutenberg Galaxy* (1962) with a discussion of the *Dunciad*. He declares that "the first age of print introduced the first age of the unconscious," p. 245.

master spirit, embalmed and treasured up on purpose to a life beyond life." Pope, in effect, shows that bad books too do not die, but
if they do not achieve the empyrean of fame they are at least con-
signed to an eternity in limbo, a place of soft, gently decaying verbal matter—"the mild limbo of our Father Tate." Pope is sounding
the great Augustan theme—it is of course a lasting pre-occupation of
humanism—of the use of knowledge: how to make knowledge live
by making it useful to the real business of living. Cibber, about to
burn his own literary productions, says they are

> Soon to that mass of Nonsense to return,
> Where things destroy'd are swept to things unborn

—and an obscure region is evoked where things not dead, but dor-
mant or only potentially alive, maintain their phantom-like existence. They lurk in a kind of lumber-room of the mind, useless and
irrelevant, in a manner comparable to the physical fate of the dead
in Rochester's powerful line: "Dead, we become the Lumber of the
World." [19] (The word *lumber*—"old furniture"—like *frippery*—"old
clothes"—is a favourite with Augustan writers, and is often given
imaginative definition by the opposite concept of *use*. Pope finds a
place for both words in the *Dunciad*.[20])

There is, I think, a strange intensity in these glimpses into a limbo
of the mind, not altogether explained by the Augustan commonplace concerning useless knowledge. Pope seems to be communicat-
ing here, however obscurely and momentarily, a sense of non-
conscious life—a form of vitality which is alien to the conscious
mind and felt to be a threat to it. It is of interest that the word
unconscious first makes its appearance in English a few years before

[19] From *The latter End of the Chorus of the second act of Seneca's Troas*, translated (*Poems*, ed. Pinto, 49). The couplet quoted above is, as Sutherland points
out, adapted by Pope from the same poem:

> And to that Mass of Matter shall be swept,
> Where things destroy'd, with things unborn are kept. . . .

[20] For a late example (1791) of *lumber* in a context concerning the use of
learning, cf. Boswell's summing up of Johnson's character at the end of his *Life*:
"But his superiority over other learned men consisted chiefly in what may be
called the art of thinking, the art of using his mind; a certain continual power
of seizing the useful substance of all that he knew, and exhibiting it in a clear
and forcible manner; so that knowledge, which we often see to be no better than
lumber in men of dull understanding, was, in him, true, evident, and actual
wisdom."

the *Dunciad*;[21] and indeed Pope's own image in Book Two of an "unconscious" pool is a suggestive one:

> No noise, no stir, no motion canst thou make,
> Th' unconscious stream sleeps o'er thee like a lake.

In this connection—Pope's poetic interest in mindlessness, which is one form of Dulness—Lancelot Law Whyte's book *The Unconscious before Freud* (1962) is illuminating: its theme is "the development of European man from overemphasis of self-consciousness to recognition of the unconscious." [22] Especially valuable in Whyte's book is his anthology of sayings from writers of the two and a half centuries before Freud. Pascal is quoted: ". . . never does reason override the imagination, whereas the imagination often unseats reason," and the remark has its value in this context. Another, which would certainly have been known to Pope, is from Dryden: ". . . long before it was a play; when it was only a confused mass of thoughts, tumbling over one another in the dark; when the fancy was yet in its first work, moving the sleeping images of things towards the light. . . ." [23] The *Dunciad* seems to have a peculiarly rich commerce with this twilight zone where intuitions have not yet been polished and clarified into an acceptable good sense. For what Pope as a deliberate satirist rejects as dully lifeless his imagination communicates as obscurely energetic—states of being densely, but often unconsciously, animated. Pope himself was undoubtedly committed to defending conscious mental alertness, vigilance, keen critical activity. Yet the poem as a whole makes us aware of the possibility of another tenable attitude, the value of what the Cambridge Platonist Ralph Cudworth called, in speaking of the mind's powers, "a drowsy unawakened cogitation." [24] In *The Castle of Indolence* (to take a slighter poem than the *Dunciad* and a far simpler case, but one not far removed in time) Thomson eventually works round to a useful moral recommending "Industry," but what is agreed to be the best

---

[21] According to the *O.E.D. unconscious* is first recorded in 1712: Sir Richard Blackmore uses it several times in his poem *The Creation,* of which the seventh Book is concerned with the operations of the human mind.

[22] Whyte's book is quoted by McLuhan, op. cit., p. 245.

[23] From an epistle To Roger, Earl of Orrery, prefixed to *The Rival Ladies* (1664) (*Of Dramatic Poesy and Other Critical Essays,* ed. George Watson, 1962, vol. i, 2).

[24] Quoted by Whyte, op. cit., p. 96.

part of the poem celebrates the allure of "Indolence." Nearly a hundred years after the first *Dunciad* Keats was to take the theme much further so as to make plain the association of Indolence, or Dulness in one of its senses, with artistic creativity.

v

I take my last ambiguous image of Dulness from a part of the poem which has hardly been the most popular or appreciated: the second Book. This Book, which describes the heroic games of the dunces, is the most notorious part of the poem, perhaps the most notorious part of all Pope's works. Here the satire against the book-sellers, critics, patrons, and Grub-street writers takes the form of making them go through ludicrous actions of a humiliating and even disgustingly sordid nature. At least, this is one way of looking at it—although a way which takes a rather external view of the actual working of the poetry. For this is not, I think, what it feels like to read. What the Book communicates is a curious warmth, a gusto, even a geniality—which, notably, G. Wilson Knight has testified to and described.[25] Certainly Pope lavished a good deal of work on this Book, and most of it is admirably written. He might have been expected to have shied away from it himself when he revised the *Dunciad*. But far from that, he carefully improved it, and added to it, making it the second longest of the four Books.

First of all, what is the dominant effect of Book Two—apart from its indecency? Some of the power of its imaginative conception comes from the fact that the action now moves out of the Grub-street gar-ret into the more publicly exposed setting of the City of London, but a city fantastically simplified, seen as in dream. This is London seen as Lud's-town—or Dul-town, as Pope brings out in a couplet in the 1728 version (its leaden thud was sacrificed in the recasting):

> Slow moves the Goddess from the sable flood,
> (Her Priest preceding) thro' the gates of Lud.

[25] Wilson Knight notes that "there is a strange and happy absence of the sa-distic. The comedy is not precisely cruel: the dunces are all happy, are not shown as realizing their absurdity, and are allowed to maintain a certain physical, though ludicrous, dignity." He further comments on Pope's "delicate emotional and sensuous touch, felt in the softness, the nature-tone, of the whole atmos-phere." See *Laureate of Peace* (1954), pp. 61, 62. In his essay on the *Dunciad*, in a discussion of a passage in Book Four, F. R. Leavis remarks on "the pre-dominant feeling, which, in fact, might fairly be called genial."

"Dul-town" is inhabited not by starving poets but by vividly felt, if faceless, presences who are sometimes infantile and sometimes maniac. (The notion of an *infant* can be related to the *Dunciad's* verbal and literary concerns through its literal meaning: "a person unable to speak or use words.")

Wilson Knight has remarked on the absence of cruelty in this narrative of the games. On the contrary, every one is having a wonderful time, for within the imaginative world of the poem no one is conscious of humiliation. These du* duces are, in fact, like unabashed small children—but children viewed with the distance and distaste of the Augustan adult. The world they inhabit is, like that of early infancy, wholly given to feeling and sensation, and so all the activities are of a simple physical nature: they run races, have urinating, tickling, shouting, and diving competitions, and finally vie with each other in keeping awake until "the soft gifts of Sleep conclude the day." The poetic atmosphere is soft and delicate, the feelings expressed by the duces playful, occasionally petulant, but essentially affectionate. As a satirist Pope is of course degrading his enemies: all the characters are given the names of actual persons. Yet, as usual, the poetry is doing something more interesting than a narrowly satirical account would suggest. What it is doing, in part, is creating a world free of adult and social restraints. "Here strip, my children!" cries their mother Dulness at one point, and they strut about naked, play games, quarrel, and shout, as free of inhibition and shame as any small infant. Pope evokes the unrestrained glee of childhood, its unthinking sensuality (as in the tickling match) and the deafening noise made by children at play:

> Now thousand tongues are heard in one loud din;
> The monkey-mimics rush discordant in;
> 'Twas chatt'ring, grinning, mouthing, jabb'ring all,
> And Noise and Norton, Brangling and Breval. . . .

The world of Book Two seems in many ways a version of preliterate infancy, and to enter it is to experience a primitive sense of liberation. Not only is it innocent; it is completely without self-consciousness: again Pope's poetic concern is with a form of unconscious vitality. The comparison of the duces with small children, however, is only implicit; it does not exhaust the whole of the poetic image. The duces are, after all, not in fact children, and in so far as they are adult they call to mind the inhabitants of

Bedlam, madmen resembling small children in being without restraint and without manners. Bedlam is one of the places which
Pope is careful to include on his simplified map of London: in the
first Book it is said to be close to the "Cave of Poverty and Poetry"
which is Cibber's Grub-street residence. In this second Book the
implicit Bedlamite metaphor becomes more insistent. (One of the
prints in the early editions of *A Tale of a Tub* gives an intensely
dismal picture of Bedlam hospital: naked madmen lie chained on
filthy mattresses in a large cell, while being peered at through grills
by members of the public.)

Let me give an example of a dunce who combines qualities of
infantility with the manic energy of a madman. This is Blackmore
in the shouting competition:

> But far o'er all, sonorous Blackmore's strain;
> Walls, steeples, skies, bray back to him again.
> In Tot'nham fields, the brethren, with amaze,
> Prick all their ears up, and forget to graze;
> Long Chanc'ry-lane retentive rolls the sound,
> And courts to courts return it round and round;
> Thames wafts it thence to Rufus' roaring hall,
> And Hungerford re-echoes bawl for bawl.

It is as if this dunce has grown to a figure of Brobdingnagian size,
or as if the City has shrunk to the dimensions of a toy-town with
a child standing astride over it. Aubrey Williams's account of
this passage is a good example of his method. He shows that the
place-names mentioned here are chosen to mark Westminster's
boundaries, so that the voice of Blackmore the "City Bard" resounding all over Westminster represents the invasion of the West End
by dulness.[26] His commentary is helpful and entirely convincing,
but such an account may have the effect of shielding us from the
full impact of the image as Pope has conceived it. For the image
of deafening, gigantesque noise—as of a giant *shouting* over London
—is, though comic, a disturbingly powerful one; and although it
has an allegorical meaning which we should know, the image itself
in all its rude force ought, it seems to me, to come first. This after
all is what one remembers after reading the Book: the games themselves, not what they "stand for"; the poetic fiction is primary.

No doubt most readers of Pope will never do other than shrink

[26] Op. cit., pp. 36–8.

from this second Book. But if one is willing to explore it, one beneficial result might be a clearer perception of Pope's extraordinarily rich, but undoubtedly very strange, sensibility. It seems possible that the impression of an unusual degree of creative release given by such parts of the *Dunciad* as these is due to Pope's being able to indulge intense feelings of an infantile nature by taking advantage of the permissive decorum of mock-heroic. There is a quality of complicity in the writing—"Heav'n rings with laughter" (ii. 121), and the mirth seems to include both poet and reader—that makes it hard to bear in mind that, from the "satirical" point of view, such writing is supposed to show Pope making a fierce retaliatory attack on his enemies. But so often this other point of view, which occasionally finds expression in Pope's own notes, seems to belong to a quite different mood and spirit. One of Pope's notes to the second Book opens in a tone of high moral indignation: "In this game is expos'd in the most contemptuous manner, the profligate licentiousness of those shameless scriblers. . . ." But the corresponding part of the poem reads:

> See in the circle next, Eliza plac'd,
> Two babes of love close clinging to her waist. . . .

The poetry, as Wilson Knight says, has a "nature-tone," and it seems not altogether absurd to find here a certain real tenderness—of course set against the incongruously risible circumstances, but none the less a modifying element in the full poetic effect. In a similar way the account of the mud-diving and the encounter with the mud-nymphs is, as several critics have remarked, strangely attractive, and has the effect of robbing the huge open sewer of Fleet-ditch, the actual scene of the action, of its horrible offensiveness. The effect is quite un-Swiftian, not nasty in the reading. In a related way such a passage as the following achieves an inimitably Popian beauty:

> Thro' Lud's fam'd gates, along the well-known Fleet
> Rolls the black troop, and overshades the street,
> 'Till show'rs of Sermons, Characters, Essays,
> In circling fleeces whiten all the ways:
> So clouds replenish'd from some bog below,
> Mount in dark volumes, and descend in snow.

This draws its vitality from its absorption of "base" matter into forms pleasurable to contemplate and from an attitude to experience which refuses to find anything repulsive or offensive: the "disagree-ables" are evaporated.

But the element of the obtrusively childish and dirty in this part of the *Dunciad* remains an issue to be faced. Pope often seems to have been attracted to indecent or equivocal subjects, as if he de-rived a stimulus from affronting conventional good taste: indeed, of all the considerable English poets he remains perhaps the one with the greatest power to shock—no doubt partly because the so-cial restraints which make the sense of shock possible are themselves powerfully represented in his verse. However we may respond to this side of Pope, it does not seem helpful to call it "immature," since it may well have been an indispensable part of his creative tempera-ment. Indeed Pope might have been a less comprehensive poet, even a less balanced one, without it. It has been suggested that during this period "various forms of play and irresponsibility may have been a chief outlet for the poetic impulse";[27] and certainly without their disconcertingly childish side not only Pope but also his fellow Scriblerians Swift and Gay would be considerably less forceful and original writers. Ambrose Philips's undistinguished, if innocuous, little poems addressed to children (such as those written for the Pulteney girls: one is dated 1724, another 1727, the years immedi-ately preceding the first *Dunciad*) were mercilessly attacked and parodied (e.g. by Henry Carey as well as by Pope[28]), presumably because they contravened the current assumption that childish feel-ings might be indulged obliquely in comic and parodic forms but not expressed directly in all their unwitty vulnerability. For the Augustans, Pope included, mock-heroic provided the perfect pro-tective form for the expression of childish feelings, since (as I sug-gested earlier) its built-in critical apparatus served to absolve the poet from a possible charge of too outrageous an irresponsibility. Similarly such versicles as Henry Carey's and Pope's Lilliputian Odes (written, for the most part, in lines of two and three syllables

[27] William K. Wimsatt, Jr., and Cleanth Brooks, *Literary Criticism: A Short History* (New York, 1957), p. 217, n. 2.

[28] Pope refers to Philips's "Infantine stile" in his note to 1728 *Dunciad*, iii. 322. Chapter xi of *The Art of Sinking in Poetry* (1727) had dealt with "The Infantine," "where a Poet grows so very simple, as to think and talk like a child." Cf. also Pope's reference to Philips in a letter to Swift, 14 December 1725 (*Correspondence*, ii. 350, ed. George Sherburn).

respectively) take advantage of the Lilliputian fiction for writing of an undiluted frivolity.

VI

In what I have been saying I have been deliberately stressing one side of Pope's genius: the peculiar *energy* of his poetry and its power to excite. I want finally to add a few remarks on this subject from a rather different point of view.

The *Dunciad* is so often discussed simply in terms of its topics, its ideas, attitudes, literary conventions, etc., or its individual effects of wit—its grotesque metaphors, its low puns, its studiedly indecorous diction—that it might seem that the poem as a whole was fully accounted for. Yet something more fundamental seems to escape such discussions: everything that can be included under the idea of *form* —the over-all shape of the poetic experience, the contributions made by Pope's use of the couplet, the paragraph, the episode and each Book of the poem. When Pope is writing well, the verse moves with a strong purposefully directed energy, the couplets are pointed, the paragraphs draw to a climax, and the individual Books each have a true conclusion—they do not merely stop. The couplets, for example, are never allowed to succeed each other in a merely additive way; instead they are held firmly in place in the verse paragraph, and the paragraph itself often follows a large rhythmic curve which makes possible a dynamic verse movement. When read with a sympathetic mimetic co-operation, such verse has an exceptional capacity to arouse nervous excitement. However, this energy sometimes has an ambiguous effect, which may be such that an account of the poem which stays too close to its satirical paraphrasable meaning may distort the real effect of the poetry.

In his liking for exuberant or agitated movement, for vehement emphasis, and for intense surface vivacity, Pope reveals himself as baroque in sensibility; as he does in his nervous sense of tempo, especially at those moments when he gathers speed for an overwhelming climax.[29] Among English poets in this one respect his true predecessor is Crashaw, whom Pope had read carefully and used, although

[29] One of the most impressive of such climactic movements, the conclusion to the *Epilogue to the Satires, Dialogue 1*—the "triumph of Vice"—was compared by Joseph Warton to a painting by Rubens.

it is not necessary to suppose that he needed Crashaw to discover these qualities in himself: there were numerous other influences. But nowhere in seventeenth-century English poetry except in the *Hymn to Saint Teresa* and the magnificent, and in some ways curiously Popian,[30] *Music's Duel*, can one find a comparable verve and ardour, such an acute response to sensory experience, or such a flamboyantly dynamic sense of movement.

These qualities are to be found in all Pope's greater poems, not least in the work he was engaged on immediately before the first *Dunciad*: the translation of Homer. This, in its energy, its sustained "elasticity" (Pope's term[31]), and in the way in which its personages are so often posed in brilliant theatrically lit *tableaux*, can certainly be seen as an outstanding example of the late baroque sensibility in poetry. In a comparable way the fantastic action of the *Dunciad* also allowed Pope to devise forms amenable to baroque taste. Some baroque art seems designed to express movement or animation almost for its own sake; and Dulness, as imagined by Pope—anarchic, "busy, bold, and blind"—encouraged the invention of such effects as those in the passage I have already quoted:

> 'Till show'rs of Sermons, Characters, Essays,
> In circling fleeces whiten all the ways:
> So clouds replenish'd from some bog below,
> Mount in dark volumes, and descend in snow

—with its repeated swirling movement, an effect which receives a number of variations:

> Not with more glee, by hands Pontific crown'd,
> With scarlet hats wide-waving circled round. . . .

and

> As man's Mæanders to the vital spring
> Roll all their tides, then back their circles bring. . . .

The sensibility which took pleasure in these and similar effects informs the entire poem, and, despite all the personal and topical allu-

---

[30] The account of the tickling contest in Book Two of the *Dunciad* possibly owes something to *Music's Duel*. Pope perhaps remembered Crashaw's reference to tickling: "that tickled with rare art/The tatling strings" (47–8). Pope's line 212, "And quick sensations skip from vein to vein" may recall Crashaw's "then quicke returning skips/And snatches this againe" (32–3), while his phrase "the pleasing pain" (211) is reminiscent of some of Crashaw's peculiar interests.
[31] Cf. *Dunciad*, i. 186.

sions and all the brilliant local explosions of wit, sets going (in the first three Books at least) a powerful current of feeling; at times the larger movements take on a demonic momentum. This may be felt particularly in the concluding phases of the Books, which are given an emphasis as if each Book were a self-contained poem.[32] Throughout his career the endings of Pope's poems are conspicuously strong and deeply felt: indeed some of his poems sound at their conclusion an almost apocalyptic note—a desire to relate the poetic subject to ultimate ends. In the *Elegy to the Memory of an Unfortunate Lady* the poet finally anticipates his own death, the end of time for himself, while in *Eloisa to Abelard* the heroine looks forward to as far in the future as her story will be read—which may again be interpreted as the end of time. And *The Rape of the Lock* has an ending whose startling power has to do with its looking forward to the death of Belinda, and again to an eternity made possible by poetry. In the *Dunciad* the first and third Books both end on sustained climactic movements; both record, in a high incantatory strain, a visionary moment when the order of things as they are, appears to be dissolving to give place to a totally different order. In the first version Book Three (originally, of course, the final Book) ends with the uplifted strains of Settle's prophecy—in the last line of which Pope's own name is introduced—before entering upon the great Conclusion to the whole poem. And this Conclusion is an ending in the grandest possible sense: the end of Nature itself.

The Conclusion to the *Dunciad* is uninterruptedly solemn and sublime: indeed its sublimity may be felt to be somewhat disconcertingly absolute. It seems entirely in keeping with the mode of the poem that we do not, perhaps, quite know how to take it; and indeed in the first version a note by Pope introduces a sense of wavering or qualification into the reader's mind.[33] In the same version the poem ends with a couplet which "contains" the vision of "Universal Darkness" and consigns it to the realm of false dreams:

> "Enough! enough!" the raptur'd Monarch cries;
> And thro' the Ivory Gate the Vision flies.

But in the final version of 1743 the Conclusion is no longer framed by this couplet, but ends uncompromisingly with

[32] Book Two is an exception: it cannot end with a powerful climax, since it shows the dunces falling asleep—although the falling asleep is in itself an elaborate set-piece.

[33] 1728 *Dunciad*, iii. 337.

> Thy hand, great Anarch! lets the curtain fall;
> And Universal Darkness buries All.

And there is no note here to suggest that the poet is not fully committed to what his poem is saying. The Conclusion has become a final, grandiose, annihilating gesture, sublime but also grotesque—for it is surely hugely disproportionate, not really prepared for in terms of the poem's own fiction. Moreover it has the effect, not uncommon in baroque paintings, of overflowing the bounds of the frame so as to engulf the spectator. Pope is of course cornering the reader, forcing upon him an acknowledgment of his responsibility, pulling him into the world of the poem—by making the poem reach out to him. But even here, it seems to me, where Pope is at his greatest as a poet of prophecy and lament, our feelings are not simple, nor simply tragic, and in one part of our minds we move through the Conclusion with a powerful sense of pleasure: the emotional drive of the poem, its baroque afflatus, seem to require a consummation as absolute as this. Pope's imaginative desire for completeness, for making an end, is here fused with his poetic delight in images of cataclysmic destruction. It is an important part of his greatness as a poet that he could not only recognize, judge, and repudiate the anarchic but feel within himself its vitality and excitement, and communicate what he felt. So it is here in the Conclusion. The poet at once succumbs to and defies the power of Dulness; and what destroys the world completes the poem.

Appendix: The Conclusion to the Dunciad

It has apparently not been noticed that as a poetic unit the Conclusion to the *Dunciad* was probably, though in a very general way, modelled on Ovid's account of the coming of the Iron Age (*Metamorphoses,* i. 125–50).

In Book One Pope had written of Dulness:

> Here pleas'd behold her mighty wings outspread
> To hatch a new Saturnian age of Lead.   (27–8)

To which he appended a note: "The ancient Golden Age is by Poets stiled *Saturnian*: but in the Chymical language *Saturn* is Lead. She is said here only to be spreading her wings to hatch this age; which is not produced completely till the fourth book." Pope here probably has in mind Ovid's account of the four ages (Gold, Silver, Brass, Iron), so that the Golden Age of Dulness—Pope's "new

Saturnian age of Lead"—corresponds to Ovid's last, and worst, Iron
Age.

The best-known version of the *Metamorphoses* in English was that
in heroic couplets (1626) by George Sandys, whom Dryden had
called "the best versifier of the former age" (*Preface to the Fables*):
Pope had read Sandys's translation as a child and had "liked [it]
extremely" ("Spence's *Anecdotes*," ed. James Osborn, 1966, vol. i, 14).
Sandys translates the coming of the Iron Age as follows (it is not, as
it happens, a particularly good specimen of his syle):

> Next unto this succeeds the *Brazen Age*;
> Worse natur'd, prompt to horrid warre, and rage:
> But yet not wicked. Stubborn *Yr'n* the last.
> Then, blushlesse crimes, which all degrees surpast,
> The World surround. Shame, Truth, and Faith depart:
> Fraud enters, ignorant in no bad Art;
> Force, Treason, and the wicked love of gain.
> Their sails, those winds, which yet they knew not, strain:
> And ships, which long on loftie Mountains stood,
> Then plow'd th'unpractis'd bosome of the Flood.
> The Ground, as common earst as Light, or Aire,
> By limit-giving Geometry they share.
> Nor with rich Earth's just nourishments content,
> For treasure they her secret entrailes rent;
> The powerful Evill, which all power invades,
> By her well hid, and wrapt in Stygian shades.
> Curst Steele, more cursed Gold she now forth brought:
> And bloody-handed Warre, who with both fought:
> All live by spoyle. The Host his Guest betrayes;
> Sons, Fathers-in-law: 'twixt Brethren love decayes.
> Wives husbands, Husbands wives attempt to kill.
> And cruell Step-mothers pale poysons fill.
> The Sonne his Fathers hastie death desires:
> Foild Pietie, trod underfoot, expires.
> *Astraea*, last of all the heavenly birth,
> Affrighted, leaves the blood-defiled Earth.

(I have quoted from the edition of 1640, page 2.) There is no doubt
that Pope used Book One of the *Metamorphoses* elsewhere in the
Conclusion, since his note to lines 637–8—

> As Argus' eyes by Hermes' wand opprest,
> Clos'd one by one to everlasting rest;

—refers to the source in *Metam*. i. 686–7, 713–14.

Ovid's description and Pope's Conclusion share a concern with a rapid decline or degeneration in human life. In structure too they have a good deal in common: like so many of the great set-pieces in the *Metamorphoses,* this one proceeds by enumerating circumstances line by line, working by accumulation to a climax—a procedure adapted here by Pope. But only the first twenty-six lines of Pope's Conclusion (627–52) are modelled on Ovid: his final four lines, in which Dulness is apostrophized, are his own invention:

> Lo! thy dread Empire, CHAOS! is restor'd;
> Light dies before thy uncreating word:
> Thy hand, great Anarch! lets the curtain fall;
> And Universal Darkness buries All.

The fact that Sandys's verse paragraph also fills twenty-six lines suggests that Pope used Sandys, rather than the original Latin, as a structural model. Moreover Pope's lines 649–52 are close in substance and tone to the last four of Sandys, and in the case of one line (650)—which was, in fact, added only in the final version—has one identical word, also in the final position:

> *Religion* blushing veils her sacred fires,
> And unawares *Morality* expires.
> Nor *public* Flame, nor *private*, dares to shine;
> Nor *human* Spark is left, nor Glimpse *divine!*

Of course the effects made by Ovid's description and Pope's Conclusion are very different. Pope transforms Ovid's description by substituting his own more abstractly metaphysical circumstances and building up to a far grander climax. But quite as important is the placing of each passage within the poem as a whole. In Pope's hands the Ovidian set-piece is removed from its place within the seemingly endless sequence of the *Metamorphoses* to a position right at the end of a long poem, unsoftened (in the final version) by any narrative framework, and left to make its full impact in all its massive abruptness.

Pope's Conclusion (unlike Johnson's in *Rasselas*) is a conclusion in which *everything* is concluded. And just as the whole poem works up to the great Conclusion, so the Conclusion itself works up to the immensely resonant last line:

> And Universal Darkness buries All.

The line had an earlier form, in which Pope tried out "Dulness" and "cover" in place of "Darkness" and "buries." Sutherland also notes three lines in Pope's *Iliad* which anticipate it (iv. 199, vi. 73— he wrongly cites 199—and xii. 80); and Constance Smith in a note, "An Echo of Dryden in Pope" (*Notes and Queries*, N.S. xii, 1965, 451), suggests as a closer parallel, line 117 in Dryden's "Last Parting of Hector and Andromache" from *Iliad*, vi:

> And Universal Ruine cover all

—only this parallel having the words *Universal* and *cover* (which Pope had used in the 1728 *Dunciad*). Two other parallels that I would add are from Crashaw's *Music's Duel*, 156:

> A full-mouth *Diapason* swallowes all

and from Creech's translation of Manilius's *Astronomicon* (1697, p. 52):

> *Earth* would not keep its place, the *Skies* would fall,
> And universal Stiffness deaden All.

There are no doubt other examples of this form of verse-sentence, with a similarly placed verb and a final *All*. These lines are all concerned with striving to accomplish something absolute and final— to swallow, cover, deaden, bury, *all;* their quasi-erotic energy is very characteristic of baroque sensibility. Among the poets who use this form of line, however, Pope achieves unquestionably the greatest effect. In his final version of the *Dunciad,* by virtue of its perfect phrasing and by being placed last in a long poem, the line reaches what seems an ultimate degree of intensity.

The Satiric Adversary

by John M. Aden

Quisquis es, o modo quem ex adverso dicere feci.
—Persius, *Satire* I

Of the devices of formal satire, few are used more sparingly or
more effectively by Pope than that of the *adversarius,* or interlocutor of the satiric dialogue. Though neither Pope nor his Roman
predecessors made extensive use of it, its advantages proved considerable, especially in the rhetorical design of the satire, and particularly for Pope, who capitalized them beyond the example of
his models. The dialogue itself permits an enlivening of the satiric
discourse, a diversification of style, tone, and statement; promotes
dramatic immediacy; and affords at least the appearance of objectivity. Where the interlocutor is friendly, the poet benefits by the
presence of a second satirist on the scene. Where he is antagonistic,
he furnishes concrete evidence of the satirist's provocation and specific justification of his contention, *defficile est satiram non scribere.*
When corruption is added to antagonism, the adversary provides the
satirist an especially effective means of establishing the ethical proof
so important to his rhetorical purposes, enhancing, by the contrast
he makes, the image of the satirist as *vir bonus,* manifestly superior
to the dull, vicious, or naïve fellow contending with him.

Some account of the use of this formula in the Roman *satura* will
help to further its definition and provide a context in which Pope's
performance can be measured and appreciated. Horace, who used it
more than any other, used it little. Of his eighteen satires (*sermones*),

"The Satiric Adversary." From *Something Like Horace,* by John M. Aden
(Nashville, Tennessee: Vanderbilt University Press, 1969), pp. 3–26; the essay appeared originally in somewhat different form as "Pope and the Satiric Adversary"
in *Studies in English Literature,* 2 (1962), 267–86. Reprinted by permission of the
publisher.

only five, or something less than a third, are dialogues between Horace and a specific, participating interlocutor or adversary: II. i (Trebatius), II. iii (Damasippus), II. iv (Catius), II. vii (Davus), and II. viii (Fundanius). Though *Satire* II. v is a dialogue, the satirist is not involved, except as creator of the fictional conversation between Ulysses and Tiresias. The fact that with one exception (I. ix. *Ibam forte via Sacra*) Horace employed no dialogue (and hence no adversary) until his second book is interesting, suggesting as it does his own late recognition of the possibilities of the form. Even I. ix is not fundamentally a dialogue, but rather the *report* of a dialogue between the persecuted satirist and a bore who has cornered him. The dramatic immediacy of the piece is undercut by its narrative frame in the imperfect tense. But Horace had caught the idea and continued to experiment with it in the second book.

In II. i he conceives, in Trebatius, a brilliant example of the friendly adversary, in this case a close-mouthed, discreet, and somewhat cynical professional advisor, who, though opposing the satirist, does so for his own good. In II. iii he hits upon the principle of a more vulnerable adversary, Damasippus, the chap who had found salvation in Stoicism and wanted Horace to share in its benefits. But, as happens in almost all Horace's remaining examples, the dialogue machinery barely manages to sustain itself, for Damasippus dominates the discourse and delivers a long stoic lecture repeated from his master Stertinius. Much the same thing happens in II. iv, for example, where Catius, the Epicurean, is allowed to dominate the satire with an extended monologue on the gastronomic niceties of the day.

In II. vii the dialogue is with Davus, Horace's slave, who receives his master's permission to speak out on the occasion of the Saturnalia. Here the interlocutor more nearly approximates the hostility implied in the term *adversary*, but the pattern of interior monologue emerging from the conversational frame recurs in II. viii, where Fundanius, a friendly adversary (if an adversary at all, in any real sense of the word), reports to Horace the absurdities of a dinner party (*cena*) given by Nasidienus Rufus. Dialogue has only token existence, Horace merely leading his friend out to tell about the banquet, for which purpose he takes only nine of the ninety-five lines of the poem.

Of Horace's examples, then, only three present a clear-cut adversary, those involving Trebatius, Damasippus, and Davus; and of these only Davus is overtly hostile. Damasippus turns the charge of madness against Horace only in his last brief speech, and Trebatius is friend and mentor, who opposes the satirist out of concern for his welfare (or, as it may be, out of his cynical indifference to the satirist's crusade). Furthermore, Horace's practice furnishes only one example (II. i) of a genuinely sustained dialogue, his formula tending toward the monologic structure most characteristic of Roman satire. Horace's normal procedure is by means of brief opening dialogue to trigger a protracted monologue on the part of the adversary, whom, when he has overextended himself, Horace trips up or rebuffs in a deft resumption of dialogue.

Juvenal is even less disposed than Horace to dialogue structure. Of his sixteen satires, only two involve the presence of a second person on the satiric scene—the Third and the Ninth—and of these the former scarcely qualifies as a dialogue. Juvenal's temperament, so much more positive than Horace's, was not the kind to experiment with ironic modes and techniques. Even III, though two persons are involved, is not a true dialogue, for the satirist merely reports what his friend Umbricius said to him on the occasion of his leaving the ignoble strife of Rome. Once Umbricius's speech begins, at line 21, the satire reverts to a monologue of 300 lines. *Satire* IX is a genuine dialogue, the satirist speaking four times and at intervals throughout the poem, but it does not involve an adversary, for Naevolus is a suppliant, seeking a shoulder to cry on and a way out of his predicament.

Persius is the only one of the three great Roman satirists to employ an adversary between whom and the satirist there exists genuine tension or opposition, and he is the only one to make his adversary notably naïve or intellectually corrupt. Persius, it is plain, is much more strongly disposed toward dialogue than either Horace or Juvenal, for though only two of his six satires exhibit a definite participating adversary (I and III), nearly all of them strain in that direction, making greater use of what I may call a "nonce" or purely rhetorical adversary than either his predecessor or his successor.

In I, Persius pits himself against a defender of the effete and decadent literary taste of the day, a fellow who by his protests in behalf of the new mode and against the manly and satiric bent of the old, furnishes the satirist the targets against which to let fly his arrows of disdain and rebuke. At the same time, the adversary affords the satirist manifest proof to his audience that the satirist is not merely shadow-boxing when he registers his complaints against the corrupt modern: *ecce homo*. *Satire* I is a sustained dialogue, with the satirist matching speech for speech his adversary, and the tone of annoyance and disapproval is pronounced throughout. In *Satire* III, however, Persius also regresses in the direction of monologue, dominating the discourse with the young derelict who is his adversary and eventually delivering a lecture to the slugabed, who is permitted to speak only long enough to reveal his indisposition to get up of a morning and force himself into any worthwhile activity.

Persius strengthens the image and function of both roles in the dialogue, that of the satirist in terms of his more nearly equal participation in the conversation and his more caustic attitude and speech, and that of the adversary in terms of his more noticeable antagonism or culpability. In these respects Pope more nearly resembles him than he does either Horace, whom he ostensibly imitates, or Juvenal, with whom he has very little in common at all. Like Persius, Pope keeps dialogue distinct, consistently sets the interlocutor at odds with himself (if sometimes only apparently so), makes capital of the corrupt adversary, manifests a spirit of impatience or contempt, and speaks with a bitter tongue. But he learned much from Horace too, especially in the uses of the friendly adversary and in the strategy of irony. Only occasionally does he rise to the *genus grande* of Juvenalian style, though when he does it is powerful indeed. But in respect to dialogue Juvenal had nothing to contribute.

Quantitatively, Pope's use of the dialogue-adversary technique is about par with the Roman. Exclusive of the odes (IV. i and ix) and the *Ethic Epistles,* and including those poems "Something like Horace," Pope's Horatian poems—which is to say, his formal verse satires—number thirteen. Of these, four, or about one third, employ dialogue with a participating adversary: *The First Satire of the Second Book of Horace, Imitated* (February 1732–33), *An Epistle from Mr. Pope to Dr. Arbuthnot* (January 1734–35), and the two dialogues of the *Epilogue to the Satires* (May and July 1738).

Pope's first dialogue was an imitation of Horace, composed in "two mornings," [1] when he was confined in early 1732–33 with a fever: "Lord Bolingbroke, [who] came to see me, happened to take up a Horace that lay on the table, and in turning it over dipped

---

[1] Letter to Swift 16 February 1732–33. See *Corr.,* III, 348. See also the letters to Richardson (III, 350) and Caryll (III, 353).

on the First Satire of the Second Book. He observed how well that
would hit my case, if I were to imitate it in English." [2] The adversary Pope imitated in that satire was Trebatius, "one of the most
considerable lawyers of his time," [3] a terse and unillusioned advisor
to the satirist, whose problem was what to do about the complaints
leveled against his satire. To the satirist's "quid faciam," Trebatius
replies with professional brevity: "Quiescas." He is even less vocal
to the next question. You mean give up all verse? asks Horace.
"Aio." If Horace is sleepless, let him oil himself, swim thrice across
the Tiber, and meet the night with plentiful wine. If he must write,
let him celebrate Caesar. When Trebatius adds, "multa laborum/
praemia laturus," it is hard to say whether he is venturing a sly
joke or speaking quite soberly. Upon Horace's observation that it
is not easy to gain the ear of Caesar, Trebatius remarks that even
so it is better to try than to go about offending Pantolabus and
Nomentanus or exciting hostility generally. To Horace's insistence
that he is provoked and that, come what may, he must write, Trebatius counters, perhaps with a show of sardonic humor, My boy,
you will die young! Some great one will deal you a killing frost.
When Horace appeals to the example of Lucilius, Trebatius merely
reminds him that there are laws against libel. But, pleads Horace,
if the verses be good, if Caesar approve, if the provocation be just
and the satirist blameless? Why then, concludes Trebatius, "Solven-
tur risu tabulae, tu missus abibis."

Trebatius is a good lawyer, wise in the ways of the world,
and perhaps uncommonly close-mouthed for his profession. His
contribution to the dialogue is, unlike that of most of Horace's
interlocutors, slight, amounting to about seventeen of the satire's
eighty-six verses. His remarks are not devoid of humor of a wry
kind, but they are never playful, and their humor arises more from
the chance of what is said than from any design on the part of the
speaker to be witty. Trebatius is a kind of cynical *eiron*, a foil to the
alazoneia of the eager satirist. He is one of Horace's subtlest adversaries, serving not only in the end to "authorize" Horace's satire, but

[2] Spence, I, 143. For the reasons why it "would hit my case," see Rogers, pp.
66 ff. Essentially the point is that after the scandal aroused by the portrait of
Timon in the *Epistle to Burlington*, Pope could benefit by a defence in the
manner of Horace.

[3] Pope to Fortescue 18 February 1732–33. *Corr.*, III, 351. C. Trebatius Testa
was friend and correspondent of Cicero.

in the course of the poem to intensify its indictment by juxtaposing
to Horace's idealistic principle his own expedient one.

In his adaptation, Pope retains the cautionary character of Trebatius but puts the adversary more in key with himself: witty, sympathetic, and, at heart, as much satirically inclined as the satirist.
Pope's Fortescue[4] is more personable and lively than Trebatius, and
a somewhat more talkative advisor. He speaks some thirty-four and
a half of Pope's 156 verses, or something less than a fourth of the
whole. The difference is not great, but one is sensible of it. The
real change, however, is in the personality and attitude of the
speaker.

Fortescue begins almost as tersely as Trebatius (as much as the
difference in languages would allow), pronouncing to the Roman's
Quiescas, "I'd write no more." But then, unlike Trebatius, he warms
to the problem and becomes witty where the Roman was matter-of-
fact. If Pope is sleepless and if fools rush into his head, he could
nevertheless do nothing worse than to write:

> Why, if the Nights seem tedious—take a Wife;
> Or rather truly, if your Point be Rest,
> Lettuce and Cowslip Wine; *Probatum est.*
> But talk with *Celsus, Celsus* will advise
> Hartshorn, or something that shall close your Eyes.[5]

By comparison with Trebatius' essentially sober advice, this is a
tissue of witticism and bawdy and refuses to take the question of
the satirist (*quid faciam?*) quite seriously, perhaps because it recognizes that the satirist himself is not quite serious. It jests on the
use of wives for sleeplessness and, almost certainly, on the poet's
lack of qualification for that remedy. It then wittily turns on that
jest and breaks another upon it—that, on second thought, a wife
may not be the best remedy for restlessness after all. A sleeping

---

[4] Fortescue was not designated in any of Pope's editions, which carried only
the initial L for the adversary. Warburton is responsible for the designation of
Fortescue. See *Corr.,* III. 351*n.* Warburton was not without authority, however.
In a letter to Fortescue (above, *n.* 3) Pope wrote: "have you seen my imitation
of Horace? I fancy it will make you smile; but though, when I first began it,
I thought of you; before I came to end it, I considered it might be too ludicrous,
to a man of your situation and grave acquaintance, to make you Trebatius. . . ."
Cf. also the note on the MS. reading of "Hollins," Fortescue's doctor, for Celsus
(v. 19), in E-C, IX, 133.

[5] Vv. 16–20. Hereafter line numbers will be cited in the text.

potion then! Professor Butt reminds us of the anaphrodisiac prop-
erties of lettuce and of the likelihood of whimsicality in the prescrip-
tion of hartshorn, a stimulant rather than a soporific.[6]

When he comes to Trebatius' advice, Write of Caesar, at which
the Roman may have winked in *multa laborum/praemia laturus*,
Fortescue spells out the ludicrous possibilities: "You'll gain at least
a *Knighthood*, or the *Bays*." In the time of a Walpole and a Cibber,
neither of these rewards could be taken seriously (even if Pope were
not a Catholic) and in suggesting them Fortescue is given another
function Horace did not confer upon Trebatius—that of fellow
satirist. While he pretends to counsel discretion, Fortescue joins in
the game and contributes to the satire, not only here, but in his next
suggestion:

> Then all your Muse's softer Art display,
> Let Carolina smooth the tuneful Lay,
> Lull with *Amelia's* liquid Name the Nine,
> And sweetly flow through all the Royal Line.

A vein of irony and ridicule runs through this advice, which is all
but open in its contempt for the royal household. Such audacity
was scarcely available to Horace, even had he been inclined to it.
As for Trebatius, he was incapable of it, either by temperament or
by policy.

Even when he tries to be earnest, Fortescue cannot resist slyness:
"Better be *Cibber*, I'll maintain it still,/Than ridicule all *Taste*,
blaspheme *Quadrille*" (37–38). Here he alludes to Pope's *Epistle to
Burlington* and *Epistle to Bathurst*, which, he suggests, with tongue
in cheek, it is better to forego and follow instead the insipid
panegyrism of Laureate Cibber. By now, too, it becomes apparent
that Fortescue is consistently naming the names he advises his friend
to avoid. He continues to do so in his next comment, which is, at
the same time, the most nearly serious statement he makes in the
entire dialogue:

> A hundred smart in *Timon* and in *Balaam*:
> The fewer still you name, you wound the more;
> *Bond* is but one, but *Harpax* is a Score.   [42–44]

It should not escape notice either that in the reference to Timon,
Fortescue is obliquely countering the charge that by that character

[6] Butt, notes pp. 5–6.

the poet meant the Duke of Chandos. Fortescue is adversary in name only; he is in reality the poet's ally, and we see him progress from Pope's counsellor to his advocate to his fellow satirist.

When, like Horace, Pope says, "I will Rhyme and Print" (Horace had said only *scribam*), Fortescue almost translates Trebatius: "Alas, young Man! your Days can ne'r be long." But then he lapses into his facetious mood again: "In Flow'r of Age you perish for a Song." Where Trebatius let the jest, if it were a jest, go with "O puer," Fortescue, having said "young man," instantly perceives that he speaks to a friend nearly forty-five years old, and so corrects himself with a witty play on the cliché "flower of youth," and perhaps a pleasantry at his friend's expense as well. Unlike Trebatius, he will specify the potential enemies and continue his participation in the satire he pretends to decry: "Plums, and Directors, *Shylock* and his wife,/Will club their Testers, now, to take your Life!" To Pope's plea about provocation, virtue, and friendship with the great, Fortescue explains: "Your Plea is good. But still I say, beware!/Laws are explain'd by Men—so have a care." Trebatius had merely called attention to the existence of the law. Fortescue remembers the jurists, who, he would seem to say, are more crucial to the issue than the laws. He continues:

> It stands on record, that in *Richard's* Time
> A Man was hang'd for very honest Rhymes.
> Consult the Statute: *quart.* I think it is,
> *Edwardi Sext.* or *prim.* & *quint. Eliz:*
> See *Libels, Satires*—here you have it—read.   [145–149]

Several things are noteworthy about this. For one, Fortescue gives us a glimpse of himself as a professional man in a way that Trebatius does not. He knows the cases, the statutes; at least he can make a good show at ransacking his memory and his books. He is, in other words, more real than Trebatius because more circumstantial in his self-display. And Fortescue displays his legal skill, his rhetorical subtlety in word play, as in the case of *honest,* which, though it seems to concede the point of criminal frankness associated with satire, at the same time asserts the ideas of virtue, uprightness, and sincerity. But even more important in the economy of the poem is the suggestion which this speech affords of the setting which Miss Randolph reminds us lurks somewhere in the background of the typical *satura*, though Horace's poem seems to lack it.[7] The advantage in Pope's case is considerable, placing as it does the satirist and his respected interlocutor on a familiar, easy, and dignified footing. Fortescue has a book in hand, opens it to the appropriate places, hands it to his friend to read for himself. From this arises a distinct impression of scene—the only one in the poem, though it reaches back at once and gathers in the rest of the dialogue—and the reassurances, both dramatic and ethical, which that promotes. It is as if poet and friend are come together in the friend's chambers or study, talk with the intimacy and frankness of witty companions, handle the books that surround them, and enjoy a problem and a jest together. The effect is to make seem private, and hence more candid, what is, in actuality, quite public.

The poet will leave this scene with good advice, but with something more important even than that. Fortescue's last speech, dismissing the case, is in Trebatius' low key, but adds a significant point. To Horace's proposal of a hypothetically justified case of satire, Trebatius says only that the satirist might expect to have a case against him dismissed. Fortescue tells his poet, "you may then *proceed.*" [8] He does more than exonerate the satirist; he gives him his blessing and his leave to carry on.

Pope has heightened and complicated the adversary he borrowed from Horace. His Fortescue enlivens the dialogue with his own wit, contributes more or less openly to the satire he purports to warn against, defines himself as a personality, provides an effective suggestion of setting, and, at the last, renders an opinion that doesn't just get the satirist *off,* but that encourages him to *get on*—with his work. Horace pits himself against a stubborn adversary and wrings from him a concession at best; Pope recruits a partisan, who shares his ideals, adds the force of his reputation and wit into the bargain, and sanctions his perseverance in the cause. Pope's adversary has, without sacrificing any of the tensional value of Horace's, become a powerful ally. Like Arbuthnot, Fortescue stands revealed, despite his pose, "To Virtue only and Her Friends, a Friend." [9]

[7] Mary Claire Randolph, "The Structural Design of Formal Verse Satire," *PQ,* XXI (1942), 372.

[8] Italics mine.

[9] It should not go unnoticed that Fortescue is the friend of Walpole as well as of Pope. This may be another reason Pope decided against naming him as the adversary. But the identity was undoubtedly an open secret, so that Pope could have it both ways. The advantage of such an adversary—a friend in court—is considerable and was almost certainly calculated.

I include the *Epistle to Arbuthnot* among the poems employing an adversary because, even though as originally published no adversary was identified, I believe a case can be made for Warburton's procedure in giving some of the speeches to Arbuthnot in the 1751 edition of the *Works*.[10] Normally, it is true, the epistle, as a form, does not employ an interlocutor, that presumably being a contradiction in terms. According to Acron, *epistulis ad absentes loquimur, sermone cum praesentibus*.[11] None of Horace's *Epistles* admits a participating adversary, though they often create, within the framework of the epistle, what I have called a nonce adversary, for the purpose of rhetorical question and answer.[12] In Pope, such a nonce adversary is very common, and what no doubt began as such in Pope's original wrestling with the poem may have given way to the introduction of his correspondent as, in effect, a present or participating adversary. What more likely happened is that Pope felt

[10] Butt, pp. 93–94, summarizes the changes made in the text by Warburton. Although Butt allows that the "change from epistle to dialogue may be the work of Pope," he regards it as "a change for the worse," and restores the poem to its earlier epistolary form. Rogers, pp. 70–71, traces in detail the piecemeal career of the poem's composition, from which it becomes clear that there is a sufficient confusion surrounding the origins, manuscripts, and texts of the poem to warrant an open mind on the subject of the form. See also Pope's letter to Arbuthnot 25 August 1734, *Corr.*, III, 428.

The arguments against dialogue structure boil down to the fact that (1) the poem is entitled an "epistle," (2) in none of the MSS. or texts supervised by Pope is an interlocutor designated by rubric. In favor of dialogue structure (or, more properly, of *mixed* structure) may be urged (1) the presence of quotation marks at every point later identified by Warburton as Arbuthnot's interjection (that there are quotation marks elsewhere is no hindrance, for they are all clearly associated with some identified speaker), (2) the correlation of the speeches later assigned to Arbuthnot with his advice to Pope in the letter of 17 July 1734 (see *Corr.*, III, 417, and Pope's replies, 419–420, 423–424, 428, 431), and (3) the "lead-in" to the first speech assigned to Arbuthnot. Pope has just said, vv. 73–74, "And is not mine, my Friend, a sorer case,/When ev'ry Coxcomb perks them in my face?" when the reply follows, vv. 75 ff. Since there can be no doubt that the "Friend" of verse 73 is Arbuthnot, there can be no doubt that the speech beginning v. 75 is Arbuthnot's. This identification is in all likelihood sustained in the "Friend" mentioned in the second speech, v. 102. None of the other three speeches assigned to Arbuthnot carries such an identifying vocative, but since all other quotations in the poem are assigned to some specified speaker (in the nonce category), there is reason to give these to the Friend who has spoken, in the same vein, twice before.

[11] Quoted in Horace, p. xxi.

[12] Cf. Horace's "Si quis nunc quaerat 'quo res haec pertinet?'" (I. ii. 23), "Nunc aliquis dicat mihi: 'quid tu?'" (I. iii. 19), ecce,/Crispinus minimo me provocat . . ." (I. iv. 13–14). The nonce adversary is in fact the most common form, either in epistolary or satiric writing, and is apparently the basis of Miss Randolph's generalization about the *adversarius* in formal verse satire.

the attraction of both forms, the epistle and the dialogue, and admitted a confusion of form into his poem. Not that the result is damaging, for I cannot agree with Professor Butt that the shift to dialogue is "a change for the worse," though it admittedly introduces a contradiction in technical point of view that is somewhat troublesome. Theoretically, an epistle, being a monologue, cannot be a dialogue. The fact remains that Pope seems to have made it not only possible but successful.

Partly, one supposes, by virtue of Pope's hesitancy in the decision, partly by virtue of the quantitatively small part assigned the adversary (Arbuthnot speaks only thirteen and one half of the poem's 419 verses), Pope's second interlocutor does not attain the reality of his first, remaining on the whole, rather like Trebatius, a disembodied voice.[13] This relative shadowiness of figure is amply compensated for, however, by the adversary's trenchancy and audacity, which are quite enough to bring him alive and to distinguish him from the abstracter nonce adversary. Pope must have realized all along the value of having Arbuthnot on the scene, having his own say rather than merely serving as a puppet for Pope's ventriloquism, for the former is precisely the impression the speeches assigned to Arbuthnot make, that of a present interlocutor, reasoning, sympathizing, and ultimately collaborating with the poet.

When the adversary speaks, he does so as the anxious friend, solicitous of the satirist's well-being. He exhibits none of Fortescue's facetiousness or playfulness, but when he lends himself, like Fortescue, to the very cause he decries, he does so with an edge not found in the speech of the earlier adversary. His first remark is in reply to the satirist's question whether, like Midas's Queen, he must not speak out:

> "Good friend forbear! you deal in dang'rous things,
> "I'd never name Queens, Ministers, or Kings;
> "Keep close to Ears, and those let Asses prick,
> "Tis nothing." . . .   [75–78]

The advice is good, and it is urged sincerely, but it has a sting too and a daring innuendo—"Keep close to Ears, and those let Asses

---

[13] Perhaps not utterly disembodied, for he alludes to his height ("I too could write, and I am twice as tall," vi 103). This, as we perceive, is an allusion to Pope's height too, and evokes an image of the two friends side by side, the smaller proving the more heroic.

prick." One recalls that it was "*Midas*, a sacred Person and a King," who had the ass's ears, and he realizes that it is unnecessary to await the *Augustus* to see a satirist bite his thumb at a King. The satirist is shrewd enough in this instance, however, to let a great and respected public figure do the biting for him. "'Tis nothing" is also finely ambiguous and teasing, and ought not to go unnoticed.

The adversary's next interruption is a warning against the use of personal names and a reminder that the satirist is physically vulnerable to retaliation:

> . . . "Hold! for God-sake—you'll offend:
> "No Names—be calm—learn Prudence of a Friend:
> "I too could write, and I am twice as tall,
> "But Foes like these!" . . .   [101–104] [14]

Again good advice followed by the advisor's own stroke, scarcely disguised, for the foes are the names Pope has just mentioned: *Colly, Henley, Moor* [James Moore-Smythe], *Phillips,* and *Sapho;* and "like these" admits of indefinite construction along unflattering lines. When he advises prudence, moreover, Arbuthnot is doing what every friendly adversary does, that is, more than he reckons; for he is not only counselling wisdom, but in so doing, providing a mark by which the satirist's superiority to convenience may be measured.

When Sporus is mentioned, the adversary cannot suppress his contempt, and his advice to let Sporus alone is itself an attack upon him: "What? that Thing of silk,/*Sporus,* that mere white Curd of Ass's milk?/Satire or Sense alas! can Sporus feel?/Who breaks a butterfly upon a Wheel?" By means of his adversary Pope can have it both ways, can express the feeling that Hervey is beneath contempt and yet have at him all the same, all the while gaining the sanction of an Arbuthnot.

Two further interjections by the adversary are quite brief and function merely to provide the needed questions: "But why insult the Poor, affront the Great?" (v. 360), enabling the poet to proclaim "A Knave's a Knave, to me, in ev'ry State"; and a final question, "What Fortune, pray?" (v. 390), enabling him to distinguish the means of his family from the ill-gotten gains of others.

Whether the concluding couplet of the poem belongs to Ar-

---

[14] Cf. Arbuthnot's letter to Pope 17 July 1734, and Pope's reply 26 July 1734 (*Corr.*, III, 417, 419–420).

buthnot or to Pope must remain a conjecture. Warburton assigned it to Arbuthnot, and it is certainly more effective as his than as Pope's, but lacking quotation marks in any of the editions Pope sponsored, it cannot with the same confidence be assigned to him. As Arbuthnot's, it would show the adversary persuaded by the satirist's argument and in effect, like Fortescue, endorsing it, proclaiming, moreover, that ultimate judgment of the poet belongs to Heaven, not to his enemies: "Whether that Blessing be deny'd, or giv'n,/Thus far was right, the rest belongs to Heaven." [15]

In some respects, Pope's second adversary retains the character and functions of his first: both are friendly adversaries, opposing the satirist for his own good; both participate in the satire while ostensibly opposing it; and both (if the last couplet of the *Epistle* does belong to Arbuthnot) pronounce an exoneration of the satirist. But in other respects Arbuthnot differs from Fortescue, and one is left with the impression of unique personality in Pope's friendly adversaries. Gone now is the facetiousness of Fortescue, his witty jibes at the common foe, his easy rapport with the satirist, and in its place is a bluntness, a sarcasm, and a fierceness matching that of the satirist himself. This is partly the effect, as I have suggested, of his being Arbuthnot rather than Fortescue. But it must be acknowledged an effect too of a reflex in Pope's technique with the friendly adversary, for what has happened is that the adversary has changed character along with the satirist. The friendly adversary in Pope is partly an alter ego. What really changes is the satirist, and the adversary is accommodated to the change. Pope is now more tart, more indignant—more himself and less Horatian—than he was in the Imitation, and the adversary reflects this shift in point of view. In both poems the adversary works with and for the poet, but how he does so is dictated partly by his identity as a person, partly by the satirist's peculiar disposition in each poem. As far as this affects the *Epistle to Arbuthnot*, it may provide additional explanation of the reduced scale of the adversary's participation. Pope is rather too heated on this occasion to allow his adversary much interven-

[15] Part of the difficulty surrounding the interpretation of this couplet stems no doubt from the fact that the final paragraph of the *Epistle*, like other parts of it, was one of the pieces of earlier vintage brought together to form the "Bill of Complaint" published 2 January 1734-35 as *An Epistle to Dr. Arbuthnot.* A version of these verses was written as early as 3 September 1731 and included in a letter to Aaron Hill (*Corr.*, III, 226-227). This version may also be consulted in Butt, p. 127*n*.

tion. When he does admit him, though, he has him lay about to good and solid effect.

Pope's final, and consummate, experiment with the adversary occurs in the two dialogues of the *Epilogue to the Satires,* both composed and published in the spring and summer of 1738. In these poems he makes the adversary a genuinely hostile figure, introduces a new dimension of irony, and translates the interlocutor into a symbol of the whole satiric indictment.

Dialogue I (originally titled *One Thousand Seven Hundred and Thirty Eight. A Dialogue Something like Horace*) is essentially an ironic structure in which Pope permits a corrupt adversary to dissuade (or seem to dissuade) him from a defense of satire and to talk (or seem to talk) him into an ostensible defense of Vice. The relation of the poet to the adversary is thus unique in this poem, both with respect to Pope's earlier and his later practice. In the Imitation (*Satire* II. i) Pope, following Horace, contended with his adversary, who, unlike Horace's, did not really want to dissuade the satirist anyway. In the *Arbuthnot,* though the adversary was more earnest in his efforts to dissuade, he was at the same time more ready to give vent to satire himself. In the second dialogue of the *Epilogue,* satirist and adversary are at genuine sixes and sevens.

The difference is made to arise, properly enough, from the character conferred upon the several adversaries. In the earlier defenses, the adversary was actually friendly to the poet, intelligent, and, if shrewd, nonetheless honest. In Dialogue I the adversary, who is not on Pope's side at all but a true adversary, a symbol of Pope's hostile public and a spokesman for its corrupt principles, is neither friendly, intelligent, nor honest. He is instead somewhat foppish (a Sir Courtly Wit) and presumptuous,[16] a good deal vicious, and not a little stupid: an epitome of the corruption he speaks for. Such a creature has the traits of a true *alazon,* blandly unaware of his knack for self-exposure. What more natural, then, than for the satirist to slip into the role of *eiron,* let this fellow extend himself and feel that he is triumphing, while all along the ground is shifting under him and depriving him of footing. No need to argue with a dunce when you can damn him with feigned praise.

The dialogue's effectiveness is ultimately the product of Pope's portrayal and manipulation of this vulnerable adversary. For Pope

---

[16] In Pope's own note (1751) the adversary is characterized as "an impertinent Censurer." See Butt, p. 297.

not only wins the argument, but through the personification of vice and folly in his adversary makes dramatically real the threat to virtue which he proclaims. Part of the "willing World" drawn in "golden Chains" at the wheels of Vice's "Triumphal Car" is the adversary himself, both a victim and a counterpart in the real world of the Vice symbolized in the metaphoric world of the poem. In him the audience may view Vice "her own image, and the very age and body of the time his form and pressure."

The shift to a negatively functioning adversary is marked by several external tokens. The adversary is designated by the conventional rubric "Fr." (Friend), thus generalizing him on the one hand, leaving him undiscriminated from the crowd of time-servers he speaks for, and dissociating him from the poet's acquaintance on the other.[17] Also, contrary to earlier procedure, the adversary is permitted to speak first, a gambit which not only shows him as aggressor but which reveals his character and mentality, both of which maneuver him into a position of immediate vulnerability. Finally, the proportion of the adversary's speaking part is sharply increased over previous examples,[18] the reason being the satirist's desire to let the fellow damn himself, as he does, with astonishing thoroughness.

The self-indictment begins at once. By opening the dialogue with an echo of Damasippus's rebuke of Horace (*Satire* II. iii. 1–4), the adversary displays a fashionable familiarity with Horace but no sense of the awkwardness of the comparison which he invites by it. For Damasippus is, after all, a zealot, a mere spouter of stoic doctrine, and he proves in the end, with the stoicism he dumps so facilely on Horace, the butt of Horace's ridicule. The adversary's play on Damassipus' lines is made, too, at the expense of strict accuracy regarding the frequency of Pope's publication. In a note to these opening lines, Pope says that they were "meant to give a handle to that which follows in the character of an impertinent Censurer," and there is every reason to suppose that he meant this comment to include such revelations of opaqueness and factual unreliability as we have noted already, or such others in this immediate context as the Friend's revealing comment that, when Pope does

---

[17] In the first edition (1738) adversary and satirist were designated respectively A and B. Fr. (F.) and P are substituted in 1740. The same is true of Dialogue II.
[18] 40.7 per cent of the whole number of verses. Fortescue spoke some 22 per cent of the lines in his poem, Arbuthnot 3.1 per cent of those in his. The adversary of Dialogue II speaks about 8.23 per cent of the verses in that poem.

publish, "the Court see nothing in't." Damasippus had not designated the Court as the judge of Horace's performance, but had said
only *nil dignum sermone canas:* you make no poem worth heeding.
If his standard was a fanatical Stoicism, it was at least better than
that of Pope's adversary.

But these lines about the Court deserve further notice, for the
economy of Pope's technique is nowhere better demonstrated. By
the remark the adversary intends no more than that the Court is
unimpressed with what the poet has published, but the way he says
it and the implications flowing from it are extremely damaging to
him and to the opposition he represents. For what the Court does
not approve is, among other things, the *Epistle to Augustus,* with
its reflections on the King and on the times, a disapproval, therefore,
scarcely either candid or moral. But when the adversary words it,
"the Court *see* nothing in't," he suggests yet another interpretation
—that the Court is not intelligent enough to see what it is that the
poet is doing. In their dullness they are left wondering what this
poet is writing about. "Why will not my subjects write in prose?"

The Friend continues in this vein, complaining next (of all
things!) of the poet's correctness and of his moral bias (which he
disallows to Wit), both of which he describes, along with the charge
of stealing from Horace, as "Decay of Parts." In such wise does he
betray his own and the Court's inverted values. Nor does he enhance
the image of his morals and wit by his shallow and palpable attempts at flattering the poet, "who once with Rapture writ."

In the same speech (Pope hasn't spoken yet: why should he?), the
adversary confidently commends Horace for all the wrong reasons,[19]
for his "sly, polite, insinuating stile," which, he notes, "Could
please at Court, and make Augustus smile." He suggests that the
satirist follow suit, and recommends specifically the consolation of
Sir Robert's "Groat." To the poet's protest that to do so would cost
him his laughter, the adversary makes no difficulty of suggesting
that he indulge his satiric bent on *"Scripture," "Honesty,"* Patriotism, harmless themes, which "all Lord Chamberlains allow." He
may, in fact, vent his satire on any but "Fools or Foes," a suspicious

---

[19] The reasons are wrong in terms of Pope's values. It is possible of course that
Pope might concur in the notion that Horace was guilty of such faults. Cf. the
lines from Dryden's translation of Persius's *Satire* I. 116–118, quoted in Butt, p.
299n. It should be noted that in them Persius's description of Horace seems
intended for a compliment.

and, one would think, embarrassing set of categories to defend. When the poet ironically yields to this High Argument and bids adieu to Satire, the Friend, who does not recognize when he is well off (the satirist has just consented to lay his satire by), holds out the consolatory suggestion that the poet might still attack those disgraced, already down and out, once again bidding him only spare those in place. All this is tossed off in a brisk, dancing pace that bespeaks the glib self-assuredness of the "well Whipt Cream of Courtly Sense."

Damaging as it is, however, the adversary's corrupt morality is not perhaps his most vulnerable point. What may be worse, though it is no doubt a symptom of the former, is his mental ineptitude, his touch of stupidity and dullness. He is not only a vicious man, but something of a dunce too, and perhaps Pope wants us to suppose that the two have a way of going together. Here, at any rate, is a spokesman who can accuse the satirist of stealing from Horace (vv. 7 ff.) and then turn around in the next breath and praise Horace and distinguish his manner from that of the satirist (vv. 11 ff.); who in his reply (vv. 37 ff.) to the satirist's remarks on Walpole can himself inadvertently slander the minister; who immediately on the heels of the blunder can put himself in the extremely awkward position of acknowledging the virtue of Lyttleton and of Fleury and of condemning Hervey (Lord Fanny: vv. 45–52); who can express a doctrine so crass (vv. 53–62) that even Vice would blush to own it; and who, finally, can unintentionally damn the very Court he is defending ("There, where no Passion, Pride, or Shame transport," etc., vv. 97–104).

Pope's adversary is still participating in his satire, but unwittingly now, and for that reason all the more effectively. The Friend in Dialogue I, like the *personae* of Swift's satires, is so convinced of his own and his country's normality and of the rightness of their vision that he is incapable of recognizing, or even of conceiving, such a thing as self-incrimination, to say nothing of acknowledging public wrong and ruin. Pope's adversary fulfills the parable: "Out of thine own mouth will I judge thee, wicked Courtier."

Against this corrupt symbol, to whom he stands as positive foil, looms the satirist who is the object of his vicious and clumsy blandishments—the *vir bonus,* but more than that, *vir ingeniosus* as well: a man who can draw the line between Walpole's good and his evil (vv. 27–36); who is witty enough to play the ironist with his adversary, pretending to give up satire (along with "Distinction . . . Warmth, and Truth") and to praise folly; who pretends even to come to the defense of Vice and to safeguard against common use what is rightfully the Court's alone, and who thus shames the nation's leadership, which would debase, not redeem, its stewardship.

The adversary of the second Dialogue, like his noble kinsman in I, is, with slight differences of emphasis, also a self-deceived, morally corrupt *persona*. The difference in the two is to be felt largely in the manner of their exposure. Where in Dialogue I the adversary exposes himself through his stupidity and moral confusion, that in II is tripped up or squarely answered by the poet, who opposes him at every turn, with the exception of two or three momentary instances of ironic pose. The folly of the Friend in II lies more in simple heedlessness and argumentative incaution than in outright stupidity, though he is by no means as mentally alert as he needs to be in order to engage Pope. This defect of carelessness, with its hint of mental sluggishness, is comically exposed near the outset of the poem. In the political vein of his predecessor, the Friend suggests to the satirist that he "Spare . . . the Person, and expose the Vice," with which the poet pretends to comply, only to suck in the adversary. "Ye Statesmen, Priests . . . Ye Tradesmen vile . . . Ye Rev'rend Atheists!" cries the satirist, whereupon the Friend breaks in: "Scandal! Name them, Who?/P. Why that's the thing you bid me not to do." Upon the poet's subsequent allusion to the "pois'ning Dame," the Friend interrupts again:

> Fr. You mean—P. I don't.—Fr.
>   You do.
>   P. See! now I keep the Secret, and not you.
> The bribing Statesman—Fr. Hold! too high you go.
>   P. The Brib'd Elector—Fr. There you stoop too low.
>   P. I fain wou'd please you, if I knew with what:
> Tell me, which Knave is lawful Game, which not?

Obviously the Court will have to field a better man than this if it expects to discredit the satirist. The fact that it apparently cannot is not the least of the satirist's proofs against it. Its representative, at any rate, has so far managed only to botch the job: he has revealed the slow wit and inconsistency of his ilk and has proved quite handily the satirist's contention that general satire is ineffective.

If not as obviously depraved as his brother in Dialogue I, the adversary in II nevertheless shares his double standard and, like him, dramatizes the evil the poem decries. He would have the satirist do his victims at least the favor of a dash for anonymity (v. 11). He has, as we have seen, his own taste for scandal, which ironically vitiates his complaints against the satirist. He would spare the man trying to make his way in the world ("You hurt a man that's rising in the Trade," v. 35). He would divert satire to the dead and low-life (Jonathan Wild, v. 54). His whole argument tends, in short, to the worldly comfort of no satire at all.

But while he is on the one hand a temporizer with vice, on the other he functions as the agent of the poet's strictly argumentative needs, raising the right questions to occasion the satirist's defense of his satire. That he raises them for the wrong reasons is but an added effect of the poet's art. If you must satirize, he asks, why must you use names? Why do you return over and over to the same victims? Do you complain of those in power because your friends are out? What is it to you anyway? he asks, his crassness mingling now with the poet's most quiet need. Pope continues to have it both ways. He wanted these questions, needed them, and he met them with strength and wit; but at the same time he got them posed by a fellow basically unprincipled, who, in putting them, inadvertently contributes to the satire himself. But by nothing does Pope more finely discriminate between himself and his adversary (and his adversary's constituency) than by the Friend's objection to the satirist's simile of the Westphaly hogs: "This filthy Simile, this beastly Line,/Quite turns my Stomach. . . ." (vv. 181–182). The adversary's is a morality that can stomach vice, but not the image of it.

Against this temporizing figure is balanced once again the image of the poet, standing for the right, with his "strong Antipathy of Good to bad" and his sense of "Affront," which should be the adversary's too. After the poet's great peroration in defense of satire ("O sacred Weapon!" vv. 212–253), the adversary is understandably shaken and draws back in a nervous and feeble attempt to divert the satirist's indignation: "Alas! alas! pray end what you began,/And write next winter more *Essays on Man*," that is, general, philosophic, personally innocuous satire. The satirist doesn't even bother to notice.

The Friend of Dialogue II has served the satirist as *provocateur*, Machiavel, hypocrite, courtly wit, and inquisitor more helpful than harmful. He has furthered the satire by commending moral relativism, by protesting delicacy in the face of honest scatology but acknowledging stomach enough for flattery, by prodding the satirist into the noblest apology for satire on record, and by betraying the intimidation which must always mark the corrupt in the presence of aroused virtue. From him Pope has extracted the last full measure of collaboration. And that may be one reason, among others, why Pope did not compose other dialogues in the brief time left to him. He had done about all that could be done with the form. He had taken a device scarcely defined in Roman usage—hardly known to Juvenal at all, experimented with cleverly but tentatively by Horace, and only somewhat sharpened in focus by Persius—and made of it a brilliant and versatile accessory of the satiric strategy. He diversified and intensified Horace's precedent in the use of the friendly adversary, and elaborated and extended Persius' in the use of the hostile one. He outstrips the field in the fusion of irony and virulence, in the creation of dramatic tension, and in the assimilation of the adversary into the total satiric economy.

Mr. Pope

by Allen Tate

When Alexander Pope strolled in the city
Strict was the glint of pearl and gold sedans.
Ladies leaned out more out of fear than pity
For Pope's tight back was rather a goat's than man's.

Often one thinks the urn should have more bones
Than skeletons provide for speedy dust,
The urn gets hollow, cobwebs brittle as stones
Weave to the funeral shell a frivolous rust.

And he who dribbled couplets like a snake
Coiled to a lithe precision in the sun
Is missing. The jar is empty; you may break
It only to find that Mr. Pope is gone.

What requisitions of a verity
Prompted the wit and rage between his teeth
One cannot say. Around a crooked tree
A moral climbs whose name should be a wreath.

"Mr. Pope." From *Poems,* by Allen Tate. (New York: Charles Scribner's Sons, 1960), p. 138. Copyright © 1932 by Charles Scribner's Sons. Copyright © renewed 1960 by Allen Tate. Reprinted by permission of Charles Scribner's Sons and Eyre & Spottiswoode.

Chronology of Important Dates

1688	May 21. Born in London to elderly parents.
ca. 1705	Becomes acquainted with the literary society of London.
1709	*The Pastorals* published in the sixth part of Tonson's *Miscellanies.*
1711	*An Essay on Criticism.* The poem provokes a furious attack from John Dennis.
1712	The first version of *The Rape of the Lock* published in Lintot's *Miscellany.* Becomes acquainted with Gay, Swift, Arbuthnot, and Parnell; together they formed the Scriblerus Club.
1714	The five-canto version of *The Rape of the Lock.*
1715	Publishes in February *The Temple of Fame* and in June *The Iliad,* Books I–IV. Becomes acquainted with Lady Mary Wortley Montagu.
1716	*The Iliad,* Vol. II.
1717	*Three Hours after Marriage* by Pope, Gay, and Arbuthnot performed. The collected volume of Pope's *Works,* containing *Verses to the Memory of an Unfortunate Lady* and *Eloïsa to Abelard. The Iliad,* Vol III. Pope's father dies.
1718	*The Iliad,* Vol. IV. Pope and his mother move to Twickenham.
1720	*The Iliad,* Vols. V and VI.
1725	Publishes his edition of Shakespeare in six volumes. *The Odyssey,* Vols. I–III.
1726	Theobald's *Shakespeare Restored: or, a Specimen of the Many Errors . . . Committed . . . by Mr. Pope. Odyssey,* Vols. IV and V.
1727	Pope–Swift *Miscellanies,* Vols. I and II.

1728   Pope–Swift *Miscellanies,* "last" volume, containing the *Peri Bathous. The Dunciad,* in three books, with Theobald as hero; numerous attacks by the dunces.

1729   *The Dunciad Variorum.* More attacks.

1731   *Epistle to Burlington.*

1732   Pope–Swift *Miscellanies,* "third" volume.

1733   *Epistle to Bathurst.* The first *Imitation of Horace* (Sat. II. i.). *An Essay on Man,* Epistles I–III. Pope's mother dies.

1734   *Epistle to Cobham. An Essay on Man,* Epistle IV. *Imitation of* Horace (Sat. II. ii.). *Sober Advice from Horace.*

1735   *Epistle to Dr. Arbuthnot. Of the Characters of Women.* The *Works,* Vol. II. Curll publishes Pope's letters.

1737   *Imitations of Horace* (Epistles II. ii. and II. i.). Pope's edition of his letters.

1738   *Imitations of Horace* (Epistles I. vi. and I. i.). *Epilogue to the Satires.*

1742   *The New Dunciad (i.e.,* Book IV).

1743   *The Dunciad* in four books, with Cibber as hero.

1744   May 30. Pope dies.

Notes on the Editor and Contributors

J. V. GUERINOT, editor of this volume, is Professor of English at the University of Wisconsin, Milwaukee. He received his Ph.D. from Yale and is the author of *Pamphlet Attacks on Alexander Pope, 1711–1744: A Descriptive Bibliography.*

JOHN M. ADEN is Professor of English at Vanderbilt University. In addition to articles on Pope, he is the author of *Something like Horace: Studies in the Art and Allusion of Pope's Horatian Poems.*

W. H. AUDEN, England's and America's most distinguished living poet, has collected much of his criticism in *The Dyer's Hand.* His most recent volume of poetry is *Epistle to a Godson.*

CLEANTH BROOKS is Gray Professor of English at Yale. One of the best-known American critics, his books include *Modern Poetry and the Tradition, The Well Wrought Urn,* and *William Faulkner: The Yoknapatawpha Country.*

IRVIN EHRENPREIS is Professor of English at the University of Virginia. He is the author of *The Personality of Jonathan Swift,* and the monumental *Swift: The Man, His Works, and the Age.*

EMRYS JONES has edited the poems of the Earl of Surrey in the Clarendon Medieval and Tudor Series.

MAYNARD MACK is Sterling Professor of English at Yale. Editor of the Twickenham Editions of *The Essay on Man, The Iliad,* and *The Odyssey,* his most recent contribution to the study of Pope is *The Garden and the City: Retirement and Politics in the Later Poetry of Pope, 1731–1743.*

ALLEN TATE is celebrated as both poet and critic. His critical writings include *Reason in Madness, The Forlorn Demon,* and *The Man of Letters in the Modern World.*

GEOFFREY TILLOTSON was Professor of English at the University of London, Birkbeck College, and the editor of *The Rape of the Lock* in the Twickenham Edition. He is the author of, among other books, *On the Poetry of Pope* and *Pope and Human Nature.*

WILLIAM K. WIMSATT, JR. is Ford Professor of English at Yale. A distinguished critic and theorist, his books include *The Verbal Icon, Hateful Contraries,* and, with Cleanth Brooks, *Literary Criticism, A Short History.*

Selected Bibliography

Editions

The Twickenham Edition of the Poems of Alexander Pope. 11 vols. John Butt, General Editor. London: Methuen, 1939–69.

The Poems of Alexander Pope: A One-Volume Edition of the Twickenham Text with Selected Annotations. John Butt, ed. London: Methuen, 1963.

The Correspondence of Alexander Pope. 5 vols. George Sherburn, ed. Oxford: Clarendon Press, 1956.

The Prose Works of Alexander Pope. Norman Ault, ed. Vol. I–The Earlier Works. Oxford: Basil Blackwell, 1936.

The Art of Sinking in Poetry. Edna Leake Steeves, ed. New York: King's Crown Press, 1952.

Memoirs of the Extraordinary Life, Works, and Discoveries of Martinus Scriblerus. Charles Kerby-Miller, ed. New Haven: Yale University Press, 1950; rep. New York: Russell and Russell, 1966.

Three Hours after Marriage. Richard Morton and William M. Peterson, eds. Painesville, Ohio: Lake Erie College Studies, Vol. i, 1961.

The Literary Criticism of Alexander Pope. Bertrand A. Goldgar, ed. Regents Critics Series. Lincoln: University of Nebraska Press, 1965.

Biography and Iconography

Rogers, Robert W. *The Major Satires* of Alexander Pope. Urbana: University of Illinois Press, 1955. The only reliable guide as yet to Pope's later career.

Sherburn, George. *The Early Career of Alexander Pope.* Oxford: Clarendon Press, 1935. The standard biography.

Wimsatt, Jr. William K. *The Portraits of Alexander Pope.* New Haven: Yale University Press, 1965.

Bibliographies

Griffith, R. H. *Alexander Pope: A Bibliography.* 2 vols. Austin, Texas: The University of Texas Press, 1922–27; rep. London: The Holland Press, 1962.

Guerinot, J. V. *Pamphlet Attacks on Alexander Pope, 1711–1744: A Descriptive Bibliography.* London: Methuen, 1969.

Lopez, Cecilia L. *Alexander Pope: An Annotated Bibliography, 1945–67.* Gainesville: University of Florida Press, 1970.

Critical Works

Aden, John M. *Something Like Horace: Studies in the Art and Allusion of Pope's Horatian Poems.* Nashville: Vanderbilt University Press, 1969. An excellent study of Pope's relationship to Horace.

Adler, Jacob. *The Reach of Art: A Study in the Prosody of Pope.* Gainesville: University of Florida Press, 1964. The only detailed study.

Brower, Reuben Arthur. *Alexander Pope: The Poetry of Allusion.* Oxford: Clarendon Press, 1959. The indispensable study of all the poems.

Dixon, Peter. *The World of Pope's Satires: An Introduction to the Epistles and Imitations of Horace.* London: Methuen, 1968. A useful and agreeable guide to the later poems.

Leavis, F. R. "Pope." *Revaluation: Tradition and Development in English Poetry.* New York: Norton, 1963. A famous essay which, most regrettably, I was not given permission to include.

Mack, Maynard, ed. *Essential Articles for the Study of Alexander Pope.* Rev. and enl. ed. Hamden, Conn.: Archon Books, 1968. A reprinting of almost all the important articles.

————. *The Garden and the City: Retirement and Politics in the Later Poems of Pope, 1733–1743.* Toronto: University of Toronto Press, 1969. A brilliantly illuminating study of Pope, his villa, and politics.

Maresca, Thomas E. *Pope's Horatian Poems.* Columbus: Ohio State University Press, 1966. A highly disputable but stimulating reading.

Root, Robert Kilburn. *The Poetical Career of Alexander Pope.* Princeton: Princeton University Press, 1938; rep. Gloucester, Mass.: Peter Smith, 1962. A lucid and still valuable critical study.

Tillotson, Geoffrey. *On the Poetry of Pope.* 2nd ed. Oxford: Clarendon Press, 1950. An extremely perceptive book, the best introduction to Pope.